Francis Beaumont

Twayne's English Authors Series

Arthur F. Kinney, Editor
University of Massachusetts–Amherst

TEAS 458

FRANCIS BEAUMONT
*The Knole Park portrait of Francis Beaumont is
reproduced with the kind permission of Lord Sackville*

Francis Beaumont

By Lee Bliss

University of California, Santa Barbara

Twayne Publishers
A Division of G. K. Hall & Co. • *Boston*

Francis Beaumont

Lee Bliss

Copyright 1987 by G. K. Hall & Co.
All rights reserved.
Published by Twayne Publishers
A Division of G. K. Hall & Co.
70 Lincoln Street
Boston, Massachusetts 02111

Copyediting supervised by Lewis DeSimone
Book production by John Amburg
Book design by Barbara Anderson

Typeset in 11 pt. Garamond
by Modern Graphics, Inc., Weymouth, Massachusetts

Printed on permanent/durable acid-free paper
and bound in the United States of America

Library of Congress Cataloging-in-Publication Data

Bliss, Lee, 1943-
  Francis Beaumont.

  (Twayne's English authors series ; TEAS 458)
  Bibliography: p.
  Includes index.
  1. Beaumont, Francis, 1584–1616—Criticism and
interpretation. I. Title. II. Series.
PR2434.B55 1987   822'.3   87–14922
ISBN 0–8057–6950–1 (alk. paper)

Contents

About the Author
Preface
Chronology

Chapter One
Introduction   1

Chapter Two
Early Comedy   17

Chapter Three
The Knight of the Burning Pestle   33

Chapter Four
Collaboration and Success   56

Chapter Five
The Maid's Tragedy   87

Chapter Six
The Legacy: Tragicomedy and Comedy   107

Chapter Seven
Conclusion   132

Notes and References   139
Selected Bibliography   161
Index   169

About the Author

Lee Bliss endured an early education at a random collection of schools in Buffalo, New York, Tucson, Arizona, and Boston, Massachusetts. She earned a B.A. from Stanford University in 1965 and a Ph.D. in English literature from the University of California, Berkeley, in 1972. Another diverse assembly of schools received her first teaching efforts—the University of California at Los Angeles, Scripps College, Occidental College—before she settled in 1975 at the University of California, Santa Barbara, where she is currently an associate professor. Scholarly journals have published her critical essays on plays by Shakespeare, Chapman, Webster, Fletcher, and Beaumont, and an essay on Shakespearean and Beaumont-and-Fletcher romantic tragicomedy appears in *Comedy from Shakespeare to Sheridan,* edited by A. R. Braunmuller and J. C. Bulman. Professor Bliss is also the author of *The World's Perspective: John Webster and the Jacobean Drama* (1983).

Preface

This study develops from a long-standing interest in Francis Beaumont, in the Beaumont-Fletcher collaboration, and in the larger but related question of what happened to English drama during the early seventeenth century. Perhaps anyone's first, surprised and delighted, reading of *The Knight of the Burning Pestle* sparks curiosity about its author; continued study of the period leads inevitably to the other concerns of this book. That Beaumont's work with Fletcher was enormously influential for the theatrical practice of their peers and successors is unchallenged, but for the last two centuries their names have generally been yoked in vilification, as composite cause— or partial cause—for the decay of the glory that was Renaissance drama. Beaumont has only very infrequently been considered separately, as man or playwright, and the last book on him—more biographical than critical—was published in 1914.

On the first score, I cannot be said to have satisfied my own curiosity. Even at its extreme limits, ca. 1605–13, Beaumont's career as dramatist was brief, and he remains fascinating but enigmatic. Such biographical facts as exist connect him with the social and political as well as theatrical life of the turbulent decade in which he came to maturity, and I have tried to explore some of their implications in the introduction. Associated with the most talented and original poets and playwrights of his time, as well as the best of the private and public troupes, he seems to have shared some of their attitudes and preoccupations while also proving remarkably bold in his approach to matters of genre and stagecraft.

On the basis of his two independent plays, we might wish Beaumont had continued to explore the originality and talent obvious even in such youthful work. He did not, and instead withdrew behind the collaboration with Fletcher that turned their taste for experiment to recombining elements of their theatrical heritage. As part of the first generation to write under the sway of Shakespeare's success and popularity, yet having "apprenticed" under Jonson, Marston, Chapman, and the taste and practices of the fashionable, innovative, and politically inflammatory private theaters, Beaumont and Fletcher were particularly suited to blend these traditions. With

FRANCIS BEAUMONT

Shakespeare now as colleague, they helped preside over the King's Men's successful acquisition of the Blackfriars theater and the creation of both a style and particular dramatic forms, carried on by Fletcher, that ensured the King's Men's predominance through the reigns of James I and Charles I, as well as "Beaumont and Fletcher's" through the early eighteenth century.

Analysis of individual plays tries to balance attention to the work itself with consideration of its sources—literary and historical as well as theatrical—and with the continuing experimentation that produced the distinctive "Beaumont and Fletcher" style and popularity. If Beaumont gets progressively absorbed into "Beaumont and Fletcher," this study simply records seventeenth-century reality. Although the plays in which Beaumont had a hand have received increasing critical scrutiny and praise, the virtue of a comprehensive book on Francis Beaumont is that connections between them become clearer. The dramaturgy and sensibility—whether Beaumont's or a serendipitous amalgam of Beaumont-and-Fletcher never achieved with Fletcher's other collaborators—takes on at least a degree of substance.

Research was undertaken in Santa Barbara, in Los Angeles at the UCLA Research Library and at the Huntington Library, and in London at the Senate House Library and the British Library. I am grateful to the staffs of these institutions, as well as for the continued support of the Academic Research Committee of the University of California, Santa Barbara. Part of chapter 3 appeared first in *Modern Language Quarterly* 45 (March 1984):3–21, as "'Plot mee no plots': The Life of Drama and the Drama of Life in *The Knight of the Burning Pestle*," and, in a much more altered form, portions of chapter 4 as "Three Plays in One: Shakespeare and *Philaster*," *Medieval and Renaissance Drama in England* 2 (1985):153–70. I thank the editors of both journals for permission to incorporate this material. Michael O'Connell read portions of this study and helped sharpen its argument; Jody Millward helped check the manuscript and tidy its loose ends.

Lee Bliss

University of California, Santa Barbara

Chronology

Few dates are certain in this chronology of Beaumont's life. Conjectural dates are preceded by a question mark; first publication, usually in quarto (Q) but occasionally not until the first folio (F 1), follows the play title, as does the name of the troupe for which the play was written.

1584–1585	Francis Beaumont born at Grace-Dieu, Leicestershire, third son of Francis Beaumont, justice of the Common Pleas.
1597	4 February, matriculates at Broadgates Hall, Oxford.
1600	November, enters Inner Temple.
1600–1605	*Grammar Lecture;* "Remedy of Love."
1602	*Salmacis and Hermaphroditus;* "F. B." verses prefixed to brother John's *Metamorphosis of Tobacco.*
1605	? Beaumont-Fletcher version of *Love's Cure* (? Paul's).
1606	*The Woman Hater* (Q 1607, Paul's).
1607	? *The Knight of the Burning Pestle* (Q 1613, Blackfriars); verses prefixed to Jonson's *Volpone.*
1608	? *Cupid's Revenge* (Q 1615, Blackfriars).
1609	"An Elegy on the Lady Markham"; ? verse letter to Jonson from the country; ? *The Coxcomb* (F 1647, Queen's Revels Children); ? *Philaster* (Q 1620, King's Men); ? verses on Jonson's *Epicoene* for lost quarto; ? verses prefixed to Fletcher's *Faithful Shepherdess* (Q 1609–10).
1610	? *The Scornful Lady* (Q 1616, Queen's Revels Children); ? *The Maid's Tragedy* (Q 1619, King's Men).
1611	*A King and No King* (Q 1619, King's Men); verses prefixed to Jonson's *Catiline.*
1612	Elegy for the countess of Rutland (? earlier, "Ad Comitissam Rutlandiae").

1613   20 February, *The Masque of the Inner Temple and Gray's Inn;* elegy for Lady Penelope Clifton. ? Marries Ursula Isley and leaves London for Kent.

1613–1616   Second verse epistle to Jonson, "To Mr B. J." Possibly still contributing in a minor way to a few Fletcher or Fletcher-Massinger plays.

1616   Dies 6 March and is buried in Westminster Abbey.

1640   *Poems* (not all by Beaumont); reprinted, with additions, 1653.

1647   *Comedies and Tragedies* (F 1; 34 plays + *Masque*).

1679   *Fifty Comedies and Tragedies* (F 2; 52 plays).

Chapter One

Introduction

Castor and Pollux

If ever two names were firmly wed in the minds of students of literature, they are those of Francis Beaumont and John Fletcher. Even to their contemporaries, Beaumont and Fletcher seemed the twin halves of a single literary phenomenon. In the commendatory verses prefixed to the 1647 first folio, George Lisle celebrates the merger by which "still your fancies are so wov'n and knit, / 'Twas FRANCIS FLETCHER, or JOHN BEAUMONT writ," and Jasper Maine finds this "Great paire of Authors, whom one equall Starre / Begot so like in *Genius*," to be "so knit, / That no man knowes where to divide your wit."[1] Looking back from later in the century, John Aubrey reports "a wonderfull consimility of phansey between [Beaumont] and Mr. John Fletcher, which caused that dearnesse of frendship between them," and it is to Aubrey (and his informant Sir John Hales) that we owe the most famous description of the conditions to which this "consimility" led: "They lived together on the Banke side, not far from the Play-house, both batchelors; lay together; had one Wench in the house between them, which they did so admire; the same cloathes and cloake, etc.; betweene them."[2]

Trying to sever the Dioscuri of Jacobean drama to concentrate on Beaumont may seem a profitless exercise in critical differentiation. Although early individual efforts like *The Knight of the Burning Pestle* and *The Faithful Shepherdess* are so dissimilar as to make their authors improbable yoke-fellows, Beaumont and Fletcher obviously found joint playwriting, and each other, particularly congenial. The application of sophisticated spelling and linguistic tests to establish the precise shares of each collaborator has not dispelled most readers'— and editors'—impression of a unity of tone and attitude that defies our confidently "attributing any line . . . to one or the other of the authors."[3]

Certainly the true Beaumont-Fletcher collaborations are part— indeed, quantitatively and in theatrical influence, the most important part—of Beaumont's oeuvre. Yet literary history can be deceptive. Ironically, the volume first presenting thirty-five works "by Francis Beaumont and John Fletcher, Gentlemen," contained almost nothing attributable to Beaumont. Since the first folio included only plays not previously published, and since nearly all the Beaumont-Fletcher collaborations had by then found their way into print, the 1647 collection offered Beaumont to his public only in the form of his *Masque of the Inner Temple and Gray's Inn* and rather limited contribution to *The Coxcomb*. In the title page's claim and in his publisher's epistle, Humphrey Moseley certainly laid himself open to charges of deceptive advertising.

Protests were not unknown, and seventeenth-century opinion supports attempts at distinction as well as identity. Some of the 1647 commendatory verses discriminate between Beaumont and Fletcher and praise opposite though complementary talents and personalities. Other contemporaries suggest that works by Beaumont and Fletcher can—and should—be distinguished from those of Fletcher alone or in collaboration with Philip Massinger. In a verse epistle to his cousin Charles Cotton (a friend of Fletcher's and dedicatee of *Monsieur Thomas*), Sir Aston Cokayne reproaches Cotton for not having pointed out to the printers that "almost every one" of the plays had been "After the death of *Beaumont* writ." In a later epigram, this early disintegrator of the canon upbraids the publishers for not giving each dramatist due credit: "For *Beaumont* (of those many) writ in few: / And *Massinger* in other few; the Main / Being sole Issues of sweet *Fletchers* brain."[4] Modern critics like Philip J. Finkelpearl continue to insist on dissimilarity, both between Beaumont and Fletcher and between their early joint works and the rest of the "Beaumont and Fletcher" canon.[5]

Certainly in background, as well as in the shape of his career, Beaumont differed from Fletcher. An admired poet in his own right, Beaumont early demonstrated a remarkable dramatic talent. *The Knight of the Burning Pestle* with wit and sophistication anatomizes the theatrical imagination; it can also lay claim to being the best as well as the first dramatic burlesque in English. Spectacularly unsuccessful at its opening, it is today the most frequently revived play in the whole "Beaumont and Fletcher" canon. As Fletcher's first and most important collaborator, too, Beaumont holds considerable interest. Together they worked out distinctive versions of the dramatic "kinds"—particularly tragicomedy, but the two traditional genres as well—that sustained Fletcher for another twelve years and helped shape the course of English drama after Shakespeare.

Early Life and the Inns of Court

Third son of Francis Beaumont, justice of the Common Pleas, the dramatist belonged to the younger branch of an old, distinguished Leicestershire family. His grandfather John Beaumont, Master of the Rolls under Henry VIII, had in 1539 acquired Grace-Dieu Priory, and there Francis was probably born in 1584 or 1585.[6] Neither birth nor christening records exist, but two later references help fix the date and fill in the meager outline of what is known of Beaumont's early life. On 4 February 1596/7, Francis was admitted, with his brothers Henry and John, a gentleman-commoner of Broadgates Hall, Oxford. Matriculation records list Francis as "aetat 12."[7] In April 1598 his father died and the funeral certificate describes Francis as "third sonne, of the age of thirteen yeares or more."[8]

Although not enrolled at their father's Cambridge college, the sons seem to have been slated to follow the paternal path. As member of the Inner Temple, the elder Francis had proceeded Reader and Bencher; when young Francis entered the Inner Temple in 1600, his brothers stood as sponsors. Yet Henry succeeded to Grace-Dieu, while John and Francis exhibited less interest in legal than in literary pursuits. Still, though they may have strayed from their father's hopes, John and Francis found the Inns of Court as congenial for budding authors as for nascent barristers.

The Inns of Court boasted a long, rich association with the literary and theatrical life of Elizabethan England. In the period between Wyatt and Surrey, and Spenser and Sidney, most of England's important writers were connected with them. They continued to foster poets in the 1590s, when John Donne (Lincoln's Inn), Thomas Campion (Gray's Inn), and Sir John Davies (Middle Temple) lived in the Inns's overlapping intellectual and poetic circles. In his study of John Marston (Middle Temple), Philip J. Finkelpearl finds in the Inns-of-Court milieu certain attitudes reflected in turn-of-the-century trends in poetry and drama: "youthful, self-conscious cynicism nurtured in the catalytic atmosphere of the law schools; a sense of belonging to an elite of wits in a world of gulls; a tradition of free and candid speech; upper-class condescension to the taste of

professional writers; a tradition of plain style in language." Some
of these young men sought preferment at court; like two of Beaumont's cousins, many became members of Parliament. Such an
atmosphere encouraged its members to be "critical, independent,
aesthetically innovative, and politically concerned."[9]

Beaumont's early burlesque *Grammar Lecture,* composed for some
Temple festivity, and his slightly tardy contribution to the fad for
erotic epyllia, *Salmacis and Hermaphroditus,* suggest he found this
community's attitudes and literary tastes congenial. The Inns's theatrical tradition, too, lived on. The days of the great "in house"
playwrights—who produced *Gorboduc* (1561/62), *Jocasta* (1566),
Tancred and Gismund (ca. 1568), *The Misfortunes of Arthur* (1588)—
had passed, but the Inns's own "Revels" continued, and students
attended both public and private playhouses.[10] Marston turned from
writing fashionable verse satire, which was common among Inns-
of-Court litterateurs, to writing satiric comedies for the children's
troupes, which was not. His early plays especially, in their jargon
and in-group jokes, seem particularly aimed at his fellow residents.
Ben Jonson dedicated *Every Man out of His Humour* in the 1616 folio
to this source of a valued segment of his audience, "the Nobelest
Nourceries of Humanity, and Liberty, in the Kingdome." He recalls
that even when the play was first performed in 1599, he "had
friendship with divers in your societies."[11]

Francis's brother John, who succeeded to the family estates when
Henry died in 1605, early became a poet and friend of poets. He
is probably the author of the mock-heroic *Metamorphosis of Tobacco*
(1602), whose "first-borne rimes" are dedicated to "my loving Friend
Master Michael Drayton";[12] he wrote commendatory verses to Drayton's *Barrons Wars* (1603), *Moyses in a Map of His Miracles* (1604),
and *Poems* (1605). Although in some financial and political difficulty
after succeeding Henry, John continued to write while at Grace-
Dieu. His social as well as literary position later improved with the
rise of Buckingham, whose mother Mary Villiers was a Beaumont
kinswoman; John was created baronet in 1626. Besides his historical
poem *Bosworth-field,* John Beaumont composed a good deal of occasional verse, including courtly poems to the duke of Buckingham
and members of the royal family. Despite the high praise showered
on his brother Francis, Sir John Beaumont was not unadmired in
his day. Edmund Bolton considered him one of the "Essentials"
for his proposed royal academy, and upon his death in 1627 Sir

John was buried in "Poets' Corner" in Westminister Abbey (with Chaucer, Spenser, and his own brother Francis).[13] When in 1629 his son, also Sir John and a minor poet himself, published *Bosworth-field* with some of his father's other poems, his and his brother's prefatory verses were joined by those of Drayton and Jonson.

This conjunction of eulogists suggests the range of Sir John's literary friendships; it may also prepare us for those of the brother who remained in London and, perhaps, for the kind of occasional verse he produced in his short career. Francis' earliest verses were probably those signed "F. B." prefixed to *The Metamorphosis of Tobacco;* through his brother, Francis may already have know Drayton, the poem's dedicatee. The older poet's relationship with the Beaumont brothers seems to have been both close and lasting. In the eighth eclogue of *Poems Lyrick and Pastorall* (1606), Drayton celebrates under pastoral names "those hopeful boyes," their sister Elizabeth, and the hospitality extended at Grace-Dieu to London poets, "southern shepheards."[14] Drayton's verse epistle to Henry Reynolds, "Of Poets and Poesie," speaks more warmly of "the two Beaumonts" and William Browne (an Inner Temple pastoralist) than of any other contemporary poets.[15] Although in personality and poetic taste Drayton would appear a more likely bosom friend of John Beaumont, perhaps Drayton's Ovidian narrative *Endimion and Phoebe* (1595) helped inspire Francis' first substantial work, *Salmacis and Hermaphroditus* (1602).

Literary Friendships and the Blackfriars Theater

That the more likely model for Beaumont's epyllion is the witty, cynical *Metamorphosis of Pigmalions Image* (1598), by fellow Inns-of-Court satirist and dramatist John Marston, points to the more expected locus of formative literary influences: members of the Inns of Court, but also the poets and dramatists associated with the private theaters these young law students attended and for which they sometimes wrote. Of a personal friendship between Marston and Beaumont we lack concrete evidence. Marston's plays as well as his epyllion clearly influenced the younger Templar's work, and Beaumont was almost certainly writing for the Children of the Queen's Revels, in which by 1604 Marston held an interest, before Marston sold his share to Robert Keysar and retired from the stage (ca. 1608).[16] Marston also moved in the circle of poets and dramatists

Beaumont soon joined; here Beaumont formed his closest literary friendships, those with John Fletcher and Ben Jonson.

Although their relations may have begun under other auspices, these men were connected with the Blackfriars theater and its boy players. Ben Jonson and George Chapman had written for them, though not exclusively, since about 1600, and Nathan Field began acting for them that year, including the lead in Jonson's *Cynthia's Revels* (and later in *Poetaster, Epicoene,* and *Bartholomew Fair*). After becoming a company shareholder, Marston wrote for the Blackfriars troupe; Beaumont and Fletcher were both associated with them by 1607. Bound by more than a common playhouse affiliation, these men reveal similiar literary tastes; they seem to have shared political and social attitudes and, sometimes, patrons. They admired each other's work and, individually and in collaboration, they created the kind of plays for which the Blackfriars theater became known, even infamous. Presumably they talked together; certainly they worked together, and they manned the battlements when their plays, especially the failures, appeared in printed form.

Most of these associations, and a sense of beleaguered camaraderie, had been established if not by 1603, the year *Sejanus* failed at the Globe, then by 1605, the year of its publication. Chapman's may have been the "second pen" in the stage version of *Sejanus,* whose material Jonson says he excised for publication; Chapman certainly rushed to its defense with a lengthy prefatory poem for the 1605 quarto, and he contributed verses to the 1607 quarto of *Volpone.* He collaborated with Jonson on the politically ill-fated *Eastward Ho* (1605, Blackfriars) and for his pains joined Jonson in jail. Jonson's respect for Chapman's stature appears in his prefatory verses for the 1618 publication of Chapman's translation of Hesiod and in his remark to Drummond of Hawthornden that "next himself" only "Fletcher [Beaumont?] and Chapman could make a Mask."[17] Chapman and Beaumont wrote the masques with which the Inns of Court celebrated the marriage of Princess Elizabeth to the Elector Palatine in 1613, and, in a graceful hymn to pastoral poetry's golden world, Chapman joins Jonson, Field, and Beaumont in defending Fletcher's unsuccessful *Faithful Shepherdess* (undated quarto, ca. 1609).

Having switched from the Children of Paul's to the Queen's Revels and ended his "war" with Jonson, Marston dedicated *The Malcontent* (1604) to Jonson. He collaborated with Jonson and Chapman on *Eastward Ho,* though he appears to have escaped prison;[18] he helped defend *Sejanus* in the 1605 quarto. As author and shareholder Marston knew Nat Field, and the theater itself connected Field with all these dramatists. Indeed, Field was probably imprisoned with Jonson and Chapman for *Eastward Ho*.[19] He became the company's principal actor; encomia at his death rank him with Burbage in ability. Field himself turned playwright around 1609, though he continued his acting career; he later joined the King's Men as both player and shareholder. Adoptive "son" to Jonson and Chapman, Field, too, wrote verses for *The Faithful Shepherdess;*[20] with *Four Plays in One* he became one of Fletcher's occasional collaborators.[21]

Recorded evidence for Beaumont and Fletcher's entry onto this scene comes with their 1607 commendatory verses for *Volpone,* Beaumont's addressed "To my deare friend." The prologue to Beaumont's *The Woman Hater* (performed early 1606) alludes to the troubles occasioned by *Eastward Ho,* but the lines fail to establish a personal friendship and the play was written for another company. Soon, however, these men had at least one cause in common. Beaumont's and Jonson's verses defending Fletcher's *Faithful Shepherdess* reflect a bitterness born of their own experience with the audiences who rejected *Sejanus* and *The Knight of the Burning Pestle*. A further Fletcher-Jonson connection may be indicated by the fact that one of the *Faithful Shepherdess*'s dedicatees, Sir Robert Townesend, was the patron and friend with whom Jonson had recently lived.[22]

Relations between Jonson and Beaumont seem to have remained close. Beaumont continued to write commendatory verses for Jonson's plays; he is the sole contributor to *Epicoene,* where he models his poem on Jonson's own second prologue.[23] Defending *Catiline* in 1611, along with Fletcher, Field, and John Selden, Beaumont praises Jonson as a principled dramatist who has commendably not "itch'd after the wild applause / Of common people."[24] The warm, even jocular, tone of Beaumont's verse epistles to Jonson suggests intimacy. Indeed, while much of Beaumont's occasional verse is disappointingly flat and mechanical, these two poems demonstrate a real engagement with his subject, and the graceful praise gains force from a sophisticated mastery of the heroic couplet favored by his friend. Despite Jonson's crusty remark to Drummond "that Francis Beaumont loved too much himself & his own verses," Jonson's epigram, beginning "How I doe love thee BEAUMONT, and thy *Muse,*" concludes with a degree of admiration unusual in Jonson: "where most thou praysest mee, / For writing better, I must envie thee."[25] Whether or not we credit Dryden's rather surprising assertion that Beaumont was "so accurate a judge of plays that Ben Jonson, while he lived, submitted all his writing to his censure, and, 'tis thought, used his judgment in correcting, if not contriving, all his plots," contemporary testimony supports both the closeness of the Beaumont-Jonson connection and his peers' respect for Beaumont's theatrical discernment.[26] Several of the 1647 encomiasts credit Beaumont with employing his sterner muse and firmer sense of dramatic construction to curb Fletcher's extravagance.[27]

While Blackfriars under the Children of the Revels earned a reputation for social satire and, more excitingly, for the politically inflammatory allusions that finally brought about the troupe's suppression, Jonson and Beaumont may have had personal reasons for hostility to James: his policy toward Catholics. Imprisoned for alleged political satire in *Eastward Ho,* indeed earlier called before the council to defend himself against charges connected with *Sejanus,* Jonson proved his loyalty through service for Lord Salisbury in the aftermath of the Gunpowder Plot. Yet despite some success at court, Jonson never felt his talents adequately recognized; he was also in the first decade of the seventeenth century Catholic, and in 1606 had to appear with his wife before London's Consistory Court for absence from service and Communion. Beaumont's personal beliefs are unknown, but both his parents were at various times in trouble for assisting the Catholic cause, and cousins on his mother's side were accused of aiding men associated with the Gunpowder Plot. His brother John suffered punishment for recusancy; by 1607 the two thirds of his lands and goods forfeited to the king had been awarded to Sir James Sempill (who was still profitting from them in 1615), and John was confined to Grace-Dieu.[28] Two cousins and country neighbors, Sir Henry Beaumont of Colerton and Sir Thomas Beaumont, Stanton Grange, were among the king's most vocal opponents in Parliament.[29]

While suggestive, these facts should not generate hasty assumptions about Jonson's or Beaumont's political convictions. The popularity of anticourt satire predates James's accession, and later slighting references to James, his Scots followers and indiscriminate bestowal of knighthoods, or satiric portraits of court fops and flatterers, are common to a whole group of dramatists writing for both children's troupes. What seems pointed criticism may spring as much from fashion as conviction. Censure could in this period also coexist with a high valuation for the arts of civility and courtship, political as well as social. Many of its critics clearly felt attracted to the court and displayed an eager willingness to seek its rewards and recognition. John Donne, as well as Chapman and Jonson, exemplifies this apparently paradoxical stance. Himself a writer of satire and, though nominally Anglican, in these years resisting pressure to take church office, Donne desperately sought preferment within the system of court patronage. Later, in a sermon preached before King Charles, Donne's animadversions on court calumniators seem to indict himself and his earlier colleagues: "We make *Satyrs;* and we looke that the world should call that *wit;* when God knowes, that that is in a great part, self-guiltinesse, . . . we cry out upon the illnesse of the times, and we make the times ill."[30]

Donne judges too harshly. Hypocrisy is not the sole explanation for such apparently ambivalent behavior. In the early seventeenth century the court could still be seen—or imagined—in ideal terms, as Jonson's masques demonstrate. At least until 1612, it is also true that Prince Henry represented the hope not only of literary patronage—successfully pursued by Jonson, Chapman, and Drayton—but of a morally renewed court that would recapture the greatness of Elizabeth's reign.[31] Out of economic necessity or ambition for the power—social, political, even artistic—that only the court could bestow, many of Beaumont's friends entered themselves in the competition for noble or royal patronage and sought to rise in a world whose failings they also held up to mockery.

Amateur and Professional Playwrights

Beaumont's early association with such men helps to focus an important aspect of his career, one partially obscured by a brief tenure as dramatist for the King's Men. This is Beaumont's status in the early seventeenth-century world of amateur and professional playwrights. Chapman, Jonson, Beaumont, and Fletcher appear in G. E. Bentley's list of those twenty-two men "who wrote or collaborated in a dozen or more plays for the commercial theater" and who "may be considered more or less professional, at least for a certain period of years."[32] Marston's extant oeuvre falls short of Bentley's quota, but his name would otherwise fit comfortably here: his theatrical career was, like Beaumont's, relatively short, but from 1599 to 1608 he wrote steadily for the children's companies. Separating these men from the "attached" professionals like Heywood, Dekker, and Shakespeare—whose ranks Fletcher soon joined—is the pattern of their careers and the degree of their literary and economic independence from the stage. Respected poets as well as successful playwrights, their devotion to the commercial theater was either brief or intermittent.

Marston's inheritance probably freed him of the need either to write plays or to practice a career at law.[33] By the early 1600s he was a poet of sufficient stature to join Shakespeare, Jonson, and Chapman in contributing verses to Robert Chester's *Love's Martyr* (1601), a volume honoring the knighthood of a fellow Middle Templar. In 1606 Marston also wrote a Latin pageant for the royal welcome of King Christian IV of Denmark to London, and, in 1607, *An Entertainment* performed at Ashby for Alice, countess dowager of Derby. After renewed difficulties with the authorities in 1608, he joined the church and seems to have been displeased when an unauthorized edition of his plays appeared in 1633.

While neither Jonson nor Chapman turned so decisively from the stage, both developed other outlets for their talent and other means of economic support. Both seem to have been productive dramatists around 1600; Chapman was already a poet and translator of some repute. The rate at which Jonson wrote plays for the commercial theater declined after 1604, as he acquired various noble patrons and turned much of his theatrical effort to producing masques for James's and Prince Henry's courts. Although Jonson included plays among his *Works* and, alone among the Elizabethan and Jacobean aspirants to a laureate career, strove to make stage plays "count as signs of his literary eminence," he did not consider himself as primarily a professional dramatist.[34] Chapman's search for patronage was dogged by his habit of choosing dedicatees on the verge of royal disgrace, but for a time he enjoyed Prince Henry's support. He continued to write plays, but he also joined Beaumont in composing the 1613 Inns-of-Court wedding masques and was, presumably, devoting much of his time to completing his translations of Homer.

Beaumont's career seems to combine the pattern of Marston's with that of Jonson's and Chapman's. Although his financial status is unknown, Beaumont was a gentleman by birth and, like Marston (and Donne), a member of the Inns of Court. The 1613 masque commission suggests that he maintained connections with the Inner Temple, as does Moseley's apology in the 1647 folio for having failed to obtain a portrait of Beaumont "though I spared no enquirie in those *Noble Families* whence he was descended, as also among those Gentlemen that were his acquaintance when he was of the *Inner Temple*."[35] Beaumont moved easily in country as well as London circles; he wrote verse epistles and elegies for various prominent noblewomen and seems to have shared with Jonson the favor of Sir Philip Sidney's daughter Elizabeth, countess of Rutland.[36] John and his circle of poetic friends were available at Grace-Dieu, and Drayton's eclogue as well as Beaumont's first epistle to Jonson suggest that Francis's visits were literary as well as familial occasions. A few of Beaumont's poems are fashionably Donnian and libertine; one, "The Indifferent," seems to be his contribution to the literary game of celebrating male or female inconstancy.

Initially, Beaumont's career as playwright appears to have been that of an amateur. In 1608 he briefly turned "professional" and collaborated with Fletcher on at least six plays, half for the King's Men. Around 1613 Beaumont married a Kentish heiress, Ursula Isley of Sundridge Hall, and retired from the stage, presumably to live a gentleman's life on her estates until his death on 6 March 1616. He was survived by his wife and daughter Elizabeth, and by another daughter born posthumously, Frances. The pattern of Beaumont's career is thus, like Marston's, what Bentley calls "sharply divided," and it removes him even more decisively than Jonson's or Chapman's from the "category of the regular attached professionals."[37] It also departs from that of Fletcher, who, though perhaps earlier a client of the earl of Huntingdon, continued with the King's Men and succeeded Shakespeare as their principal dramatist.[38]

The attitude of Beaumont's early colleagues toward their profession, as well as the conduct of their careers, may in a different way help clarify Beaumont's retirement. In this period attitudes toward playwriting, and the traditionally low literary status of play texts, were just beginning to change. Though some also sought non-theatrical preferment, these quasi-professional dramatists were not loath to claim their stage work. Even before Jonson's 1616 folio, with its individual play dedications, efforts had been made to erase the stigma of print.[39] Most of Marston's plays were published soon after performance with his name or initials on the title page, one third with signed addresses to the reader. Dedication of quarto printings to particular individuals is rare before 1611, when Jonson offered *Catiline* to the earl of Pembroke, but *Volpone* had been publically dedicated to the universities of Oxford and Cambridge in 1607, and special presentation copies of *Cynthia's Revels* to William Camden and the countess of Bedford in 1601.[40]

It was precisely this group of poet-dramatists, not just Jonson, that set about to transform the status of plays. No longer ephemeral entertainments, printed plays began to assert their dignity as literature worthy of a nobleman's consideration.[41] Even before 1611, Fletcher added three dedications to *The Faithful Shepherdess*, and in 1608 Chapman offered his Byron plays (and perhaps in 1605 *All Fools*, though this is probably a Collier forgery) to Sir Thomas Walsingham and his son, a family that earlier had received Chapman's continuation of *Hero and Leander*. The trend is clear, though so also is a certain ambivalence: early dedications often reveal an uneasy awareness that they are unusual. While the status of dramatic compositions and their authors gained enormously by the publication of Jonson's and Shakespeare's plays in prestigious, expensive, folio form, Jonson was still being twitted in the 1630s for claiming plays as "works."[42]

Beaumont's practice suggests a different attitude and, perhaps, a different conception of himself. His plays are undedicated; indeed, with the exception of the 1613 masque and of verses for *The Metamorphosis of Tobacco* and for three Jonson plays and Fletcher's *Faithful Shepherdess*, nothing printed in Beaumont's lifetime bears his name.[43] While this period contains much anonymous publication, not all of it attributable to authorial reticence, Beaumont seems to have gone out of his way to avoid permanent association with his work. *Salmacis and Hermaphroditus* appeared anonymously in 1602, despite the fact that previous epyllia had been signed by their authors and in some cases considered worthy offerings to potential or present patrons. That his first play *The Woman Hater* was published a year after stage performance with no authorial attribution might occasion no remark, but circumstances surrounding the remaining early quartos suggest deliberate intention. Fletcher not only claimed authorship of his unsuccessful *Faithful Shepherdess*, he accompanied its publication with the full panoply of defense: signed dedications, a self-justificatory letter to the readers, and prefatory poems by his friends. Despite Beaumont's contribution to this venture, his own unsuccessful *Knight of the Burning Pestle* reached print in 1613 with no ascription and only a dedicatory letter to Robert Keysar, the manager of the Queen's Revels children who had provided the manuscript, from the publisher Walter Burre.

The first quarto of *Cupid's Revenge* (1615) carries only Fletcher's name; double attribution did not appear until 1630. The first play to claim both Beaumont and Fletcher as authors is *The Scornful Lady*, entered for publication thirteen days after Beaumont's death. Without claiming too much significance for these facts, it can perhaps be said that not only did Beaumont suddenly, for whatever reasons, retire from the stage shortly after having attained commercial popularity and the prestige of writing for London's foremost company, but even during those brief, productive years he seems to have kept a distance from his own professional activities.

Beaumont clearly, at least publicly, turned his back on the theater, but his motives remain mysterious. Although he received an apparently substantial inheritance when his brother Henry died in 1605, he may have adopted playwriting, and a quasi-professional commitment to the Revels Children and then the King's Men, out of financial necessity.[44] In such circumstances, Ursula Isley perhaps offered a desired opportunity to leave the loathed stage. Possibly, however, Beaumont remained economically independent and turned dramatist out of interest or because that is what his circle of friends did. Abandoning this alliance might indicate disillusionment with the theater, or with the ambitious London court-oriented society in which he moved, or even political disaffection for James and his rule. A general cultural malaise did seem to set in around the middle of James's reign, and Beaumont was not alone in breaking with his past at this time. On the other hand, his choice may have resulted simply from a gentleman's sense that marriage and the prospect of heirs necessitated a change of life-style.

Even the decisiveness of Beaumont's exit from London and his theatrical occupation remains unclear. He seems to have spared little attention to his former colleagues, but this impression may be inaccurate. The second verse letter to Jonson may date from this period, as may several plays in which Beaumont's hand has been traced in a few scenes: *Beggars' Bush, The Tragedy of Thierry and Theodoret,* and *Love's Pilgrimage.* Thus he may have left abruptly, like Marston and after a similarly brief career, or he may have severed his connection more slowly and, like Shakespeare, tapered off his activities by helping out with a few final collaborations. Different as their lives as men and dramatists appear, and despite the fact that Beaumont was twenty years Shakespeare's junior, both men retired at the same time from successful careers as playwrights for the King's Men. By a further quirk of literary history, three years later they died the same spring.

Creative Partnership

Precisely because of Beaumont and Fletcher's obvious debt to Shakespeare, it has been necessary to establish their close association with Jonson and the circle of playwrights connected with Blackfriars and the Revels Children. This rather hardy band, variously in trouble with both the authorities and their audiences, created not only a social but a theatrical milieu of a particular kind, one that overlapped in attitudes, even members, with the Inns-of-Court segment of its audience. Its chief playwrights were grounded in the fashion for satire at the turn of the century and eager to write plays both socially and politically topical. In theatrical terms iconoclastic, they encouraged formal experiment and favored challenging ideas as well as stage-spectacle. In this group Beaumont and Fletcher wrote their first plays; indeed, its esprit de corps may explain the decision to try their hands at playwriting. In 1608 the company was suppressed, its dramatists went their separate ways, and the theater was turned over to the King's Men. But the friendships established at the children's Blackfriars endured, and Beaumont and Fletcher carried with them its influence when they began writing for the adults.

Beaumont and Fletcher were, then, not simply Shakespearean mimics, inadequate to their task of cloning the master's style or content. They were not "after all . . . but an inferior sort of Shakespeares and Sidneys."[45] Neither, however, were they sons of Ben. Despite Jonson's late turn to English pastoral, Fletcher's *Faithful Shepherdess* could not be less Jonsonian. Of Beaumont's early independence we have slightly more evidence. Although he is commonly said to have learned dramatic construction from Jonson, *The Woman Hater* looks as much to Marston and satiric city comedy. Beaumont's verses for *Volpone* laud "the Art" which Jonson "alone / Hast taught our tongue, the rules of Time, of Place," but these are rules to which *The Woman Hater* does not itself adhere.[46] *The Knight of the Burning Pestle* may jokingly nod to Jonson's neo-classical "rules": however wandering its action and characters, the design of *The Knight* obeys the unities to the letter. Still, although this play also mocks two favorite Jonsonian targets—popular romance literature and the audience to which it appealed—neither its tone nor its form is Jonsonian. With *Cupid's Revenge,* the young collaborators turn decisively to romance, and exotic locales and improbable action become a constituent element of their dramaturgy. They also jettison for good the unities of time and place and turn their backs on Jonson's belief that in tragedy death should not be shown onstage.

Clearly, Jonson was an admired friend but no absolute mentor. Beaumont and Fletcher came to specialize in very un-Jonsonian kinds of plays—romantic tragicomedy and tragedy, comedies based on love rather than financial intrigue. In matters of form, too, they moved in different directions. Although Jonson's early comical satires—*Every Man out of His Humour* and *Cynthia's Revels,* for instance—tend to the loose multiplicity characteristic of Beaumont and Fletcher's tragicomedies, Jonson developed a structure in which intricate plotting rests on a Plautine foundation. When Beaumont and Fletcher seek an ordering principle for comedy's multitude of incidents, they usually adopt the traditional Elizabethan double plot as solution.

Not surprisingly, as members of the first generation to begin writing under the influence of a substantial Shakespearean corpus, Beaumont and Fletcher turn to this proven and popular dramatist as well as to their own early colleagues. A variable but evident debt appears in even the noncollaborative plays written for the children's troupes; later, and continuing after Beaumont's departure, Shakespearean speeches, characters, situations—even whole plays—get recycled in the works of the "Beaumont and Fletcher" canon. Shakespeare's impress may from the beginning have been a personal one. We do not know when these men became acquainted, or whether Beaumont and Fletcher witnessed the "wit-combats" between Shakespeare and Jonson so humorously described by Thomas Fuller as between "a Spanish great galleon and an English man-of-war" reenacting the Armada's defeat: "Master Jonson (like the former) was built far higher in learning; solid, but slow in his performances. Shakespeare, . . . lesser in bulk, but lighter in sailing, could turn with all tides, tack about and take advantage of all winds by the quickness of his wit and invention."[47] By about 1609 Beaumont and Fletcher were writing for Shakespeare's company, and in 1613 Fletcher collaborated on Shakespeare's final contributions to the

King's Men's repertoire (indeed, borrowing for *The Two Noble Kins-men* from the second antimasque in Beaumont's *Masque of the Inner Temple and Gray's Inn*).

Beaumont and Fletcher's theatrical background thus encompasses two apparently dissimilar traditions: one associated with the children's theaters, where comical satire and satiric city comedy predominated; one with Shakespeare and the kinds of plays popular at the Globe. To such bifold dramatic authority Beaumont and Fletcher brought a talent for innovation: however unpopular with their first audiences, *The Knight of the Burning Pestle* and *The Faithful Shepherdess* were boldly original. These playwrights learned from their early association with the Blackfriars environment, but equally important, within it they found the freedom to experiment. Initial failure led to collaboration and fresh approaches. The joint plays turn to creative adaptation, first of Sidney's prose romance, then of more specifically theatrical materials. They adjusted elements of their particular private-theater background to their fondness for Shakespearean motifs and the demand, after 1608, for plays also suitable to a popular, public stage. Out of the inventive ways in which they merged their dual theatrical heritage, the Beaumont-Fletcher partnership developed its distinctive and influential dramaturgy.

Chapter Two

Early Comedy

Tantalizing Hints: *Love's Cure*

We do not know how soon after moving to London and the Inns of Court Beaumont met Fletcher, or when they decided to try composing plays. Apparently it was early, for they seem to have worked together before writing independently the plays whose commercial failure sent them back to the collaborative drawing board. The first evidence of partnership indicates little more than its existence: the remnants of a Beaumont-Fletcher play beneath what has come down to us as *Love's Cure, or The Martial Maid.*

The nature, date, and provenance of the original collaboration must remain conjectural. *Love's Cure,* first printed in the 1647 folio, has been heavily revised by Philip Massinger, probably after Fletcher's death, along the lines of a Spanish play first printed in Valencia in 1625, *La fuerza de la costumbre,* and of Leonard Digges's translation of the Spanish romance *Gerardo* (1622). The main plot of *Love's Cure* is thus Massinger's, as may be the Spanish locale. Internal evidence, however, suggests that in some form this play existed a good twenty years earlier. References to the seige of Ostend (1601–4) would have been most pertinent then, and they also suggest that the original play's historical setting was a contemporary one.[1] Lazarillo, a braggart soldier with a hungry page in Middleton's *Blurt, Master Constable* (1602, Paul's boys), probably inspired his namesake in *Love's Cure.* Bobadilla, a servant in *Love's Cure,* may borrow his name from Jonson's captain in *Every Man in His Humour* (1598, Chamberlain's Men) and his comic development from Chapman's *Gentleman Usher* and *Sir Giles Goosecap.*[2] If we accept Cyrus Hoy's distribution of scenes, Beaumont and Fletcher remain in the farcical humor associated with these characters as well as in the low-comic plot, where a cobbler, a botcher (mender), and a smith briefly become the Watch under a corrupt constable's direction.[3]

Love's Cure's aristocratic main plot turns on sex reversal and transvestism: a brother brought up by his mother at home as a girl;

a sister whose father raised her as the subtitle's "martial maid" and
who has just fought heroically at Ostend when the play opens. The
Beaumont-Fletcher original may have dealt with similar themes and,
if Hoy is correct, Massinger used more of their work than just the
comic citizens. Certainly scenes of sexual confusion, of passion ov-
ermastering reason, and of nature pitted against nurture figure prominently in their later plays. Hoy assigns to Beaumont and Fletcher
at least one of the main plot's comic scenes, and to Beaumont some
of *Love's Cure*'s most vivid speeches.

Beaumont seems largely responsible for the sideplot involving
Vitelli, the romantic hero, and his unfaithful mistress Malroda.
When the corrupt constable bargains to become Malroda's bawd,
he proudly defends his free choice of evil. Justified by a "vicious"
world, the constable's "chiefe felicity / Is wealth the nurse of sensuality," and he defines his goal with a gross vigor worthy of Marston: "he that mainly labours to be rich / Must scratch great scabs,
and claw a Strumpets itch" (3.1.83–86). More interesting, in light
of the young playwrights' later work, is Vitelli's answer to Malroda's
tirade against him as one who first corrupted her and now wishes
to discard her. This passage, too, is probably Beaumont's, and it
is the only time an aristocratic character connected with the main
plot deserts its high-flown rhetoric and pat love-versus-honor conflict to explore fundamental human complexity. Publicly Vitelli
tries to shift all blame back on his accuser, but in a lengthy Chap-
manesque "aside" he considers with horrified awe his own contradictory nature: he can "with rationall discourse sometimes / Advance
my spirit into Heaven, before / 'T has shook hands with my body";
yet the power of lust forces him to "blindly / Suffer my filthy flesh
to master it, / With sight of such faire fraile beguiling objects"
(3.3.58–62).

If the original Beaumont-Fletcher collaboration underlying *Love's
Cure* dates from ca. 1605, Beaumont may here reflect an awareness
of contemporary explorations of this dilemma as well as echo his
colleagues' styles. Rational man's helplessness in the face of powerful
urges, a traditional theme revivified by Montaigne's recently translated essays, becomes a central concern in plays like Shakespeare's
Measure for Measure, Marston's *Dutch Courtesan*, and Chapman's *Widow's Tears*. The situation in which two men visit the same whore—
herself jealous of the suitor who deserts her for a socially acceptable
marriage—suggests Beaumont may have had the Malheureux-

Franceschina-Frevill triangle of *The Dutch Courtesan* explicitly in mind when composing Vitelli's scene.

The Woman Hater

The Woman Hater appeared anonymously in 1607 as having been "Acted by the Children of Paules" (most likely in the first half of 1606, before the summer plague restrictions on playing and that troupe's collapse). In first performance it was probably Beaumont's alone; yet since recent scholars agree that some scenes in the printed text are either original Fletcher or heavily revised by him, the young friends apparently still consulted each other.[4] The way in which these scenes are distributed, however, suggests that *The Woman Hater* is Beaumont's in conception and, largely, in execution. It remains the first dramatic composition that can be discussed as his.

Critics generally agree that in the private theaters' "comedies of humour and . . . satires Beaumont found his model for his first play,"[5] though we should also note the impress of Shakespeare, the one purely public-theater playwright whose influence marks both Beaumont's and Fletcher's work from the beginning. In fact, *The Woman Hater* offers its audience a curious, though quite skillful, mixture. Verbally fresh and witty, frequently original (and when not, often inventively adaptive), it demonstrates Beaumont's grasp of stageworthy material and comic pacing. With more success than might be expected in an early work, it tries to hold together its multiple and largely heterogeneous plots. It also abounds in recognizable character types and dramatic devices as well as in direct borrowings and parodied speeches whose originals at least some auditors would recognize. In *The Woman Hater* Beaumont explores both his individual talent and the traditions familiar to him and to his audience; he also begins to establish the sophisticated ironic tone, as well as the bold use of his heritage, that mark his best work.

From the beginning the play openly recognizes—even capitalizes on—its immediate dramatic environment. The prologue mocks its author as well as its audience, and much of its humor assumes some theatrical experience. Plays of the late 1590s and early 1600s made frequent, often inventive, use of theatrically self-conscious Inductions and lengthy, explanatory prologues, and, of course, such prefatory speeches and scenes continued to appear on both public and

private stages. Yet Beaumont now declares that, "Gentlemen, Inductions are out of date, and a Prologue in Verse is as stale, as a
blacke Velvet Cloake, and a Bay Garland" (prol. 1–2). Fashionably
impudent in itself, the assertion becomes wholly tongue-in-cheek
if Beaumont had already begun planning *The Knight of the Burning
Pestle*. There, the "out of date" Induction expands to dominate the
play.

The Woman Hater's prologue goes wittily about its preparatory
function. It proclaims not only what today's play is but, to forestall
criticism, what it is not. Audiences at the private theaters were
frequently accused of intolerance for any but a few favored kinds of
drama, and Beaumont ostentatiously offers to outflank such critics
by announcing that he will eschew the usual "lascivious Scenes"
and satire of particular individuals. Such catch-penny devices are
dismissed as unethical and "vile." The possibility of informers with
"Table bookes" in the audience also renders satiric jibes foolhardy
in practical terms, as Beaumont acknowledges in his timely wish
to avoid the punishment that threatened the authors of Blackfriars'
Eastward Ho (1605): "the deare losse of his eares" (prol. 11–12).
Unlike Jonson's usual practice, however, Beaumont in his prologue
claims no didactic justification for his play; like Marston, Beaumont
defends himself by emphasizing his work's status as entertainment.

Further clarification follows. *The Woman Hater* lacks the fully
developed tragicomic pattern of Beaumont and Fletcher's later collaborations, since real danger does not threaten until late in act 5,
but it already "wants deaths . . . yet brings some neere it."[6] Beaumont knows the assault on Oriana's honor will strain expectations
created by earlier comic developments; he admits he "dare not call
it Comedie, or Tragedie; 'tis perfectly neyther: A Play it is" (prol.
12–13).[7] Forewarned, we are also reassured: this "Play" will lean
toward comedy, for it was "meant to make you laugh." And, though
it may lack personal satire, Beaumont promises that in some things
The Woman Hater will follow the "common Roade: a Duke there is,
and the Scene lyes in *Italy,* as those two thinges lightly wee never
misse" (prol. 17–18). The prologue closes with a final sly, general
guarantee. However modish, this play will not indulge in satiric
city comedy's "ordinarie and over-worne trade of jeasting at Lordes
and Courtiers, and Citizens," for its author claims "hee did never
thinke, but that a Lord borne might bee a wise man, and a Courtier
an honest man" (prol. 19–20, 23–26).

Having given its warnings and defined the audience as one to share its "in" jokes, *The Woman Hater* takes little care to follow its prologue's disclaimers. Satiric thrusts at common targets pepper Beaumont's play: new knights and up-start courtiers, royal favorites, government informers. It also jests evenhandedly—in this, perhaps, unusually—at "Lordes and Courtiers, and Citizens," for though its lords "borne" may prove finally "wise" and happy, a good deal of noble folly is exposed along the way. Indeed, in the play's first scene, trying to guess why the Duke is up at four in the morning, his sycophantic courtiers suggest that he intends to cure "corruptions in the common wealth" and, perhaps, "to walke the publique streetes disguised, / To see the streetes disorders" (1.1.12, 24–25). The allusion to other disguised princes by contrast helps to characterize this play's ruler; unlike Middleton's Phoenix or Shakespeare's Vincentio, Beaumont's Duke cares only for private, romantic matters. Wise enough to see through his flatterers and young enough to enjoy toying with them, he encourages their ingratiating suggestions to increase the shock of his real, most un-"waightie," concern: "a wench" (1.1.29).

The rather flat-footed humor of 1.1 establishes the play as, at least in part, romantic comedy and, despite a lengthy disquisition on court flattery, the Duke's primary function as lover rather than statesman. The crudity of "wench" melts under the Duke's raptures, for, unbeknown to her, he adores Count Valore's sister Oriana. A Petrarchan enthusiast, the Duke sees her as a maid to whom princes must "lowly kneele," one who holds sway not only over his life but over "the generall fate / Of all mortalitie" (1.1.39–40). The main plot will move toward uniting these would-be lovers; obstacles to comedy's nuptial denouement come not from parental opposition but from the malice of the play's title character, the woman-hating General Gondarino. The Duke, Oriana, and Gondarino come together when Oriana, eager to experience fashionable society, ignores her cynical brother's advice and leaves home to gain "fine sights at the Court" (1.3.11); on her way, she is driven by a hailstorm to seek shelter in Gondarino's house. Gondarino's passionate antifeminist suspicions are stirred by her sudden visit and by the subsequent arrival of the Duke, fleeing the same storm. Seeing a conspiracy of lovers and prodigious sexual misconduct everywhere, Gondarino thinks he is being used as their pander and gets his revenge by asserting to the Duke that he has himself enjoyed the "strumpet."

The surprising initial credulity of Oriana's brother as well as the Duke gives way to more reasonable doubts. To make good his claims, Gondarino has Oriana moved to another house, in reality a brothel. He tells Oriana he will clear her name; he in fact intends to use her new abode to convince the Duke of her typically feminine looseness and hypocrisy. When the Duke and Valore prove more resistant to mere verbal slander than he had expected, Gondarino urges them to put her to the extreme test themselves. They do, and they watch "above" while one of the Duke's companions threatens Oriana with death unless she submit to his lust. Oriana, of course, chooses death before dishonor, shames the men, and demonstrates the purity and nobility of mind that qualify her to become the Duke's bride. Her immediate reward lies in selecting Gondarino's punishment, and the torment she devises turns the play from its brush with mortality back toward farce. Bound to a chair, Gondarino must endure being "wooed" and fondled by the ladies summoned to aid Oriana.

The Oriana-Gondarino-Duke story provides the play's main narrative thread, and in it Beaumont makes intelligent use of common materials. He opens with what looks to be a familiar dramatic premise, the "disguised prince" gambit, and then turns it, like a good joke, to a different end. This plot's comedy and motive force derive from Gondarino's woman-hating obsession. The idea for a misogynist central character, his verbal indictment of all women and final punishment at their hands, may have been inspired by the denouement of the popular prose romance *Aurelio e Isabella*.[8] Gondarino is also a recognizable humour character who builds on the development and continued popularity of such figures in numerous private-theater plays. Yet Gondarino is so vividly drawn, his torment under Oriana's wooing so acute, and the malice to which his egoism drives him so extreme, that he escapes being merely derivitive and seems as much an "original" (even perhaps precursor of Morose in Jonson's *Epicoene*) as a copy of what others had already done. Gondarino hates all aspects of women, but especially their unstoppable verbosity, and one of the play's funniest scenes portrays his growing hysteria under the garrulous old Country Gentlewoman's solicitations for help in petitioning the Duke (4. 1). On the darker side, a disturbing unnaturalness underlies his ruling humour and makes Gondarino (as it does Morose) more than a simple comic type.

Gondarino's maneuvering dominates the aristocratic main plot, but this is only one of the drama's many actions. Beaumont uses another humour character as the nucleus of his primary subplot. Here Lazarello's obsessional desire to dine on the head of an umbrana fish propels him into the streets of Milan in a determined, repeatedly frustrated, search for this gustatory nonpareil. Beaumont's treatment of Lazarello may owe something to the farcical subplot of Marston's *Dutch Courtesan* (a play perhaps already raided for *Love's Cure*), but the story of Lazarello's peripatetic quest derives principally from one of the lighter works by the Italian humanist historian Paulo Giovio. This sixteenth-century doctor, bishop of Nocera and member of the Medici popes' "Roman Academy," is today best known as father of the Renaissance portrait gallery and encourager of Vasari; his contemporary fame rested on his *Historiarum sui temporis libri XLV*. England also appreciated his essay on mottoes and devices (translated by Samuel Daniel, 1585), *A Short Treatise upon the Turkes Chronicles* ("Englished" by Peter Ashton, 1546), and, apparently, *De Piscibus romanis* (available in numerous Latin editions as well as Carlo Zancaruolo's Italian translation of 1560).[9] Giovio's anecdotal treatise "On Roman Fishes" includes the story of Tamisius, a witty parasite given to gluttony, who seeks the head of an umbrana fish. Each "owner" of the fish head gives it away as gift or payment for debt; with Herculean labor Tamisius follows it all over Rome before he finally partakes of his goal at the house of the last recipient, a harlot.

Giovio's treatise makes an unusual source, given Beaumont's (and Fletcher's) later preferences, but its domestication illustrates Beaumont's talent for refashioning disparate borrowed materials into strikingly fresh creations. Native antecedents include Lazarello's name and association with hunger, probably first taken from Middleton for *Love's Cure*. He is salvaged from that apparent failure (no record of performance exists), advanced in status to courtier-parasite, and expanded on Giovio's model into the nucleus of an extended dramatic action (indeed, one developed almost as fully as the aristocratic love plot). The instinct proved a wise one: the 1648 quarto's second issue (1649) reflects his popularity, for it adds the subtitle "The Hungry Courtier."[10]

Beaumont also capitalizes on Giovio's hint of Herculean effort: Lazarello's search is raised to the mock-heroic level and linguistically embellished with allusions to contemporary tragedies. Most of *The Woman Hater*'s funniest parodies sprout from Lazarello's mouth. Hamlet with his ghostly father, Antony's speech on joining Cleopatra in the Elysian fields, Othello's "farewell" to his profession (developed, after the initial allusion, on the verbal model of Slitgut's "farewell" to the horn in *Eastward Ho,* 4.1), all get recycled to fit Lazarello's passionate dedication to his beloved fish head. This endlessly verbal gourmand presses into service most of the (outmoded) literary languages of his day—Petrarchanism, Euphuism, the rhetoric of chivalric romance. He may be a classical parasite in type, but he has been brought very much up to date in his speeches.

In adapting Giovio's anecdote, Beaumont develops links between his apparently dissimilar primary plots. Their physical connection is artificial, engineered by the constant removal of the fish head to locales where other characters gather, for their own reasons, until all arrive at the brothel's denouement. Thematic parallels arise from Lazarello's monomaniacal determination. His humour controls all his responses, and in this he resembles Gondarino in the main plot. Funny and harmless fool that he is, Lazarello also helps to deflect, or control, emotions aroused by the frustrated Gondarino's vicious revenge on Oriana. If Gondarino's disproportionate hatred threatens frightening consequences, Lazarello's equally unbalanced piscatory devotion helps right the play's comic balance.

Structurally useful as a low-comic parallel to Gondarino, Lazarello's humour relates him in other ways to the romantic plot. Beaumont also sees Lazarello's potential as foil to the Duke, and he elaborates his source's obsession into an amorous quest. When overcome by emotion, Lazarello erupts into "inspired" verse, and these moments are frequently juxtaposed to the Duke's own effusions. Beaumont sets up this echo-effect early. The Duke closes 1.1 and his prose discourse on flatterers with an abrupt shift to poetry and to love: a description of "faire *Thetis*" who "hath undon the bares / To *Phebus* teame," prefaces an invocation to the "bright *Paphian* Queene" to inspire Oriana's "heart with love, or lessen my desire" (1.1.84–92). The next scene opens with a characterizing soliloquy in which Lazarello envies princes the abundance and variety of their tables; almost immediately, he bursts into his own lengthy invocation: "O thou Goddesse of plentie / Fill me this day with some rare delicates . . ." (1.2.17–30). This travesty of the Lord's Prayer introduces an idolatry that soon develops along extravagantly Petrarchan lines. Lazarello repeatedly compares the fish head to a coveted woman and his adoring pursuit to a knightly lover's service. Eager to prove his heroic worth, he wishes his object were "set downe in the owter court, / And all the Guard about it in a ring,

/ With their knives drawne," and "I to be let loose, onely in my shirt, / To trie by valor" the right to "my deere Saint" (3.2.48–53, 76). When the Mercer tries to detain him for the "wrong" dinner, Lazarello actually draws his rapier to fight his way offstage. The parodies of Othello and Antony fall into place as the comically "appropriate" language for this deranged courtier's anguish when he finds his love has again been spirited away.

The aristocratic plot's obsession with Oriana's chastity also finds its parodic counterpart in the Lazarello action. Apparently seeking Oriana, the Duke to his surprise discovers her at Gondarino's house and becomes immediately suspicious of the idealized mistress of his heart. Lazarello applies the same "courtly" sexual morality to his beloved. Pursuing his quarry, he ecstatically anticipates seeing his "loves face, the chast virgin head / Of a deere Fish, yet pure and undeflowred." The object of his affections is precious because "Not known of man," untouched by "Pandars" or "Court hand"; as a devoted lover, he can only pray that "it be thought lawfull then for me, / To crop the flower of thy virginitie" (1.3.217–28). Lazarello's ardor remains a skewed version of a romantic hero's. He protests later to Count Valore that his love is both "gentle" and "chast"; he seeks his goal not "For any mallice, or for privat ends," but as one moved by "pure love, and free from servile lust" (2.1.357–66).

Both noble-minded lovers finally attain their goals at Madonna Julia's brothel. Both undergo trial—the Duke by the suspicions that lead him to test Oriana, Lazarello by the bombastic transport he terms "a jealous furie" but his page more accurately characterizes as a condition in which "your owne imaginations have made you mad" (4.2.146–48). Analogies between Lazarello and the Duke must, of course, break down. Lazarello marries a whore to gain his end; he is thus finally paired not with his prince but with the Mercer, who has also married a prostitute. Oriana accepts death as the price of refusing whoredom and wins a Duke. Yet as amorists Beaumont has linked Lazarello and the Duke—in attitude, rhetoric, and jealous imagination. For most of the play Lazarello provides an hilarious running commentary on the romantic plot's high-minded concern with love, honor, and the proper relation between the sexes.

If in its two most developed actions *The Woman Hater* hedges on the prologue's denial of "over-worne jeasting at Lordes and Courtiers," its other two plots add Citizens to the play's democratic list of targets. Though only briefly sketched, the story of the Mercer's gulling offers a theatrically familiar satiric portrait of contemporary urban life. Links with the main plot and subplot appear rather forced. With some straining the Mercer, too, could be said to be in love, for he passionately reveres and pursues learning (which he seems to equate with sorcery, divination, and a generally mysterious but desired control over events). Appealing to this folly by posing as a scholar-magician, the Pandar promises access to both knowledge and an heiress; by a trick he secures the Mercer's marriage to one of Madonna Julia's prostitutes. The Mercer's house also provides another destination for the umbrana head, and his gulling another set of characters to increase act 5's confusion at the brothel. A less mechanical connection lies in the Mercer's contribution to the final mood of reconciliation and fulfillment, for his essential good humor, like Lazarello's, helps balance Gondarino's malice and final refusal to accept his proper place in society. Upset that his scraps of learning have not prevented a humiliating marriage, the Mercer yet chooses to believe Francessina's declaration that she intends to be a good wife, and he determines to take the whole fraud as "good honest mirth." He promises the wedding feast will include her friends as well as his; he even extracts from his defeat a timely moral: the "chiefe note of a Scholler . . . is to governe his passions" (5.3.22–23).

This citizen is kindly dealt with by the play, convicted of silliness but not of malice or baseness. The other tangential subplot treats more harshly of political folly in both citizens and courtiers. The intelligencers show themselves ambitious for power, money, and influence; they enjoy being feared by their neighbors. By profession informers feed off the state, twisting scraps of overheard conversation into proof of treason, and Valore uses such general moral terms when in 5.2 he dismisses them from his service and the play's happy ending. Yet the introduction of real-world judgments and consequences works against the comic decorum of this plot's generally farcical treatment. Earlier, in the eavesdropping scene Valore has for his own amusement set up, the intelligencers wrench disconnected phrases into a plan whereby Lazarello, who only wants his fish head, intends to "burne the Palace, kill the Duke, and poison his privie Counsell" (3.2.106–7). The comedy of their extravagant misprision seems modeled on Dogberry and the Watch in Shakespeare's *Much Ado about Nothing,* a popular aspect of that play.[11] A conventional emphasis also determines Beaumont's treatment of

Lucio, the man to whom these bumbling spies report. In 1.1 merely a sycophantic companion to the Duke, Lucio burgeons into a pompous would-be statesman. In 5.1 and 5.2 Lucio becomes a "type" whose most famous representative is Polonius, though his self-important verbosity and confident inversions of justice probably draw more immediately on Chapman's fatuous Governor in *The Widow's Tears* and, possibly, on Marston's "all wise" Duke Gonzago in *The Fawn.*

The different judgments awarded at the play's end to Lucio and to the intelligencers mark the failure of this plot's complete integration. Like the Mercer, Lucio remains a comic figure. Another harmless fool rather than the dangerous, self-deluded politician he would be if he could, he is let off lightly, "dispatch[ed]" to his study to continue his labors against the state's overthrow. Securely wrapped in his own self-esteem, Lucio remains oblivious to the mockery in Valore's dismissal: "Goe, and mayest thou knocke downe Treason like an Oxe" (5.2.110–24). The unprincipled informers at times escape their comic "type," however, and Valore's righteous condemnation in 1.3 and especially 5.2 introduces an unexpectedly sharp, topically satiric, note that unsettles the resolution of this miniplot and, to some extent, that of the play itself.

It is just this astringent tone, most prominently associated with Valore, that roughens *The Woman Hater*'s smooth surface yet also connects it with some of the more interesting—and troubling—satiric comedies of Beaumont's contemporaries. Of course Gondarino, too, threatens any consistently light, comic mood. The ferocity of his passion and the vicious stratagem to which it drives him push beyond the usual humour character's merely eccentric egotism. Yet the play holds Gondarino at a distance. To the other characters, he is not one of "us," and—like Shylock or Malvolio or Morose—once outflanked by the group Gondarino can be expelled and forgotten. Through Valore, Beaumont makes self-consciously part of his play observations that question the integrity of the very characters the generic form asks us to accept and admire.

To the extent possible with four plots, Valore dominates the play. Beaumont has made him nearly ubiquitous: central to no plot, he is affixed to three. Valore sets the intelligencers in motion; he travels about town with Lazarello, ostensibly to introduce him to the umbrana head's current owner; he advises Oriana to avoid the court and, as both brother to the heroine and privy counsellor to the

Duke, he plausibly appears at Gondarino's house and again for the
testing of Oriana at the brothel. Although Gondarino and Lazarello
have occasional soliloquies, Valore's meditations seem often to be
addressed directly to us; they draw us into the play while fostering
our acceptance of his viewpoint and centrality. With the exception
of the main plot's protagonists, Valore also seems to direct much
of the play's action. He "presents" characters to us (as with his
capsule descriptions of Lazarello and then the intelligencers in 1.3),
tells others what to do or where to go, and finally "dispatch[es]"
his actors, dismissing Lucio and the informers from the play and
urging his sister to accept the Duke's sudden proposal.

As mocking observer and directorial intelligence, Valore resembles the witty young gentlemen—satirists, pranksters, successful
manipulators—who preside over *The Widow's Tears* and *The Dutch
Courtesan*. They denounce many of the same fashionable satiric targets; more important, they seem to share a fundamental cynicism
about human nature, and their running commentary darkens the
plays they inhabit. In 1.3 real disgust fuels Valore's vitriolic description of the court's selfish, brainless ladies and worthless non-
entities jacked-up into knights and gentlemen. Yet he also accepts
this world and his own participation in it; he has employed the
blood-sucking informers before. Here, as with Marston's and Chapman's young satiric-commentators, the keen penetration of others
that lends his observations force turns back to undermine his own
stature as moral center.

Valore deflates himself in 1.3. His scathing account of the court,
over which as privy counsellor he in part presides, leads smoothly
into his shrewd analyses of Lazarello and the intelligencers; it does
not prepare us for his setting these characters in motion, or for the
explanation which follows. Left alone and "idle," he analyzes himself
as a bored young gentleman who needs external amusement. Unable
to occupy his own time, since no "Scholler," he needs not only
others' company but their envy to satisfy his ego (1.3.54–75). Valore
closes 1.3 with what may also be the play's rationale, but after such
admissions it sounds rather hollow: "This day I am for fooles, I am
all theirs. . . . But for a foole, our wisdom oft amends, / As
enemies doe teach us more then friends." He confesses to preferring
"base company" in which he can, without "much labour," appear
the "wisest ever" (1.3.229–36).

Valore also qualifies our acceptance of the Duke as romantic hero.

If Lazarello provides a low-comic parallel to the Duke's pursuit of his virgin mistress, as more nearly equal in social status and attitude Valore represents a different kind of foil. The expository opening presents a telling sequence: the Duke toys with his foolish companions, then offers a remarkably acute—and self-serving—analysis of why princes tolerate, even advance, their flatterers. He seems to mock his own "care" for his subjects and for the business of ruling well. This impression is not dropped, left behind as a bit of incidental political satire; instead, it is reintroduced with Count Valore in 1.3. In complacently accepting his own self-analysis, Valore repeats the Duke. Valore's concern with present amusement makes us wonder if the Duke's decision to walk the early morning streets as a lover is any more serious than the guessing-games he plays with his flatterers.

These young aristocrats exhibit a surprising degree of self-knowledge, but their cool analyses produce no results. Both prefer to play with those they should discipline. Valore's principled skepticism leads him to share his prince's doubts about Oriana, though the Duke has at least a jealous lover's excuse to mistrust a woman he does not really know. Indeed, Valore immediately suspects the Duke, too, for he assumes him capable of assignations and bastard children. Imagining his sister as the partner in such a degrading liaison, while momentarily shocking, presents no real difficulty. Valore believes Oriana's protestations only on the rational grounds that she has just met the Duke for the first time and is not behaving as a mistress. In 1.1 the Duke carefully delineates his concerns as private, romantic, and apolitical, but he does not remain beyond the audience's censure.[12]

Despite the superior "commentator" status Valore seems to claim, then, neither he nor the Duke is presented as the play's spokesman or moral center. One critical description of the play—a "Jonsonian comedy of humours that satirizes the prodigality of the aristocracy"[13]—seems inadequate as a full account of this multifaceted drama and its democratically distributed mockery. Yet *The Woman Hater* does at times rather disconcertingly remind us that its carefree laughter rests on the responsible figures' neglect of the duty they know accompanies privilege. Valore at last properly dismisses the intelligencers from his service, and the Duke, though unable to trust Oriana's integrity without visible proof, finally offers her his admiration as well as his hand in marriage. These gestures

help create the appropriate happy ending, but they are not introduced as evidence of any fundamental new maturity of character.

The Woman Hater never becomes a serious political play or, after
its opening scenes, even a consistently satiric one. To a considerable
degree it maintains its light comic tone. The whole Lazarello plot
receives farcical treatment, and its well-paced, inventive elaboration
of an already fantastical premise provides one through-line of increasing hilarity. The threat of death-or-dishonor appears only as a
final surprise thrill, and it is confined to seventy lines of a scene
that closes with reconciliation and the Duke's proposal of marriage
(5.4). The main plot also wisely relegates both Valore and the Duke
to peripheral status. Beaumont partially circumvents the effect of
their characterization by concentrating instead on the struggle between Oriana and Gondarino. In the central battle of the sexes
Beaumont exploits the comic potential of inverting conventional
roles. Here Gondarino's antifeminist obsession finds its match in
the intelligent, self-confident, persistent Oriana. Although the
framing sexual morality is relentlessly conservative, and she is finally
outmaneuvered and trapped into a traditional virgin-martyr role,
Oriana for most of the play looks toward the self-reliant, mischievous
women of later Beaumont-Fletcher comedies and, ultimately, to the
Restoration heroine they helped to fashion.[14]

Oriana wants to see the court, not merely hear her brother denounce it, and this willful curiosity leads her to pick Gondarino's
house as shelter. She wants to hear for herself this local character's
famous rudeness to women. Oriana's conduct throughout demonstrates an independent, commonsensical idea of virtue and what
constitutes true propriety.[15] When her waiting woman suspects they
have been housed in a place "no better then it should be," Oriana
insists on plain speaking rather than coy euphemism: "Out with it,
'tis not true modesty to feare to speak that thou doest thinke"
(4.2.276, 279–80). She values personal integrity over social form
and thinks honesty the guardian of virtue. They may indeed be in
"one of these same bawdy houses," but " 'Tis no matter wench,
wee are warme in it; keepe thou thy minde pure, and upon my
word, that name will doe thee no hurt" (4.2.281–84). In this belief
Oriana is, of course, naively idealistic; in a play so strongly influenced by the ethos of satiric city comedy her directness and adherence
to principles rather than the accidentals of "proper" behavior is
singular. When Gondarino, the Duke, and Valore arrive to test her,

they come heavily disguised because "this house . . . is not to bee visited in our own shapes" (4.2.288–89).

While others depend on conventional social responses to what "fate"—or the plot—offers, both Oriana and Gondarino imaginatively use and manipulate circumstances. Gondarino sees how to turn the Duke's sudden jealousy against Oriana and, though tormented by the Old Woman petitioner's garrulity, he transforms his reluctant support (to shut her up) into proof that he does not categorically hate women and should be trusted. While Gondarino's opportunism remains close to the conventional villain's, Oriana invents a new code of conduct. Faced with his slanderous opinion of her whole sex, she takes the initiative to punish him with his own antifeminist stereotype: she becomes talkative, amorous, aggressive. She turns upside-down the tradition of male wooing and instead chases Gondarino all over his own house, forcing upon him the language of courtly compliment and the threat of her undying devotion. Thus in some of the play's funniest sections, Oriana's self-conscious violations of decorum in language and behavior parallel and intensify the comic effect of outrageous disproportion in the Lazarello subplot.

The Oriana-Gondarino struggle offers well-turned comedy of manners and includes a (lightly held) moral. Although Oriana determines to stick with "this fellow, I will torment him to madnes" (2.1.397), her aims go beyond her own—or her sex's—revenge for his calumny. She intends her shocking antics to restore Gondarino to his natural role. Her own impropriety will force him back into what Nature "first entended" him for: "A man" (3.1.80–81). This salutary comic purging of one excess by its opposite also determines the punishment the Duke allows Oriana to dictate at the play's end.

The act 5 baiting ostensibly repeats in wittily exaggerated form the pursuit and wooing of act 3, and it would doubtless prove very funny staged; yet the circumstances have altered. Between these episodes, events have darkened the play's tone. Oriana's playful independence offers a healthy alternative to both Gondarino's and the Duke's conventional (though theoretically opposed) stereotypes of women, but she prevails with no one. Gondarino is not cured of his unnatural hatred and self-sequestration. Instead, he is driven to the stratagem by which he hopes publicly to destroy her. Unable to see Oriana's bold behavior as innocent or to believe her frank declarations, the Duke agrees with Gondarino that she must be subjected to the ultimate test, put "too'it without hope or pittie" (5.2.52). Representing two sides of the same sexual code, Gondarino and the Duke between them force Oriana to become—or demonstrate that she is willing to be—a woman on their terms.

The open world of comic possibilities and individual freedom suddenly narrows to a choice between dishonor and death in what Oriana calls "my tragedy" (5.4.74). She proves she shares the Duke's ideas of purity and honor and wins him as her reward, but we see how vulnerable and ineffectual are the refreshing qualities that provided us with such fun in act 3. And because Oriana has not been able to purge Gondarino's humour, has indeed hardened his dislike into vicious hatred, the final punishment for his slander becomes merely punishment, Oriana's and the ladies' revenge. The scene is one of public humiliation, and society's representatives join ranks to ridicule and expel the man who will not join them.

That Gondarino deserves worse than he gets, that his fate hilariously suits his limited "character," does not wholly obscure his tormentors' cruelty or the analogy with bear-baiting that the stage action suggests: tied to a chair, he must face the ladies who "fall off in couples" and "charge" him (5.4.132–33). He asks for the dignity of banishment; instead he gets a lady on his knee, ruffling his hair and scolding him as she would a child. The *Women Hater* finds its way to a happy ending, but the prologue's description of it as neither comedy nor tragedy is not inaccurate. Its resolution remains clouded by disturbing intellectual and moral ambiguities as well as by the briefly introduced threat of death.

Chapter Three
The Knight of the Burning Pestle

Literary and Dramatic Setting

Despite some disturbing undercurrents, *The Woman Hater*'s tone is largely controlled by its witty, mischievous heroine and comic exploration of the battle between the sexes. In the amatory skirmishes between rakish young gentlemen and well-born ladies of independent minds and means, we can see the model for several light romantic comedies written with Fletcher for both public and private companies: those to which Beaumont may have contributed a few scenes—*The Captain* (1609–12, King's Men?) and *Beggars' Bush* (1612–14, King's Men?)[1]—as well as those in which he participated more fully—*The Coxcomb* (?1609, Queen's Revels) and *The Scornful Lady* (?1610, Queen's Revels).[2] Yet other aspects of *The Woman Hater* point more immediately to *The Knight of the Burning Pestle*, probably Beaumont's next, and only surviving unaided, play.[3]

The Woman Hater's prologue combines witty allusion to the contemporary theatrical scene with good-natured mockery of both its author and audience; the play itself demonstrates Beaumont's talent for lightening his satire with linguistic parody and farce. Beaumont's ability to travesty literary languages effortlessly and apparently at any length—Petrarchan effusions, mock-heroic descriptions, extended euphuistic analogies, courtly vapidities worthy of Osric—makes *The Woman Hater* a verbal delight. Lazarello's part in particular becomes a showman's feast of words, for beyond the comedy of his frustrated quest, Lazarello's claim on our laughter lies in his language—its abuse of decorum, given its object, and the contagious exhilaration of his devotion to *copia* as he rapturously piles one incongruous, extravagant comparison or description upon another. *The Knight of the Burning Pestle* is remarkable both for the full flowering of this talent and for Beaumont's discovery of how to harness his peripatetic multiple plots and casts with a more coherently structured interplay of literary and dramatic conventions and styles.

In *The Knight* Beaumont explores the imagination and its relation to desire in its institutional home, the playhouse. To examine the ways in which the actors, their play, and the spectators function— or fail to function—together to create a shared imaginative experience, Beaumont introduces an audience in conflict with the theater to which it has come for entertainment. The Blackfriars children are about to present a city comedy called "The London Merchant" when two citizens, George and Nell, climb onto the stage to join the gallants on stools; dissatisfied with the intended fare, they demand something more to their taste. With the help of their apprentice (and amateur actor) Rafe, they make up a "play," scene by scene, out of the stock characters, situations, and rhetorical style of their favorite literature, chivalric romance. The Citizens intend their play to exalt both their class and their guild; for "The Grocers' Honour" the boy-Prologue substitutes a bawdy new title, "The Knight of the Burning Pestle," but he cannot stop these would-be playwrights. The actors refuse to cede to the Citizens' improbable and indecorous mishmash of events, but they are forced to allow "The Knight of the Burning Pestle," starring Rafe, to be staged in an impromptu fashion between the scenes of their own production.

Beaumont found in native traditions his model for presenting the uneasy relations between theatrical fiction and its fiction-starved audience, for behind his central conceit lie both dramatic convention and the reality of unruly audiences. Prologues and Inductions instruct the audience about the nature of the coming play; Inductions, particularly, mediate between the physical and temporal space of the spectators and the imaginative world they are asked to help create. They expand the prologue's address into a scripted, though supposedly spontaneous, miniplay; they offer everything from simple exposition, to allegorical figures who watch or direct the action, to literary harangue or lengthier versions of the kind of joking self-defense found in *The Woman Hater*'s prologue. An Induction may initiate a fully developed "frame play," where the opening characters return after the interior fiction has been resolved. This audience of actors-playing-spectators may also remain on stage to comment on, even join, the play's fiction, as they do in Robert Green's *James IV* (ca. 1591, Queen's Men) and Anthony Munday's *The Downfall of Robert Earl of Huntingdon* (1598, Admiral's Men).

In the early seventeenth century, Inductions became less popular on the public stage, though private-theater playwrights used them to develop a critical, self-conscious relationship with their audience. Yet whatever their form, Inductions also served a very practical purpose: they allowed time for a noisy, inattentive audience to settle down. Numerous complaints by other dramatists suggest that Dekker's burlesque advice to the ambitious gallant all too accurately reflected common practice. So that all eyes should turn his way and his clothes receive their fullest audience, the would-be cynosure is urged to enter just as the play is about to start and "presently advance himselfe up to the Throne of the Stage." Those with a personal grudge against the author should exit spectacularly in mid-play, accompanied by as many friends as possible. If forced to endure a whole performance, the restless sophisticate may "turne plaine Ape, take up a rush and tickle the earnest eares of your fellow gallants, . . . mewe at passionate speeches, blare at merrie, finde fault with the musicke, whew at the childrens Action, whistle at the songs."[4] Indeed, Beaumont has his own words on this subject: in *The Woman Hater,* a bored Count Valore considers attending "a Play; where, when I first enter, you shall have a murmure in the house, every one that does not knowe, cries, what Noble man is that; all the Gallants on the Stage rise, vayle to me, kisse their hand, offer mee their places" (1.3.65–69).

Audiences could be more than merely impolite. While some saw the theater as primarily a stage on which to display their clothes, wit, and sophisticated disdain, others demanded not only to be entertained but to dictate the form in which that demand would be met. The most famous description of the theater's defeat by its own customers comes from a near-contemporary of Beaumont's, Edmund Gayton, in his *Pleasant Notes upon Don Quixot* (1654). Having declared academic plays unsuitable for the "common stage," because "men come not to study at a Play-house," Gayton goes on to observe that

if it be on Holy dayes, when Saylers, Water-men, Shoomakers, Butchers and Apprentices are at leisure, then it is good policy to amaze those violent spirits, with some tearing Tragaedy full of fights and skirmishes . . . the spectators frequently mounting the stage, and making a more bloody Catastrophe amongst themselves, than the Players did. I have known upon one of these *Festivals,* but especially at *Shrove-tide,* where the Players have been appointed, notwithstanding their bils to the contrary, to act what the major part of the company had a mind to; sometimes *Tamerlane,* sometimes *Jugurth,* sometimes the Jew of *Malta,* . . . and at last, none of the three taking, they were forc'd to undress and put off their Tragick habits, and conclude the day with the merry milk-maides.[5]

Plays and behavior suggest that Gayton describes the rowdier of the public theaters, the Red Bull and Fortune, and Shrovetide was a particularly saturnalian holiday. Still, such an attitude continually threatened the authority of both playwright and actors. Nor was it confined to the public houses or their penny-entry sailors, apprentices, and watermen. Despite higher admission prices at the private houses, the audience's mood was not so very different. Jonson's verses for Fletcher's *Faithful Shepherdess* sarcastically describe the Blackfriars audience that rejected this play as a "wise, and many-headed *Bench* . . . Compos'd of *Gamester, Captaine, Knight, Knight's man, / Lady,* or *Pusil,*" all "rank'd in the darke / With the shops *Foreman*" as well as the *"brave sparke."*[6] The Induction to John Day's *Ile of Guls* (1606, Blackfriars) dramatizes a similar audience's fractious insistence on its own taste: three gallants voice contradictory demands—for satire, bawdry, and bombastic history—and one threatens to leave early. In another instance, through one auditor's dissatisfaction and a juggler's sleight-of-hand, the advertised moral drama *Spectrum* is "replaced" by the comedy actually presented, *Wily Beguiled.*[7]

In *The Knight,* then, Beaumont drew on forms of a theatrical convention familiar to his audience: the fashionable critical Induction that combined literary instruction with satiric portraits of its own audience;[8] and an older, largely public-theater tradition in which characters from the frame plot could join the play's action yet retain their identity and rapport with the audience. Beaumont expanded the Induction to provide continuing commentary on the actors' offering as well as a competing play. His conception depends on the resulting onstage confusion, yet his very success in exploding narrative expectations and continuity may explain the play's initial failure. An audience must both understand and accept what *The Knight's* publisher called the play's "privy marke of *Ironie*" (dedicatory epistle, 5). Constant oscillation between levels of illusion demands a complex, simultaneously imaginative and critical, participation. However admired today, *The Knight* apparently asked more—or gave less—than its first customers deemed satisfactory.

Beaumont also refused to provide the pleasures of a consistently clear satiric focus. Initially, in the Induction proper, all seems weighted against the Citizens. The grocer and his wife lack any sense of how to behave as audience, and through them Beaumont wittily "girds at Citizens" even before the "London Merchant" begins (Induction, 8). As soon as the boy announces the play they object: George rightly suspects that any Blackfriars drama about businessmen will offend him. The Citizens insist that their own taste be satisfied and further convict themselves as they reveal its nature. The satire is there, to be sure, and its class bias clear. Yet Beaumont's mockery is genial, its target ultimately human nature rather than strictly citizen folly. Boorish behavior and the demand that the playhouse serve private preference were hardly uniquely citizen failings. Indeed, one of the Induction's surprises, for a Blackfriars audience, would have been its substitution of imperious shopkeeper for the usual rude gallant or Inns-of-Court man. And if the Blackfriars audience laughed at the Citizens' attempt to replace satiric city comedy with chivalric romance, it might have sensed that here, too, the author's aim was a bit uncomfortably inclusive.

Certainly the chivalric romances—both the home-grown variety and those rendered from Spanish (usually via French or Italian intermediaries) by the Anthony Munday translation factory—were publicly derided by men of letters as escapist literature appropriate only for those lacking culture or critical judgment: tradesmen, apprentices, women.[9] Yet it was not merely servants and shopkeepers—the increasingly literate nongentle audience for printed books[10]—who devoured the chivalric romances. In their heyday they were read by everyone, and even the respectable authors who condemned the romances show a close knowledge of their contents.[11] Herbert S. Murch has established Beaumont's familiarity with a number of such works;[12] his private-theater audience, too, had been brought up on the romances of the 1580s and 1590s, and he could depend on it recognizing his parodic appropriations. Allusions in Marston's *Dutch Courtesan* and the collaborative *Eastward Ho,* both for Blackfriars, suggest a similar assumption.

Though they continued to be read, however, the vogue for chivalric romance had waned. The Citizens' preference is not aberrant, just out of date. Stylistically, too, these romances had come to seem old-fashioned. Most continuations of the original stories (book after book of the hero's and then his sons' adventures), as well as the translations, were hack work. The Renaissance's rather free idea of "translation" also meant that each redactor had updated the text for his own time and market: fourteenth- and fifteenth-century Spanish tales burgeoned in size as a late sixteenth-century taste expanded sentimental outpourings and added elaborately euphuistic rhetorical flights.[13] At a time when prose style was shifting from the highly oratorical to the plain, when Donne and Jonson were revolutionizing the euphonious "sweet style" of Elizabethan lyric poetry, and when the city comedy of the children's theaters had begun to reflect the time, class, and mannerisms of its audience, the Citizens' enthusiasm for the language of popular romance complements their belief in its marvels and exotic adventures.

Beaumont thus gains for his comedy of contrasts not only the impossible action of romance, but also its wholly artificial rhetoric. Rafe begins his stage career literally "by the book," *Palmerin de Oliva* (mistitled *Palmerin of England*); later, more delightfully, he imitates the assigned style in adapting new events to his role. Romance's formalized rhetoric and archaic vocabulary, declaimed from the stage as living dialogue, offers its own humor and plays off the language as well as the concerns of "The London Merchant." It finds its polar opposite and measure in George and Nell themselves, two of the most linguistically fully realized tradesmen in Renaissance drama.

The Knight's citizen playwrights intend to update their favorite form, but their idea of making chivalric romance "contemporary" is to substitute one of themselves as aristocratic hero and then treat its events as real by enacting them. Comic because so literal and personal, they are also representative. Through them Beaumont slyly dramatizes the motive force behind a whole literature glorifying merchants and tradesmen that had developed in the 1590s with such prose tales as Thomas Deloney's *Jack of Newbury* (for clothiers) and *The Gentle Craft* (for shoemakers). A subtype devoted itself to fulfilling the fantasies of the lowly apprentice, in works ranging from the ballad "The honour of a London prentice" (where an apprentice fights in a tournament and marries a king's daughter) to the Thomas Heywood play named by the Citizens, *The Four Prentises of London*.

The public theaters were associated with satisfying this taste for shapeless romantic drama as well as citizen success-stories, and many of the plays in George and Nell's list of preferences could have been found there. No "legend of *Whittington*" remains, though a Stationers' Register entry of 8 February 1605 exists for a play on this popular rags-to-riches tale. The "story of Queene *Elenor*" probably refers to Peele's *Edward I; Bold Beauchamps*, now lost, was in a 1663 allusion attributed to Heywood. *Jane Shore* refers either to *King Edward the Fourth*, possibly by Heywood, or to a lost play by Day and Chettle mentioned in Henslowe's diary in 1603.[14] Finally, "the life and death of sir *Thomas Gresham* . . . with the building of the Royall Exchange" appears to be a Citizen reworking of the title of part 2 of Heywood's extremely popular *If You Know not Me, You Know Nobody. With the Building of the Royal Exchange: And the famous Victorie of Queene Elizabeth, in the Yeare 1588* (Q 1606). The tellingly misremembered title allows the boy-Prologue his chance for retaliation. To their demand for "something notably in honour of the Commons of the Citty," he offers his own demeaning parody of plays on citizen triumphs: "what doe you say to the life and death of fat *Drake*, or the repairing of Fleet-privies?" (Induction, 25–28)

The Induction's jokes are good fun and allow the private theater its jibes at the opposition playhouses. The Citizens' lack of sophistication—as audience, as readers, as playwrights—is fundamental to Beaumont's larger concerns, however, not simply a hook on which to hang topical theatrical or social satire. In dramatizing the way a "folk" mentality operates on the romantic adventure material it loves, *The Knight* is also not without dramatic precedent. George Peele's *Old Wives Tale* offers a performed tale of marvels and knightly adventures, an audience of runaway pageboys, and the story's teller, the elderly countrywoman Madge who seems to conjure her narrated story into stage reality. Shakespeare's *Midsummer Night's Dream* presents both an unappreciative audience and the intellectual confusions of its craftsmen actors' attempt to stage the old romance tale of Pyramus and Thisby.

Yet Beaumont's idea for his Citizens' literary credulity and for the form they give their play may also have come from a recent nondramatic burlesque of many of the same romances—Cervantes's *Don Quixote*. A number of critics have argued for separate creation, inspired by the reaction in both Spain and England against the literary fashions of the 1590s, and much specific parody can be

traced to the romances that are clearly one target of Beaumont's
satire.[15] Yet larger matters of conception remain—the particular
juxtaposition of social classes and styles, both literary and personal;
the Citizens' and their apprentice's at least intermittent belief in
the reality of the world of chivalric romance, and, hence, its rep-
resentability. Moreover, two of the scenes re-creating this world in
a modern setting seem too close to episodes in *Don Quixote* to be of
serendipitously independent origin: Rafe's insistence that the Bell
Inn is a castle and that as a knight and guest he owes no reckoning
for his lodging, and Rafe's defeat of the "giant" Barbaroso and release
of the barber's "captives," the syphilitic customers undergoing the
standard Renaissance treatment for venereal disease. The latter example seems to conflate two incidents in *Don Quixote:* the "chival-
rizing" of Mambrino's helmet and Quixote's freeing of what prove
to be criminals deservedly confined to a chain-gang. If Beaumont
did know *Don Quixote,* then among the galley slaves he would have
found Ginés de Pasamonte, whose confident assertion that his au-
tobiography cannot be completed because he is still alive sounds
very like the mad literalism of Beaumont's Citizen "authors" and
may also have inspired Rafe's attempt to gain narrative closure by
staging his own death-scene.

Cervantes's influence cannot be proved conclusively, for Beaumont
mentions neither author nor work by name. Indeed, the quarto's
dedicatory letter from its publisher Walter Burre "To His Many
Waies Endeered friend Maister Robert Keysar" specifically denies
the play's indebtedness: "Perhaps it will be thought to bee of the
race of *Don Quixote:* we both may confidently sweare, it is his elder
above a yeare" (ll. 21–23). Although no Stationers' Register entry
exists and the quarto lists neither dramatist nor printer, *The Knight's*
title page dates it 1613. Burre's claim to have received the text
from Keysar and "fostred it privately in my bosome these two yeares"
(ll. 12–13) offers a possible date of composition and suggests that
his dismissal of *Don Quixote* refers to Thomas Shelton's English
translation of part 1 of Cervantes's work, published in 1612.[16]

For both Beaumont's play and a knowledge of *Don Quixote* in
England, however, such dates are misleading. Allusions to perfor-
mance by a boys' company, and the fact that sometime in 1606
Keysar became master of the Children of Blackfriars, suggest that
The Knight was performed by this troupe and explain Keysar's pos-
session of the manuscript. George's remark that "This seven yeares

there hath beene playes at this house" (Induction, 6–7) points to Blackfriars as the playhouse and 1607 as the date of performance (rather than Whitefriars in 1611), since Blackfriars had been revived and reopened in 1600.[17] His request for a scene in which the Sophy of Persia christens a child (4.27–30) seems a clear reference to an episode in Day, Rowley, and Wilkins's *Travailes of the Three English Brothers,* produced and published in 1607, and the mention of "Moldavia" (4.54) would have been topical in 1607, when a prince of Moldavia visited London.[18] Composition and performance in 1607 seem a reasonable conjecture and one that places *The Knight* close to the Beaumont play it most resembles in spirit, *The Woman Hater.*[19]

A date of 1607 does not exclude the possibility of Cervantes's influence. Part 1 of *Don Quixote* was published in Madrid in January 1605, and other Spanish editions appeared in Brussels in 1607 and in Milan in 1610. Shelton's 1612 dedicatory letter says he completed his translation "some five or six yeares agoe" and "in the space of forty daies"; an Irish Catholic political exile trying to eke out a living in Brussels and Paris, Shelton used the Brussels edition.[20] Shelton's version could have circulated in manuscript, then, as early as 1607, though his epistle fails to establish its availability in England. Certainly some version of Cervantes's narrative passed through London literary, and especially theatrical, circles well before Shelton's translation reached print. By 1607 other dramatists knew enough of its contents to refer to its most famous episode, Quixote's tilting with windmills: George Wilkins, in *The Miseries of Enforced Marriage,* and Thomas Middleton, in *Your Five Gallants.* Ben Jonson alludes to Don Quixote in *Epicoene* (1609) and again in *The Alchemist* (1610). Such passing references may derive from verbal reports, of course, but they suggest that someone who knew these dramatists had read the book.[21]

The Knight, however, unlike the other early dramas, seems to reflect substantive, conceptual inspiration.[22] Postulating the circulation of Shelton's translation soon after its completion offers one explanation for Beaumont's apparent familiarity, nor would manuscript circulation be unusual, given contemporary practice. Other possible avenues of acquaintance existed: the 1604 peace with Spain and renewed diplomatic and business contacts; the large number of courtiers and gentlemen accompanying the 1605 English embassy to Valladolid and the record of at least one member's purchase of popular Spanish books; the existence of an English audience, admittedly small but including some of Beaumont's friends and acquaintances, capable of reading *Don Quixote* in the original.[23] Yet if in some form *Don Quixote* provided partial inspiration for Beaumont's play, as is likely, the young dramatist certainly approached Cervantes's work as inventively as he did the conventional dramatic Induction.

The Knight of the Burning Pestle

In *The Knight of the Burning Pestle,* character, plot, episode, and allusion all do double or triple duty. The play looks outward, to its contemporary audience and its theatrical and nontheatrical sources, and inward, to its own operation as a dramatic mechanism and its status as an imaginative construct. Competing interior plays threaten to dismantle attempts at larger formal unity, yet Beaumont's control over his apparently clashing plays and players finally allows a complex, richly textured effect to emerge from *The Knight*'s surface chaos. What looks to be a battle royal between art and life becomes not only an investigation of their interrelations but also a generically appropriate occasion of festive release.

The play's satiric thrust is strongest in the opening Induction, though throughout *The Knight* the Citizens' lack of literary or theatrical sophistication repeatedly betrays them to our laughter. Beneath the farcical exaggeration, Beaumont also suggests the darker implications of this citizen "aesthetic." Misunderstanding the relation of audience to stage, not to say the nature or function of art, these inexperienced playgoers enact the destructive potential of the untutored imagination. Insisting that the stage gratify each transitory wish, they demolish the independent aesthetic status of the playwright's work and overturn Renaissance ideals of the theater's moral efficacy. These citizens create as well as destroy, but they do not want "art," since plot, character, construction are all irrelevant—even obstacles—to the immediate gratifications they seek. Alternating scenes of spectacle and violence constitute the only desiderata, and the presence on stage of their own Rafe fulfills their highest hopes for a visit to the theater. In a fantasia on "every man his own playwright," Beaumont shows the Citizens turning the stage into a three-dimensional projection of the mind's own fleeting, infantile, aggressive, and narcissistic urges. In the formless mass of unconnected incident dictated, to their eminent satisfaction, by

George and Nell, and in their utter disregard for both the shape and content of the playhouse's own offering, Beaumont exposes the damning congruence among his Citizens' deficiencies in taste, imagination, and moral sensibility.[24] That they are willing to pay, as well as threaten, to get what they want completes Beaumont's anatomy of art's corruption by commerce.

Yet such a description violates the play's mood and final effect. The Citizens' behavior and taste may illustrate a Jonsonian analysis of the serious artist's plight—the demands of his craft pitted against those of the paying customers—but Beaumont's satire is pursued without Jonson's rigor or contempt. Determined to direct "The London Merchant" as well as his own play, George bullies and threatens the actors; he is also endearingly affectionate with his wife, proud of his apprentice (and solicitous, since he intervenes to pay the Host of the Bell Inn and later spares Rafe the requested morris dance as "too much for the boy"), and eager to honor his country as well as his guild. Nell's almost stream-of-consciousness responses betray latent sexual preoccupations and an all too overt demand for violence as well as spectacle, yet she displays a maternal care for the actors who try to please her. Poor "fatherless" Rafe is her chief concern, but she dispenses candy and homey medical advice freely, and she tips the boy who dances between acts 3 and 4 even though he cannot tumble or eat fire. Although she shares her husband's dislike of the runaway apprentice in "The London Merchant," she defends Jasper when he is accused of lying about his departure from Venturewell's service. Honesty requires that spectators bear witness: "I *George,* but yet truth is truth" (1.375).

The comic irony undermining Nell's good-hearted assertion—epistemological certitude from a woman consistently incapable of distinguishing fact from fiction—points to Beaumont's primary interest in his citizen audience. It is not simply a matter of class, of their having come to the wrong theater for the kind of play they want. Having scored his satiric thrusts, Beaumont is less interested in George and Nell's taste in plays than in their naiveté as playgoers. Their interruptions make literal and comic the metaphor of an "interaction" between drama and audience. They heighten our consciousness of plays as artistic mechanisms, contrived structures that rely not only on shared generic conventions but on a whole set of assumptions about the nature of the theatrical experience itself.[25] Having George and Nell stage "The Knight of the Burning Pestle"

in the interstices of "The London Merchant" increases their usefulness: they become audience to two plays, one of which they invent.
At the same time, Beaumont adds levels of creativity in the resulting
improvisations of Rafe and the cast of "The London Merchant."
Dramatic fact and fiction begin to blur for us, too, and while we
laugh at the onstage confusion, Beaumont turns some of his mockery
back on his own, supposedly more sophisticated, spectators. He
recaptures, for his play, drama's proper office as the mirror that
shows us ourselves.

As audience, George and Nell exhibit precisely the mis-responses
to art feared—and represented—by the rude mechanicals in *A Midsummer Night's Dream*. Exercising both too much and too little imagination, the Citizens flip-flop between under- and overdistancing;
they never find that degree of suspended disbelief needed to establish
the special time and space in which drama can operate. Nell refuses
to let actor disappear into character, stopping "The London Merchant" to comment on the prettiness of the child who plays Humphrey and to ask if he was once one of "Maister *Monkesters* schollars"
(1.94). Almost simultaneously, she projects an historical reality for
the character Venturewell, whose speech convinces her that he must
have been "an old stringer [fornicator] in's daies" (1.103).

Having mounted the stage and argued with the boy-Prologue,
the Citizens from the beginning violate the play's privileged space,
and they continue to misunderstand this most basic convention.
They willingly imagine the stage as wherever the dialogue says it
is—Waltham Forest, the Bell Inn, Cracovia or Mile-End—even
when they have dictated the location. Yet they also treat its action
as present, "real" within its believed fiction but also physically
happening in their own nontheatrical world. Thus George can pay
the Host of the Bell Inn or give Rafe money to tip the King of
Cracovia's servants; when Jasper threatens to kill Luce, Nell can
urge George to "raise the watch at *Ludgate,* and bring a *Mittimus*
from the Justice for this desperate villaine" or, later, "crave a word"
with Merrythought to criticize his behavior to his wife (3.92–93,
532). Temporal conventions, too, puzzle the Citizens. At one point
Nell marks time by her own physical experience: her very sense of
the stage-play's reality compels her to tell Mistress Merrythought
of a prior incident in "The London Merchant," one that happened
"even in this place . . . within this halfe houre . . . my husband
was by" (1.368–70). Elsewhere she accepts completely the temporal

(if not spatial) dictates of the fiction: she interrupts the Host's demand that Rafe pay for his lodgings to ask Rafe, "how hast thou slept to night?" (3.136).

The Citizens' ignorance of other, only slightly less elementary, conventions leads to further crimes against "The London Merchant." The whole concept of plot is foreign to George. He repeats his demand to see more of Rafe, even to have Rafe intervene in "The London Merchant" to punish Jasper, because the boy's protest that "the plot of our Plaie lies contrarie, and 'twill hazard the spoiling of our Plaie" carries no force with George: "Plot mee no plots" (2.258–60). George's idea of art has a purity all its own: fiction is about the "fabulous," by definition unrealistic. "Plot" assumes some unity of action and depends on the laws of cause and effect to relate coherently the separate incidents of the story it dramatizes. The story George makes up for Rafe exhibits neither narrative sequence nor probability. When an incident goes "wrong" and Jasper beats Rafe, George seeks explanations in the realm that inspired him: Jasper is "inchanted" (2.315). The player's appeals to decorum— behavioral or artistic—fail for the same reason. If drama satisfies by creating desirable rather than probable worlds, then, over the boy's protests, apprentices can court ladies and Rafe can die at the end of a comedy.

Inexperienced in particular conventions, inveterate personalizers of experience, the Citizens misapprehend "The London Merchant" as well as interrupt it. With the exception of Merrythought and its inversion of the "Prodigal Son" play's usual moral, "The London Merchant" is a conventional little romantic comedy;[26] its signals for generically appropriate response are writ large in every speech. For George and Nell, however, drama is fresh and real, and, partly because the play's story and characters are close to their own experience, they consistently misread those cues. They see not sympathetic young lovers but a rebellious apprentice and a girl who naughtily refuses her father's guidance and runs away from home. What they would censure in life, they reject in art. They side with prudent Mistress Merrythought over her spendthrift husband because they know the practical value of having "a peny i'th purse" (1.360). Nell ignores the play's larger claims on her spirit, and her pragmatic medical advice for fictional chilblains suggests the level of her response. She distrusts Merrythought as irresponsible, yet accepts his incidental observations. Not Merrythought's principle, the importance to life of mirth, but his illustration strikes her as valuable: when the old man says a tailor's failure to sing at his work betokens his dishonesty, Nell counsels, "Marke this *George*, tis worth noting" (2.440). She finds a predictable love story as mysterious as life: "*George*, do'st thou thinke in thy conscience now 'twil be a match [between Humphrey and Luce]? tell me but what thou thinkst sweet rogue" (2.8–9). Soon both try to predict events by applying real-life experience to art—the likely consequences of Luce's tender feet or the confusing darkness of Waltham Forest at night.

The multiple levels of George and Nell's difficulties with "The London Merchant" are reflected, transposed, in their own dramatic composition, although they have no doubts about what they want to see or whether their scenes of spectacle should take precedence over "The London Merchant." Comic in their self-assurance, as dramatists they also begin to charm us. George willfully tramples on many of the most basic dramatic conventions, but he cares about his theatrical undertaking and, in his own way, is eager to get it right and please his audience as well as himself. He displays a rudimentary sense of the existence of theatrical decorum, even if its finer points elude him. Because he feels a "stately part" requires "stately musicke," Rafe "must needs have shawmes" (Induction, 94, 97). George's desire for an art that glorifies everyday life finds its verbal expression in the high rhetorical style he prefers: the "huffing part" of Rafe's audition before the gentlemen (Hotspur's speech on honor from *Henry IV*, part 1), and the language of romance with which Rafe transforms the quotidian world to fit his knightly career. This is what George wants: "Well said *Rafe*, some more of those words *Rafe*" (1.246). Yet he can also demonstrate reasonable critical standards for execution, as when he praises Rafe for "cleane action and good deliverie" (2.194).

Finally, though George's "play" has lacked plot or structure, at the end he discovers at least one dramatic principle: the need for closure. As "The London Merchant" winds up its action, George is left stranded: "I do not like this . . . every bodies part is come to an end but *Raphes*, and hee's left out" (5.265–66). George requests help—"make [an end] on him as you have done of the rest, boies" (5.269–70)—but Nell intervenes. Despite its indecorum "in a Comedy," Beaumont playfully allows a sense in which her suggestion, the only real-life "end" she knows, is fitting. The plotless story of Rafe's adventures bears no seeds of its own resolution; as a loose, chronicle history, however, it finds a natural termination in the death of the adventurer himself. George's final remark is comic in again refusing the standard of probability (since the boy also objects to the lack of "occasion" for this sudden death). It is also funny because as unanswerably true for his kind of play as for life: "is not his part at an end, thinke you, when he's dead?" (5.275–76).

The Citizens' creative efforts, more than their responses to "The London Merchant," illustrate the doubleness with which Beaumont treats these characters. Demanding, ill-educated and inexperienced, sublimely egotistical—in some ways they seem beyond the reach of art. Yet these are no Puritan censors, stopping the actors because they wish to suppress playing. Rather, like eager children the Citizens and their apprentice crave theater, fiction, the exercise of their imagination. Ignorant of the etiquette of theatergoing, capable themselves only of ill-constructed, ridiculously self-glorifying fantasies, their enthusiasm and engagement are nevertheless contagious.[27] What they *have* grasped is something even more fundamental than conventions of behavior or dramatic genre: theater as a place where the imagination seeks its own ends, satisfies its hunger to transform everyday reality and explore its own metamorphic powers. Their creative instincts and models may be crude, but the primary impulse is the one on which theater—its players, playwrights, audience—rests.

The Knight's exuberant vitality thus arises not only from the Citizens' energy, especially in comparison with the tameness of the play they interrupt, but also from Beaumont's skill in suggesting that he has brought life on stage and freed it to shape its own desires. Neither interior "play" holds much intrinsic interest; their juxtaposition and interaction do. Imaginative verve, the spontaneity and adaptability of audience and actors, men as shapers of fiction—these create the play's sense of freedom. As script apparently dissolves into improvisation, what we watch begins to be as unpredictable and mysterious as George and Nell find "The London Merchant." We behold the apparent shapelessness of life itself, but also the irrepressible human impulse to impose significance and intelligible form.

The boy-Prologue's capitulation in the Induction seemed to promise alternating scenes from two different plays: one written and presented by theatrical professionals; one invented on the spot by

the audience and an enthusiastic but amateur actor. The players
soon discover that they must do more than donate costumes and
willingly break off whenever the Citizens become restive. When
Rafe enters "The London Merchant," the actors are put on their
mettle. Initially, they cede the stage to Rafe. Mistress Merrythought
improvises a cry of fright and a reason to flee: "here be Gyants"
(2.104). Yet this knight needs a damsel to rescue, and she is brought
back and her diction corrected, from "forrest" to "Desart." Rafe
needs her for his play; the Citizens feel the love story needs Rafe
to right its injustices. Their demand that Rafe punish Jasper threatens the integrity of "The London Merchant," but, for a time, the
players gamely accommodate Rafe while continuing their own script.

The initial compromise soon breaks down, and the players apparently turn from their own production to revenge themselves on
their citizen tormentors. Whether the Bell Inn is improvised, or
was Mistress Merrythought's destination in the now derailed "London Merchant," remains unclear.[28] The players' inventive use of it
gets Rafe offstage so that two long scenes of the original script can
be completed, interrupted only by George and Nell. The players
then create new parts for themselves and two scenes for Rafe's knightly
romance—"The Reckoning at the Bell Inn" and "Barbaroso's Cave"—
meant to ridicule Rafe and his sponsors before the gentlemen spectators. (George and Nell, of course, miss the point and think Rafe
acquits himself admirably.) Rafe does not return to "The London
Merchant." Nell's intervention is routed by Merrythought's bawdy
song, presumably the actor's impromptu but in-character "answer"
to her scolding. The players have had their revenge, and they too
have acquitted themselves well: their improvisations are much more
fun than the play they push to completion in acts 4 and 5. Dramatic
responsibility for Rafe passes back to the Citizens—"You shall have
what you will sir," says the boy (4.26)—and the players restrict
themselves to enacting, mockingly, the minor characters needed for
the disparate scenes the Citizens now request (Princess Pompiona,
the incompetent crew Rafe drills at Mile-End).

The players depart from their text only in midplay, to second
with their own methods the boy-Prologue's struggle against audience incursions. The real challenge to the theatrical imagination
belongs to Rafe, *The Knight*'s farcical figure of the dramatist and
his plight. George and Nell may feel "The Knight" to be their play
and Rafe merely their agent; in fact, they have only a vague and

confused idea of what they want to see. Actor-hero of "The Knight," Rafe becomes of necessity its self-appointed dramatist: he must create dialogue and motivation to give life to the skimpy situational cues provided by an audience that is, quite literally, both his master and "customer."[29] As if the Citizens' erratic "direction" were not sufficient test of Rafe's improvisational prowess, he also faces the same difficulty as the players. His fictional "space" must be shared with, or absorb, the characters and plot of "The London Merchant."

An ardent amateur actor with at least *Henry IV,* part 1, *Mucedorus,* and *The Spanish Tragedy* in his repertoire, as well as an avid reader of Iberian romance, Rafe brings more theatrical experience and sense of narrative shape to his task than do George and Nell. He has a tyrannical audience to please, but he also feels responsible, as fledgling dramatist, to his new craft. While "The Knight" dramatizes the requested compendium of favorite episodes from different kinds of literature, Rafe labors manfully to impose narrative coherence— a sense of "plot" beyond the Citizens' ken—on these disjunctive events. In his first scene, Rafe gives the story of his adventures a clear expository beginning that neatly incorporates an explanation of the boy-Prologue's mockingly suggested title. He instructs George and Tim in the rhetorical style appropriate to their roles as squire and dwarf. Since he understands the conventions of knightly romance, Rafe exceeds George and Nell's request and provides an amatory motive for his adventures: "*Susan* my Lady deere, / The Coblers Maid in Milke-streete, for whose sake, / I take these Armes" (3.312–14). In "Cracovia" he is unruffled by Princess Pompiona's advances (though also perhaps insensible to the boy player's mockery). Embroidering on George's demand that he uphold the honor of English grocers by tipping the King's servants, Rafe "remembers" an entire night of services for which they deserve reward.

The last three stipulated episodes crown Rafe's efforts, even though they return him to London and his "real" apprentice status. For his speech as May Lord he shifts his style, as well as his costume, and delivers a formal descriptive praise of spring and invocation for English hearts to rejoice and go a-maying. The fourteener couplets even turn bits of *The Spanish Tragedy* to festive uses. The mustering of his men at Mile-End and prose address to the troops further demonstrate Rafe's range and versatility. A travesty of euphuistic analogy and alliteration, the oration ridicules the whole idea of citizens aspiring to military honor; it also illustrates Rafe's infectious love of language and, in its way, an artistic propriety that suits patriotic speech to a tradesmen audience. Finally, required to die "upon no occasion," Rafe attempts to rationalize this absurdity: his allegorical story of Death's arrival and pursuit explains both his demise and the forked arrow through his head. More impressively, in his death scene (now iambic pentameter), Rafe endeavors to give retrospective narrative coherence to his theatrical life as apprentice-errant. He emphasizes motive and temporal sequence, even implies a causal relation between later activities and earlier demonstrations of worth: "I then returned home . . . and by all men chosen was / Lord of the May . . . . After this action, I preferred was, / And chosen Citty Captaine at Mile-end" (5.295–300). Rafe knows plays should be *utile* as well as *dolce,* so he attaches, desperately and hilariously, a moral lesson: "therefore be warn'd by me, / My fellowes every one of forked heads" (5.318–19). He even tries to satisfy the boy-Prologue's objection that death violates the comic order. Rafe's "end" is fittingly comic beyond his understanding, but in his own contribution to decorum he stresses not "tragic" finality but his soul's ascent to its immortal resting place.

Rafe has returned as a spirit to tell of his death and soul's flight (cribbing, now more appropriately, from Andrea's ghost in *The Spanish Tragedy*). His tale—and his literal "resurrection" when he gets up, bows, and exits—recall Jasper's mock death, return (his model is Banquo's ghost), and revival in "The London Merchant."[30] Though one interior play ends in marriage and one in death, they have accomplished a rapprochement in tone, duplicating with variation comedy's triumph of life over annihilation. This parallel points to further connections, unrecognized by the Citizens, that help bind two apparently disparate dramatic actions into one aesthetic whole. Each features a plucky apprentice-lover who meets with adventures that test his worth. Within "The London Merchant" Jasper, like Rafe, champions true love over monetary or social concerns. In a gesture out of Rafe's romances, Jasper casts aside the mucky pelf of his small inheritance: "From earth thou art, and to the earth I give thee, / There grow and multiply, whilst fresher aire, / Breeds me a fresher fortune" (2.144–46). In good romance fashion he is immediately rewarded with the casket of gold. A few lines later Rafe echoes this proper trust in the powers that be when he consoles the now penniless Mistress Merrythought: "fortune will give us more / Upon our next adventure" (2.190–91).

In siding with Mistress Merrythought and Venturewell in "The London Merchant," George and Nell respond oppositely to the plays they watch. The values central to romance, with which they wish to identify, are precisely those they reject in "The London Merchant": daring over caution; love over economic or social interests; idealism and aid to the distressed over distrust, hoarding, or any form of principled self-interest. They should favor Jasper, but they do not, and their failure to see the two plays' larger unity of spirit stems from the same misunderstandings about art that lead to more local confusions. In this they condemn themselves; through their continued resistance to the professional play's festive, forgiving ethic, Beaumont also ruefully if wittily acknowledges the limits of his own craft.

Yet just as *The Knight* becomes more—and more positive—than a satire on citizen taste and morals, it is also quite obviously not simply the presiding dramatist's admission of failure. Aesthetically, Beaumont's success lies in the coherence of *The Knight* itself, the artful thematic and structural integration of its disparate plots and characters. Yet as celebration as well as exploration of theatrical performance, *The Knight* must offer more than a humorous, well-crafted enactment of the playhouse's defeat. In the *genius loci* of "The London Merchant" Beaumont creates a figure who helps establish his play's artistic unity while suggesting the fruitful potential of his medium with even the most willful, recalcitrant audience.

"The London Merchant" inverts a genre usually devoted to extolling thrift and prudence. If, freed of everyday limits, George and Nell are spendthrifts of the imagination, in this they complement Merrythought's economic prodigality. Each exaggeration reminds us of its folly, but each also has something to say to the imaginatively, socially, and economically constrained world beyond the theater. George and Nell stop the players before "The London Merchant" even begins, yet their rude intervention ironically liberates not only their own creative potential, but also that of Rafe and the professional actors. Merrythought in his play promotes carefree, communal mirth—a sort of green world of the spirit. Through his presence and Jasper's schemes, "The London Merchant" works to release—or better, create—the generosity, forgiveness, and unity of feeling necessary to realize that ideal.

Set apart by his singing humour and notable inactivity in the love plot of "The London Merchant," Merrythought becomes an

almost free-floating embodiment of comedy's festive spirit—Lord
of Misrule but also priest of well-being. He stands for those fundamental values comedy reminds us are necessary to both individual
and social content.[31] The wine and food that exhaust his purse are
means to the good fellowship and satisfaction with one's lot that he
extols in his "philosophic" hymn to mirth: *"Tis mirth that fils the
veines with bloud . . . Let each man keepe his heart at ease, / No man
dies of that disease"* (2.444–47). As he later reaffirms in the face of
loss, "This is it that keepes life and soule together, mirth, this is
the Philosophers stone that they write so much on" (4.326–27).
From an apparently irresponsible, principled prodigality that would
be intolerable outside the theater he also derives comedy's quite
sensible recipe for a life worth living: he counsels his sons not to
hoard but to "Bee a good husband, that is, weare ordinary clothes,
eate the best meate, and drinke the best drinke, bee merrie, and
give to the poore, and beleeve me, thou hast no end of thy goods"
(1.388–90).

Although Jasper's maneuverings produce his play's happy outcome, at the end Merrythought dominates the stage. He has forgiven
his wife and Venturewell and, more important, converted them
from values that destroy the heart's ease. By singing for her entrance,
Mistress Merrythought suggests she will no longer be a "vext thing";
by forgiving Jasper, Venturewell escapes the "weights" that "Will
sinke me to my grave" (5.211, 250–51). Merrythought's influence
seems also to have reached beyond "The London Merchant." Rafe's
knightly role already endows him with the proper virtues, since
even the apprentice's version emphasizes spirit over substance, service over self-interest. As the requested episodes move Rafe closer
to home and "real life," his contributions increasingly project the
ideal, if more mundane, community Merrythought's philosophy
envisions. Rafe's speech as May Lord urges all English hearts to
rejoice. It celebrates a season of peace, plenty, and renewal; it pic-
tures an entire society, its usual class consciousness suspended, at
play. The humorous patriotism of his exhortation at Mile-End also
reflects this communal spirit. Finally, the way Rafe suits his "death"
to the end of a comedy suggests he has been listening even when
offstage. Merrythought's sunny optimism is contagious, and Rafe's
final words echo the snatch of song with which Merrythought refused
to fear death: *"When earth and seas from me are reft, / The skyes aloft
for me are left"* (1.415–16).

Of the characters in "The London Merchant," only Merrythought interacts with the Citizens and, at times, touches them—as Jasper and Luce do not—to the proper response. There is no marked playhouse triumph here, no clearly educative pattern making George and Nell at play's end the people and audience they so evidently were not at the beginning. Yet although she may disapprove of his imprudence and chastise him for his treatment of his wife, Nell feels the appeal of Merrythought, his fiddlers and songs, on his first appearance. Her myopic perception usually prompts only the most literal reactions, but Merrythought's praise of mirth moves her to bless the "fine old man" and wish George could be "so merry" (2.458–60). Merrythought later sings insults at his wife and Nell, and Mistress Merrythought departs cursing while he turns to "frolicke": "fill the good fellowes wine" (3.553). Surprisingly, though "almost molten with fretting," Nell immediately imitates this convivial courtesy when George returns with her drink: "Fill the Gentlemen some beere *George*" (3.Interlude.5).

The Citizens are not wondrously transformed, yet as the play progresses we see more clearly another side of their willingness to use the profits of trade to buy a desired self-image on the public stage. Their money may threaten to corrupt both players and theater; it also lends itself to more positive uses. Nell's offer to share her beverage, George's eagerness to tip the King of Cracovia's servants or pay Rafe's tab at the Bell Inn—these can be seen as merely additional attempts to flaunt the honor of London grocers. In the context of the parsimony central to Venturewell and Mistress Merrythought in "The London Merchant," however, they suggest an instinctive generosity more akin to Merrythought's ideal than to the frugal burgher ethic the Citizens ostensibly defend.

Finally, when "The London Merchant" has concluded and its actors have stood patiently by while Rafe dies, Merrythought's request for song may also include the now satisfied George and Nell in the comic resolution: he refers ambiguously to "all we, thus kindly and unexpectedly reconciled" (5.330–31). The players' last chorus echoes Merrythought's earlier philosophic song, now made exhortation: we are enjoined to *"Learne of"* them and their play to share his spirit, to create the happy communal music of *"a quire of hearts in one"* (5.338, 335). Nell's sudden attack of "manners"— the invitation to her house for wine and the tobacco she earlier denounced—completes   festive   comedy's   signs   of   closure.

Irrepressible, Nell gets the last word; magically, those words suggest a theatrical efficacy we had despaired of. Despite the apparent failure of "The London Merchant," the whole playhouse experience seems to have elicited its audience's best side and created a generous community that mirrors the inner play's own ideal.

That final harmony becomes *The Knight*'s epilogue. Beaumont nods both to his dramatic form and to us. Nell's invitation supplies the appropriate ending to his comedy; in its sense of arbitrariness, it also refuses to make sweeping claims for the coincidence of dramatic conventions with life as it is lived beyond the theater. In this Beaumont is true to the doubleness of effect—and authorial reticence—with which his play has operated throughout. Any single stance evaporates beneath *The Knight*'s shifting point of view. The Citizens' disruptive commentary and substitute play indict their moral and artistic sensibility. The players, once they enter Rafe's dramatic fiction, easily ridicule the Citizens' aspiration to gentility by placing its fantasy form—its language, situations, social pretensions—in a real-life context of country inns and syphilitic patients. At the same time, Rafe's imagination shames them by amending and elevating their crude reality, and the Citizens' use of romance for private glorification also expresses a less ignoble yearning to see themselves as participants in that idealized, golden world traditionally reserved for an aristocratic audience. The satire cuts both ways, and if George and Nell seem laughable aspirants to a chivalric milieu, their detractors can ill afford to sneer. Beaumont allows Nell and Rafe some pertinent remarks on the current fate of romance's ideal of service accompanying privilege: "our Knights neglect their possessions well enough, but they do not the rest," says Nell, and Rafe agrees there "are no such courteous and faire well spoken Knights in this age" (1.233–36). The patched and tub-sweated "knights" with which the players mock Rafe's heroic rescue at Barbaroso's Cave contribute to a satiric point they do not intend.

Focus for much of *The Knight*'s satiric humor and source of its burlesque romance, the Citizens' theatrical and literary naïveté also brings a kind of ironic realism to Beaumont's play. Their untutored responses to "The London Merchant" point up the arbitrary, contrived nature of this ostensibly more realistic offering. However well-constructed, it is as much an idealizing fiction as the flagrantly impossible, disjointed series of adventures the Citizens prefer. Its plot bears little relation to the London life they know; its working out depends on generic conventions that tidily organize life's un-predictable vitality. Drama can mirror the truths of our condition—here not the improbability of grocers-errant or economically suc-cessful prodigals, but the complementary qualities of generosity and contentment they represent. Yet not only will its effect always be hedged by the audience's capacity for imaginative apprehension; *what* it mirrors will also be, of necessity, partial. The juxtaposed endings of *The Knight*'s interior plays make a comic but telling point. "The London Merchant" moves through unlikely and sur-prising repentances to reconciliation and festive harmony, the nat-ural completion of its comic pattern. George and Nell's refusal to recognize conventions of plot or genre leads "The Knight of the Burning Pestle" to an equally natural but opposite fulfillment: the "plot" of a man's life, the "part" he plays, ends only with his death.

At the end, city comedy and romance come together in spirit, even as their proponents share the stage they have contested; yet they also remain distinct, poised in final mutual commentary. So it is with the art and life on whose clash Beaumont has built his play. In a sense, the dramatist has wittily co-opted life and forced its representatives to do his bidding: the framing fiction of audience disruption has served, paradoxically, as Beaumont's means to create an artistic whole out of his characters' strife and their plays' frag-mentation. At the same time, he allows fractious life its own in-tegrity. It is both creative and anarchic, drawn to the theater and the life of the imagination, yet subversive of the very shaping power through which it seeks expression. Rather than remind us of his overarching direction of events, Beaumont maintains his Citizen frame. "Nell" does not dissolve, as is usual in dramatic epilogues, into the actor who for the sake of author and players begs his audience's applause. "Nell" completes the play's comic pattern but also escapes it. She departs to the life that interests her more than art, perhaps carrying the theater's lesson into the world but also still absorbed in her private concerns and probably no more fit an auditory for her second visit to a play than for her first.

Chapter Four
Collaboration and Success
Dates and Provenance

Although *Cupid's Revenge* is a tragedy, written for a boys' troupe, and *Philaster* a tragicomedy composed for the King's Men, these plays form a natural pair. Together they also inaugurate the serious collaboration and theatrical success of two promising but as yet undistinguished playwrights.[1] No plaudits or other evidence of popularity remain for Beaumont's *Woman Hater; The Knight of the Burning Pestle* was both brilliantly original and emphatically a commercial disaster. Fletcher's very differently independent *Faithful Shepherdess* was probably written in the same year as *Cupid's Revenge*, 1608, and for the same troupe, though priority remains unclear.[2] Its prefatory verses and epistle bear ample testimony to its failure to enthrall the public.

Certainly these were troubled times for the Blackfriars boys and their playwrights. Two politically offensive plays, capping a rich list of skirmishes with the authorities, drove King James to dissolve the Children of Blackfriars in March 1608; in August the theater was surrendered to Burbage, who held the lease, and the King's Men. The boys' fortunes in 1608 are particularly hard to trace. They may have been playing in the provinces during the summer; they were back at court for the Christmas season of 1608–9 as the Children of Blackfriars, and under some arrangement with Burbage they may have continued intermittent playing at Blackfriars during the winter and spring of 1608–9. In autumn 1609 they seem to have taken over the Whitefriars theater and by Christmas were playing at court as the Children of Whitefriars; in January 1610 they regained their old name and patronage as the Children of the Queen's Revels.[3] Public performances in London by any troupe can only have been infrequent, for this was the worst plague year between 1603 and 1625. From 28 July 1608 to 7 December 1609 the weekly mortality bills seem sufficient to have kept the theaters largely closed.[4]

Cupid's Revenge reached print in 1615 as having been acted by the
Queen's Revels children. On the basis of topical allusions as well
as dramatic criteria, James E. Savage concludes that it preceded
Philaster, and his evidence for composition in "1607, or the early
part of 1608" is, in the main, persuasive.[5] If performed before the
March 1608 ban on playing, *Cupid's Revenge* would have begun its
life at Blackfriars; it apparently moved with the company to Whitefriars in 1609, while its authors began writing for the old theater's
new tenants. Accepting Savage's date for *Cupid's Revenge,* John H.
Astington argues that it was in fact this play's success that convinced
the most prestigious London adult company to enlist Beaumont and
Fletcher's talents when it took over the Blackfriars theater.[6]

While the young dramatists still wrote for their old troupe,
association with the King's Men produced not only the most famous
Beaumont-Fletcher plays but also Fletcher's work with Shakespeare
and later with Massinger and others when Fletcher succeeded Shakespeare in the company. The history of English drama in the seventeenth century in part depends on Beaumont and Fletcher's shift
between troupes and on the success of their first major collaborations.
Between *Cupid's Revenge* and *Philaster* they refined their influential
tragicomic form, and for that form they found a newly appreciative
audience at Blackfriars, at the Globe, and at court.

Cupid's Revenge

In his first comedies Beaumont favored an inventive use of literary
sources within an increasingly bold reworking of theatrical conventions and genres. *Cupid's Revenge* launches a new venture. As the
basis for their joint labor Beaumont and Fletcher selected a single
nondramatic source, Sidney's *Arcadia,* and a tragic mode. Such a
decisive break with past practice suggests a continued willingness
to try different forms and subject matter, as well as a determined
pursuit of success.[7] Given Beaumont's burlesque of chivalric romance
in *The Knight of the Burning Pestle,* Sidney's *Arcadia* might seem a
surprising choice, yet to the extent that *The Knight* takes the romances themselves as target, beyond the Citizens' attempt to turn
them into drama, Beaumont's parodies concentrate on the popular
hack-work translations and their imitators.

An apparent revival of romance—particularly the sophisticated,
pastoral, Sidneian sort—may also have made the *Arcadia* appealing.

One of Sidney's and later Shakespeare's sources, Heliodorus's *Ae-thiopian History,* enjoyed a current popularity: the fourth edition of Thomas Underdowne's translation appeared in 1605, with another issue in 1606. *The Arcadia* itself was reprinted in 1605, and at Blackfriars a politically topical version of Sidney's main plot, John Day's *Ile of Guls* (acted early 1606), got its author in trouble and some of the company jailed. The first part of Gervase Markham's prose continuation of Sidney, *The English Arcadia,* appeared in 1607. Giambattista Guarini's *Il Pastor Fido,* in the crude "Dymock" trans-lation of 1602, spawned a "Pastorall Trage-comedie" by Samuel Daniel which was presented before the queen at Oxford in August 1605; Daniel's title, *The Queenes Arcadia,* suggests he may have had Sidney in mind as well.[8] The adaptations are undistinguished, but they suggest a fashion, especially at the private theaters and among Inns-of-Court men. Ironically, given *The Knight*'s satiric treatment of attempts to stage *Palmerin* and *Amadis de Gaule,* when Beaumont and Fletcher follow their source as closely as in *Cupid's Revenge,* they prove only slightly more adept than George and Nell at dramatizing prose narrative.

The two main plots of *Cupid's Revenge* are drawn from a series of stories loosely linked by the figure of Plangus in the revised, "New" *Arcadia.*[9] Out of book 2, chapters 13–22, Beaumont and Fletcher attempt to forge a single dramatic sequence illustrating Cupid's punishment for sacrilege. Sidney's two-paragraph tale of Erona, daughter of the King of Lycia (chap. 13), with additions expands to provide the play's framework. Offended at the Lycians' lewd and superstitious worship of Cupid, Erona convinces her father to let her pull down and deface the god's statues. Cupid's swift punishment (within a year in the story's time scheme; the next sentence in Sidney's narrative) takes the form of Erona's sudden, ungovernable passion for her nurse's son. Despite her father's persuasions and threats, even a faked execution of the young man, Erona persists in loving against degree, and the King of Lycia dies of a broken heart.

The play's second plot adapts the story, begun in chapter 15 of the "New" *Arcadia,* of Plangus, son of the King of Iberia and another ill-fated lover. Caught by his father in an adulterous affair, Plangus so successfully pleads the lady's innocence that the widowed king becomes infatuated and marries her himself when her husband dies. Although his new stepmother wishes to continue their liaison, Plan-gus refuses and earns her hatred; aided by an ambitious servant, the queen gains her revenge by turning the king against his son. Condemned to death by his father, Plangus is rescued by an armed revolt of his friends and followers, but he refuses the crown and instead chooses voluntary exile. The evil servant is caught trying to poison Plangus and executed, but in Plangus's absence the queen convinces the Iberian king to name her own son heir.

In Sidney's telling, the story here gives place to other tales; it is resumed and completed in chapters 20–23. There the queen, finally named as Andromana, continues both to rule her husband and pursue her own desires, though the objects of her affection have now become the *Arcadia*'s heroes, Musidorus and Pyrocles. Imprisoned by Andromana to satisfy her lust, these two princes are saved by the queen's own son acting out of love for Zelmane, a young princess in love with Pyrocles. When Andromana's forces by mistake murder their prince, the queen kills herself with her son's dagger. Zelmane disguises herself as a page to live out her hopeless love in service to Pyrocles, and she reveals her sex and name only when, oppressed with many griefs, she is dying in his arms. It is in her honor that Pyrocles in the "New" *Arcadia* takes the name Zelmane when he adopts his Amazon disguise.

Beaumont and Fletcher's major changes aim at blending these stories and simplifying Sidney's busy canvas. The two families are combined and the setting restricted to Licia; the King, now called Leontius, is given a son (Leucippus) as well as a daughter (Sidney's Erona, renamed Hidaspes). All three are guilty of offending Cupid, and the play's action becomes a family tragedy, unified by the continuity of (some) characters and by Cupid's direction of their fates. The object of Hidaspes's sudden passion, now a dwarf rather than her nurse's son, is put to death and she, not her father, dies of grief. Leontius and Leucippus survive to assume the roles of Sidney's King of Iberia and Plangus. The evil queen is renamed Bacha and made the instrument by which Cupid completes his vengeance; her heir becomes a daughter, Urania, who can enact with Leucippus Sidney's story of Zelmane's selfless love for Pyrocles and thus contribute a poignant, unearned death to the finale's general carnage.

While the primary narrative material used in *Cupid's Revenge* comes from one, fairly localized, section of the revised *Arcadia,* names and characterizations reveal a wide-ranging acquaintance with both the "Old" and "New" versions of Sidney's romance. Beaumont and

Fletcher take their queen's name from the story (bk. 2, chap. 22) of Baccha, reputed to be "the most impudentlie unchaste woman of all *Asia.*" Other names—even those for servants, choric lords, and the dwarf Zoylus—are transferred from minor figures who appear briefly in more widely scattered episodes of books 1–3. One character, Bacha's machiavellian servant Timantus, comes from the other end of Sidney's story, books 4–5.[10]

Such borrowing from relatively insignificant figures suggests that, while sticking to the *Arcadia,* Beaumont and Fletcher wished to avoid the direct allusiveness of Day's *Ile of Guls,* whose version of Sidney's main plot retained the well-known names. The only inappropriate names in *Cupid's Revenge* are the king's and princess's. The choice of "Hidaspes" for Sidney's "Erona" remains mysterious: the one significant non-Arcadian name, it comes from Heliodorus's *Aethiopian History,* but there Hydaspes is the black King of Ethiopia. A Leontius appears in the *Arcadia,* but only to die avenging a friend's death in battle (bk. 3, chap. 7). Having decided on a plot that would extend Sidney's story of Erona through Cupid's punishment of her whole family, however, the dramatists had to create the family as well as its fate. "Leontius" provides a suitable designation to unite and personalize the two unnamed kings in chapter 2 whose stories are blended in the play.

If names and plot details for acts 3–5 are lifted from elsewhere in the *Arcadia,* in characterization, Beaumont and Fletcher use an analogously composite method. For both Leontius and Leucippus, behavior and personality derive largely from the more developed figures in Sidney's main plot. The king must be sufficiently foolish to allow his daughter's sacrilege and to marry his son's scheming mistress. Leontius is thus made an absurdly doting father in act 1 and his later courtship of Bacha modeled on that of Sidney's King Basilius, whose wooing of the disguised Prince Pyrocles furnishes some of the *Arcadia*'s funniest scenes. Leucippus's plight combines that of Plangus pursued by his new stepmother and that of Pyrocles and Musidorus imprisoned by the lustful Andromana; with Urania, Leucippus also absorbs the story of Pyrocles and the disguised Zelmane. In character, too, Beaumont and Fletcher's prince borrows from the *Arcadia*'s principals. Heroic friendship, a central theme in Sidney's work, gains prominence in *Cupid's Revenge* with the addition of the stalwart soldier-companion Ismenus, and his relationship with his cousin Leucippus is patterned on that of Pyrocles and Musidorus.

In theory complex, the only person in *Cupid's Revenge* to experience conflicting loyalties and a change of heart, Leucippus does not in fact transcend this additive approach to characterization. In act 1 he encourages his sister's folly—indeed, it seems a mutually planned sacrilege; in act 2 he jokes callously with his mistress Bacha. Upon his father's marriage, Leucippus suddenly recognizes the error of his ways and Cupid's power, and in acts 3–5 he becomes a noble-minded victim, credulous with his enemies and as much too good for this evil world as the saintly Urania.

The problem with Leucippus is, magnified, the play's, for it too is a rather broken-backed affair. Despite efforts to knit different stories by means of overlapping characters and themes, plotting remains sequential and the seams show. Clearly, *Cupid's Revenge* is Hidaspes's in act 1, though her death is held off until 2.5; at the end of act 1 Leontius suddenly wonders why his son has been absent from court, and act 2 becomes largely expository again, setting up the relations among Leucippus, Bacha, and the king. With Bacha established in 3.1 as now a scorned-woman and revengeress (and the existence of Urania made known), the play begins to work out its second set of consequences. The misjudgments are complementary. Where Beaumont and Fletcher need to be more daring in turning consecutive narratives into drama, they hold back and too slavishly follow their source. The result is drama at its most mechanical in matters of plot, dramatic construction, and to some extent in characterization. Where they are original, often in adapting material from elsewhere in the *Arcadia,* they are frequently too inventive and fail to see that they undermine what they have already borrowed.

At first glance Beaumont and Fletcher seem to attack straightforwardly the task of dramatization. They create three courtier-lords who provide continuity, exposition, and commentary. Bringing Cupid onstage in a spectacular descent contributes theatrical interest, and there was ample precedent for his appearance in the private theaters. While usually the familiar mischievous boy and incidental to the plot (as in Lyly's *Gallathea* and Jonson's *Cynthia's Revels* for Paul's, or Sharpham's *Cupid's Whirligig* for the Children of the King's Revels), in Lyly's *Loves Metamorphosis* (Q 1601, Paul's) Cupid is a major deity and his punishment of offenders central to the play. *Love's Metamorphosis* ends happily, however, while Beaumont and Fletcher's powerful god, angry at being scorned by those "whose

lives / Are but my recreation," carries out his vow to make the
whole kingdom "wretched" (1.3.7–8, 20; cf. 2.1.3–4). Their conception of Cupid as at best indifferent to men's happiness, at worst
a violent, even sadistic avenger, may show the influence of an apparent unrelated chapter in the *Arcadia*. Between the stories of Erona
and Plangus, Sidney offers the clownish Miso's old wives' tale that
vividly warns against Love by portraying him as a monstrous, "hang-
man" god who lures men and women to destruction. In *Cupid's
Revenge,* the god's curse produces its effect immediately, and making
Hidaspes's object a dwarf—"the most deformed fellow i' the Land"
(1.4.15)—suggests Miso's view of love as well as the playwrights'
striving for sensational effects. [11]

Cupid not only echoes the choric lords, defining Hidaspes's offense
and confirming that it will be punished; he also reappears to gloat
over his success and tell us he will use Bacha to chasten Hidaspes's
father and brother. Nor is he alone in announcing why and how he
operates: this is a play of rampant overexposition. Nearly every major
character favors unambiguous self-declaration, either to others or to
us. Demanding permission to marry the dwarf, Hidaspes tells her
father not to "looke / For reason or obedience in my words: . . .
My inflamed bloud heares nothing but my will" (1.5.70–75). Leucippus explains his repentance and predicament to Ismenus before
the interview with his stepmother that amply demonstrates both.
Though she plays her own game with Leucippus and Leontius, Bacha
admits to us that her motives are greed and lust, not love (2.2.71–
79). In asides she analyzes her behavior; scorned by a suddenly
"godly" stepson, she tells us exactly how she will effect her revenge
(3.2.81–84, 243–53). When not explaining themselves, they are
busy defining others. We are more than once prepared for both
Urania's goodness and her comic accent; Bacha seeks Timantus's aid
because, she informs us, she sees in him "A fellow voyde of any
worth to raise himselfe, / And therfore like to catch at any evill /
That will but plucke him uppe" (3.2.231–34).

Such elaborate exposition places the audience in a privileged position, sharing information with gods and villains that other characters lack. Our knowledge of Bacha's hypocrisy and intent to exploit
first Leucippus and then his father must make both seem gullible
fools. Her asides in 2.2, when despite the king's wrath she learns
she may yet turn events to her advantage, draw us into her confidence
and create comic undercurrents in a scene of apparently dangerous

confrontation. Our attention is redirected to her wit, to how she will extricate herself. When a rather dense but helpful Leucippus catches her hint on tactics, his hyperbolic praise of her chastity tips the scene's balance toward comedy. This emphasis Beaumont and Fletcher pursue in developing other aspects of their material.

Using Basilius as model for the love-sick Leontius may have been prompted by Sidney's own juxtapositions: in the *Arcadia,* chapter 15 recounts the tragic tale of the King of Iberia's doting submission to his new wife and attempt to have his son killed; chapter 16 presents the elderly Basilius's helpless passion for the disguised Pyrocles and ludicrous attempt to woo "her" by pretending to be young and dashing. In *Cupid's Revenge* Beaumont and Fletcher prepare for Leontius's antics by having Cupid single out the blaspheming children's father as ultimately responsible and, hence, worthy of a special punishment: "his madde love, shall publish that the rage / Of *Cupid,* has the power to conquer Age" (2.1.12–13). Certainly Sidney is willing to laugh at his characters, to present Basilius as a fool in love; indeed, even his noble princes are driven to hilariously unheroic postures by their disguised pursuit of Basilius's daughters. Yet Sidney's main plot is tragicomic, and his narrative voice controls the humor and keeps it good-natured. Basilius's folly is temporary; it is heightened into farce by his behavior but also by our knowledge that he has mistaken the sex of his beloved. Moreover, the object of his passion is unsuitable but not unworthy: in the end Pyrocles will make an entirely fitting husband for Basilius's daughter.

Beaumont and Fletcher's appropriation fits their characterization of love yet also subverts any single or cumulative tragic effect. There is no genial humor here, only a fool manipulated by a scheming woman and his own evil servant. Perhaps because their previous experience lay with the satiric comedy typical of the children's troupes, they seize on and expand this potential in Sidney. The result is two long scenes of hard-edged comedy at the play's center: one of Leontius dressing himself before his mirror, obsessed with the size of his feather, the cut of his clothes, and the fit of his false teeth (2.4); the other of his actual wooing of Bacha (2.6). In each, coarse, reductionist asides—first by Timantus, then by both Timantus and Bacha—keep Leontius the butt of our laughter. Not merely pitifully self-deluded, he is transformed into something grotesquely inhuman, looking "like Winter, stucke here and there with fresh flowers" (2.4.13–14). This tone dominates the play's middle acts, sustained by the choric lords' own commentary on Leontius's folly and Bacha's lust ("I knew her when I have beene offerd her to be brought to my bed for five pound"—3.1.13–14) and by scenes of Bacha's success in provoking Leontius's jealousy (3.4).

In different ways, both Leontius and Leucippus lose dignity as they become puppets of Bacha's and Timantus's manipulations. As Ismenus points out later, trying futilely to warn Leucippus against trusting Timantus, "Take heede, Children and Fooles first feele the smart, then weepe" (4.1.165–66). He articulates one danger in this presentation when he assures Leucippus that "if I lov'd you not, I would laugh at you, and see you run your neck into the noose, and cry a Woodcocke" (4.1.216–17). Tragedy, in the middle acts, evaporates into murderous farce. Even the repentant, "godly" Leucippus becomes comic facing Bacha's advances: in this tables-turned situation the ex-roué becomes suddenly too innocent to see the sexual invitation behind her opening coy remarks. His responses appear childlike and confused: "They that can answere must be lesse amazde, / Then I am now: you see my teares deliver / My meaning to you" (3.2.173–75). Bacha controls the game, alternately mocking and threatening him. Indeed, the whole bizarre love-triangle is developed initially along city comedy lines—the sexual adventuress scheming her way into a profitable marriage and then wooing the embarrassed ex-lover, now stepson. The farcical presentation of Leontius's folly oddly brackets and distances the scene of Hidaspes's death (2.5).

The play's comic treatment of its ostensibly tragic material is intermittent but pervasive, and it undermines both unity of tone and dramatic coherence. The rescue of Leucippus appears in Sidney, but Beaumont and Fletcher change the prince's supporters from friends and followers to a group of unnamed, comically presented, citizens. The rescue itself is reported, but they are given one scene as they gather outside their shops (4.3). Similar local disturbances occur with the play's minor good characters. Urania's comic-rustic dialect seems a misguided way of establishing her innocence of courtly ways, especially since we are elaborately cued to find her funny. Ismenus, too, is exposed to our laughter. Insisting on following Leucippus into exile, Ismenus becomes tongue-tied when asked his reasons; his sudden inability to declare his loving friendship is presented comically rather than as an example of manly reticence.

A more general confusion of tone accompanies each appearance of the choric lords who open the play, then reappear to report events and offer their opinions. Political temporizers whose self-interest has produced the courtly wisdom of "heare all, and say nothing" (2.3.39), they play no active part in the story. Their one opportunity, which they reject, is the rescue of Leucippus. Yet despite their peripheral plot status, they dominate or appear prominently in six scenes; though they largely disappear after 4.4, their cynical prose has left an indellible mark. Their appropriate milieu is satiric comedy, and they add to the timeless romance world of Sidney's tragic tales a contemporary, very Jacobean spirit. They prove to be rather self-centered young gallants than political advisors; to these hangers-on, love does not exist and sex is a casual commodity, a subject for smutty humor. They see pride and blasphemy in Hidaspes's request and her father's acquiescence, but they also make sport of the probable consequences: a "plague" of chastity brought on by a ruler who is "old and past it," though their own promiscuous lives will suffer "hard meate" if women should grow honest (1.1.117, 111).

The Woman Hater's cynical young men—its courtiers, Count Valore, even its Duke—thus get recycled into *Cupid's Revenge,* and they bring with them even more problems for tragedy than for a play only in part meant as romantic comedy. In beginning *Cupid's Revenge* by treating as a joke the situation that ultimately results in seven deaths, they initiate a confusion exacerbated by later comic moments. They also muddy the play's moral bearings, giving us jumbled signals about how to interpret events as well as about what kind of play to expect. Until Cupid himself declares the severity of his wrath, an offense against this deity would seem a comic predictor, as it had in other "Cupid" plays; with the lords' jests as cue, we expect the prim young enforcers of chastity to learn comedy's lesson in self-knowledge and the acceptance of sexual maturity. We soon learn both Hidaspes and the lords are wrong. The lords see her faults, but the promiscuity they laud hardly presents an inviting alternative. We are offered only desperate extremes; no middle possibility of sexual temperance is admitted by anyone. The lords confess that they have loved "wickedly . . . for endlesse pleasures," that although "our women were new still as we needed 'em: yet we like beasts still cryde" (1.1.120–24). The predicted Lenten season is deserved, the natural consequence of heedless indulgence: it "comes of fulnes, a sin too frequent with us" (1.1.146–47).

To add to our confusion, Cupid's previous punishment for a lesser slight was to enforce exactly the constancy and temperance humanity here admits to being incapable of exercising on its own. As one lord sarcastically reports, "what followed? Women kept their houses, grew good huswives . . . wore their own faces . . . and which was most lamentable, they lov'd their husbands" (1.1.129–33). What had looked like pride and excessive austerity in Hidaspes in fact takes on a certain attractiveness. Yet Hidaspes's usurpation of Cupid's prerogative now brings an opposite curse. What we see of love in the play is not the expected plague of fidelity but passion out of all control—irrational, unnatural, destructive of the self as well as literally fatal. The Priest of Cupid in his song promises an ideal: sensual love free of the *"frozen honour"* of social hypocrisy, but also one in which *"Men shall be true, and women shall beleeve"* (1.2.21, 26). What we hear from the hardened young gallants and what we see of Cupid's influence suggest that the priest has mistaken his god.

Cupid's Revenge offers a perplexing deity, one who demands worship but whose imperatives are at different times contradictory. He controls this play's world but, except that it is clearly unwise to offend him, he provides no helpful moral guidance. According to his own laws he aids or destroys those who are his "recreation"; his justice remains arbitrary and inscrutable. The choric lords offer criticism freely but no human standard of values, sexual or otherwise, from which to take our bearings. In Zoylus's execution they see only a threat to themselves (2.3), and they will adopt whatever behavior seems expedient: "though my owne nature hate it, if all determine to be knaves, Ile try what I can doe upon my selfe, . . . I will not have my throat cut for my goodnes" (3.3.10–13).

To offset murderous egotism and self-serving pragmatism, *Cupid's Revenge* proposes a rather mixed assortment of dramatized alternatives: Urania, the citizens, Ismenus, and Leucippus. As romantic lover Urania represents contrast but no realistic ideal. Her love alone is selfless; yet though not exactly grotesque, it is hopeless, immobilized by her disguise as a boy and refusal to declare herself. For her, too, love is fatal: she is pining away in Leucippus's arms even before being granted the opportunity to die on the sword meant for him. The citizens demonstrate a political honor and loyalty conspicuously lacking in their social superiors, but they appear in only one scene and their success is nullified by Leucippus's refusal of the crown and by the further machinations that lead to his murder.

The devoted friendship between Ismenus and Leucippus quite obviously sets up a positive moral value, yet it remains as ineffectual
as the citizens' loyalty. Ismenus survives, and the dying Leucippus,
Hamlet-like, does what he can for his kingdom by handing it over
to his cousin. Yet while the traditional political coda effectively
signals the final exhaustion of Cupid's wrath, it carries less weight
if we try to read it as proof of the triumph of good over evil.

Leucippus himself contributes to the ending's sense of moral
indeterminacy. The dramatists not only use him to focus the action;
they also make him another martyr-hero, spiritual twin to Urania
even if not her lover. Pressing Leucippus into such disparate service
in the play's two halves entails more than a swift conversion; as
Beaumont and Fletcher present it, repentance creates a psychological
regression that weakens Leucippus's authority and stature. The
movement is an awkward one, from experience to the innocence of
an adolescent bewildered by reality's violation of ethical precept. In
acts 4–5 he emerges as prototype of those later honor-bound young
men who, torn between conflicting loyalties and beliefs, become
both suicidal and fondly trusting. In 4.1, where he wishes for death,
and especially 5.4, with the lovelorn page Urania, Leucippus has
already taken on the tone, even the language, of Philaster.

Though they borrow from the *Arcadia*'s tragicomic main plot,
Beaumont and Fletcher take none of its trust in a mysterious but
benevolent Providence. The world of *Cupid's Revenge* is a nightmare
come true, and Ismenus and Leucippus can only respond with horrified disbelief: "I am sure we dreame: this cannot be" (4.1.73).
Unable to bear a god and a world that promote human suffering,
Leucippus turns to insistent faith, in villains like Timantus as well
as in the heavens' necessary goodness. Blame must be internalized,
lest it threaten fundamental cosmological explanations. Leucippus
is, in the play's scheme, punished for having offended Cupid, but
until almost the end he persists in the more conventional belief that
his affair with Bacha is the source of his persecution and his father's
subjugation. Converted, he needs his gods to represent chastity and
veracity. He assures Ismenus that "they above . . . are intirely
truth" and now punish his sin in lying about Bacha (3.2.27); the
gods are "just" and will in their own "blessed time . . . mercifully
. . . ease my griefe" (3.2.110–13). "What ever Fortune comes,"
he can "bid it welcome, / My innocencie is my Armor" (4.2.103–
4).

Like the Priest's song, Leucippus's assertions do not tally with the nature or purposes of the only god we have seen or with the world he rules. Bacha is merely Cupid's agent, and the corrupt court more nearly mirrors this god's glib amorality than does the saintly Leucippus. An impassable gulf widens between the prince's belief in ultimate justice and what the play's action shows. He may trust the "Heavens [will] defend me / As I am innocent," but Cupid is unforgiving and, in any case, unlikely to look favorably on a heart now committed to chastity (4.1.189–90). Urania unwittingly reminds us of our privileged knowledge when she prays for her mother: "Feth a she be no good, God may her so" (4.1.98). The god of this play never does "make" Bacha good; he needs her vicious for his own purposes. Blind to the nature of his world, Leucippus refuses to punish Bacha when he can: "Leave her to heaven brave Cousen, / They shall tell her how she has sind against em" (5.4.150–51). Cupid has cozened this world even more effectively than his agent, and the play's prevailing fatalism and uncertainty is more accurately captured by the prayer of one of the three lords: "Thou angry power, whether of heaven or hell, / That layst this sharpe correction on our Kingdome . . . O heare me, and at length be pleas'd, be pleas'd / With pitty to draw backe thy vengeance" (4.4.26–30). Pity is hardly Cupid's distinguishing characteristic, and he refuses to accept Leucippus's execution, on his father's order, as "sacrifice for all"; he postpones the occasion of this death until it can garner three more.

This mixed view of the gods, the tension between what is claimed of them and the nature they seem to demonstrate through events, persists, though more fruitfully, in later Beaumont-Fletcher plays. When the gods remain offstage, effective ambiguity can replace flat contradiction. *Cupid's Revenge* entertains incompatible explanations without gaining real complexity, and this philosophical irresolution intensifies the local effect of inconsistency in characterization and clashing modes of dramatic presentation. Comedy and tragedy mix without achieving an effective or harmonious blend; instead, comic scenes and types repeatedly undermine the gravity of the situation and erode any sense of tragic inevitability. Technically tragedy, *Cupid's Revenge* more nearly approximates the "mungrell Tragy-comedie"—ill-sorted compound of "Horn-pypes and Funeralls"—that Sidney deplores in *An Apologie for Poetrie*.[12] Eugene Waith rightly observes of *Cupid's Revenge* that if "all the characters were

saved from death and if the play ended in repentance and reconciliation, its total effect would be very little different."[13]

A new departure, *Cupid's Revenge* introduces numerous elements
of the joint style—from specific incidents that appear in other plays
(like the citizen rescue of a prince), to the types and patterning of
characters. It also reflects both men's continued interest in blending
genres, in creating fresh kinds of plays rather than merely repro-
ducing variations on children's-troupe staples. Despite its apparent
commercial success, however, Beaumont and Fletcher seem to have
shared posterity's dissatisfaction with the play: they do not repeat
its form, nor do they again become so hamstrung by their sources.
Yet what they had found most congenial in Sidney lay at a more
basic level than plot, and some features of his romance lingered to
help shape the pattern of subsequent collaborations. They develop
their own version of Sidney's partly pastoral, partly courtly and
aristocratic environment. More important, they learn what Sidney
himself discovered in revising his own work: a "timeless" thematic
structure, allowing for sharp tonal juxtapositions between scenes,
replaces plot as the primary organizing principle. The seemingly
endless proliferation of stories and characters in the "New" *Arcadia*,
the alternation between the "present" of Basilius's retreat and tales
of the heroes' and others' past adventures, make thematic sense
despite violations of chronological order and apparently constant
digression from the events of the main story. Finally, Sidney's witty,
sophisticated, self-mocking narrative tone provided a model for which
Beaumont and Fletcher continued to seek dramatic expression.[14]

Tragicomedy and Fletcher's *Faithful Shepherdess*

Although *Philaster* shows some influence from the pastoral romance *Diana*, the play derives fundamentally from a more sophisticated and bolder reworking of the Arcadian material used in *Cupid's
Revenge*.[15] *Philaster*'s aesthetic advance rests on the lessons learned
there, but also on another work of the same year as *Cupid's Revenge:*
Fletcher's adroit though commercially unsuccessful pastoral tragicomedy, *The Faithful Shepherdess*. Though it models its title, and in
the quarto issue its combative defense of tragicomedy, on Guarini's
Il Pastor Fido, Fletcher's play is in fact quite original. Whether
written before, after, or simultaneously with *Cupid's Revenge, The
Faithful Shepherdess* shows Fletcher transmuting much of the same

material into a more limited but also more clearly articulated and controlled generic blend.

In some ways *The Faithful Shepherdess* seems a critique, or at least companion piece, of the courtly corruption and awkwardly combined genres of *Cupid's Revenge*. Fletcher's play celebrates fidelity and chastity, two virtues turned on their head in the tragedy's dramatization of the power of sensual love. Some of the main character types of *Cupid's Revenge* appear, elaborated in pastoral terms. The "gullible old king" and "faithful friend" are absent, but the rest are now more easily seen as "a gamut of love extending from spiritual devotion to bestial sensuality," and the play fixes its moral hierarchy by providing the ideal against which all are measured, the title shepherdess Clorin.[16] A shifting configuration of lovers rather than true narrative sequence, the play's thematic patterning, too, probably owes something to the reading of the *Arcadia* that produced *Cupid's Revenge*. *The Faithful Shepherdess* is more successful dramatically in part because Fletcher has narrowed his scope (temporally, in obeying the unity of time, and in the smaller cast's integration into a single "plot"); he has also found a dramatic model for the structure of events. Both direct allusion and more diffuse imitation show that Shakespeare's *Midsummer Night's Dream*—the night in the magical wood of acts 2 and 3—stands behind *The Faithful Shepherdess*. In tone, too, the Shakespeare of *Midsummer Night's Dream* reinforces Sidney as a model. The kind of mixed mode *Cupid's Revenge* seems to strive for, against genre, with a different emphasis and a smaller canvas Fletcher catches as he learns how to introduce tragic potential while subordinating it to comedy's final reconciliations.

Fletcher discovered in practice what the printed text's epistle "To the Reader" defends in theory: a conception of tragicomedy as a sophisticated blend of genres that results not in the awkward yoking that Sidney scorned but in a new genre with its own distinctive style and effect. That this form was new, and his own audience unprepared to understand what it was offered, is clear from the play's initial failure and from Fletcher's own wish that his explanatory epistle "had bene the prologue" (ll. 2–3).[17] To answer his Italian critics, Guarini had developed a justification of his unorthodox mixture;[18] from Guarini Fletcher borrows his definition of the new genre's latitude in subject matter, character, and style:

A tragie-comedie is not so called in respect of mirth and killing, but in respect it wants deaths, which is inough to make it no tragedie, yet brings some neere it, which is inough to make it no comedie: which must be a representation of familiar people, with such kinde of trouble as no life be questioned, so that a God is as lawfull in this as in a tragedie, and meane people as in a comedie. (ll. 20–26)

Fletcher's epistle helped to establish the term, as part of the English critical vocabulary, and to legitimize "tragicomedy" as a theatrical form. Tragicomedy became, indeed, one of the most popular seventeenth-century genres, and although few adopted Fletcher's pastoralism, his emphasis on erotic themes proved to be, if not original, influential.

The result of Fletcher's delicate combination of gods and shepherds, lyricism and earthy humor, threatened loss and (in the middle section) farce, is a sophisticated double view of love. We are made to feel love's unique and individuating importance, the intensity and power that to the lover makes every obstacle tragically significant; at the same time, we are asked to share the dramatist's appreciation—acknowledged, as it were, over the heads of the characters—of humankind's mortal folly in love. Fletcher lets us share sympathetically his characters' torments, as we largely do not in *Cupid's Revenge*, while yet distancing them by exaggeration and poetic stylization: the characters' purposefully heightened emotions are simultaneously both real and remote.[19] This is a complexity of response fully achieved with *Philaster*, but in the rarefied pastoral idiom, using some of the components of *Cupid's Revenge*, Fletcher seems to have worked out the way to manage truly tragicomic effects.

Despite its virtual uniqueness in Jacobean drama, then, *The Faithful Shepherdess* should be seen in relation to Beaumont and Fletcher's other work. It looks forward to the essential shape of the plays to come; it displays a kinship in attitude extending beyond the Arcadian material that at the time occupied them both. Different as it is from Beaumont's plays, *The Faithful Shepherdess* suggests why this particular collaboration was so effective and, perhaps, why it produced plays of such seamless jointure. Each liked dramatic experiment, especially the innovative mixing of genres and conventions. In *The Faithful Shepherdess* Fletcher also demonstrates his share in the taste for emphatically theatricalized emotion and action that incurred later charges of sensationalism and decadence.[20] Fletcher's young shepherd Perigot, for instance, stands midway between Leucippus and Philaster as a romantic hero whose naiveté threatens repeatedly to make him merely ridiculous. Thoroughly confused by various twists in the plot, Perigot twice stabs his beloved with his sword. The reprise of his action in *Philaster* proved so successful that the woodcut on the 1620 quarto depicts the wounded heroine, and the play's alternate title was "Love lies a Bleeding."[21]

The Faithful Shepherdess also reveals a Fletcher who helped create the disturbing, morally ambiguous world of *Cupid's Revenge* and the later work with Beaumont. Fletcher wisely keeps his presiding diety offstage, yet Pan's representatives—his priest, the forest Satyre, the River God—appear, and they muddy the philosophical waters for both characters and audience alike. The Priest of Pan counsels purity and chastity, and Clorin's prominence, the Satyre's instinctive worship of her, and her ability to command nature's curative power all seem to support the idea of a moral nature with which man need only align himself to find his proper path. Yet elsewhere Fletcher presents a richly Ovidian world. Pan does not direct this play's action because he is otherwise engaged: notwithstanding his injunctions about human conduct, he is reveling with his paramour. The River God falls in love with the mortal Amoret and woos her in some of the play's most gorgeous verse. Satyre, at least temporarily, shifts his allegiance from promiscuous Pan to chaste Clorin, but he offers her the same tribute intended for Pan—the fruits of nature's "lusty spring"—and reminds her that the "lusty blood" of his proffered grapes is "the learned Poets good" as well as Bacchus's "crowne" (1.1.51, 76–78). This paradoxical, polymorphous nature refuses simplification; instead, despite attempts to order it into socially acceptable form, it gives us back our own contradictions. Fletcher explores the premises of his models, both romantic comedy and pastoral, and pays tribute to the values they celebrate. Like Sidney and Shakespeare, he also acknowledges the difficulties and complexities pastoral's Golden World can so easily ignore.[22]

If his own initial effort failed, Fletcher learned his lesson and did not again venture a purely pastoral play. Tragicomedy, however, had begun to flourish, and in the early years of James's reign others experimented with ways to adapt this form to the English tradition. G. K. Hunter has pointed out that sixteenth-century Italian tragedy had had little appeal in England because its conventions emphasized the personal and passionate; eschewing the political conflicts favored by Elizabethan tragedy, it appeared inadequate and incomplete.[23] The same absence of a political dimension marked the new Italian pastoral tragicomedy, and *Il Pastor Fido* earned contemporary accusations (from Ben Jonson, for instance) of triviality. The first real translation of Guarini's tragicomic ideal into the context of the English professional theater was Marston's *Malcontent* (Q 1604), popular on both the public and private stage. Marston, like Fletcher, borrows Guarini's erotic emphasis, but he sets it in a quasi-historical world of political tyranny and court intrigue. Love and politics affect all relationships, yet their very intermingling means that steadfastness in love can help resolve political problems and turn revenge tragedy toward expulsion of the incorrigible, forgiveness of the repentant. Although Marston's influence on Beaumont and Fletcher is clear from *The Woman Hater* through *A King and No King,* he was not alone in seeing the newly fashionable tragicomedy's potential. Guarini's ideal, often blended with satiric comedy, found a suitable soil in both public and private theaters. In *Philaster* the young collaborators set about their own "Englishing" of the new form.

Philaster

Freed of *Cupid's Revenge*'s slavish adherence to one source, Beaumont and Fletcher again become original and eclectic. A summary of the raw materials for *Philaster*—"plot-situation from Perez, character-types from Sidney, and an emotional situation" from *Hamlet*[24]—suggests the range of sources but not the decisiveness of the return to dramatic models. The characteristic tragicomic vision derives largely from prose romance; the influential form discovered with *Philaster* results from reexamining theatrical practice. Marston's *Malcontent* offered one precedent—in setting, political concerns, and nontragic resolution. In substantive matters, Beaumont and Fletcher find their own way. In their first play for the King's Men they work out their dramatic structure by inventively blending comedy and tragedy, and the generic exemplars through which they filter the characters and relationships established in *Cupid's Revenge* and *The Faithful Shepherdess* are Shakespearean.[25]

The most immediately obvious source is *Hamlet*. The initial handling of the dispossessed-prince *topos* and the usurping king's guilty conscience both evoke Shakespeare's play. Beyond its commercial viability as a story line, we may also sense Beaumont and Fletcher's special affinity for this play and its themes. John F. Danby perhaps overestimates *Hamlet*'s determining effect, but he rightly sees that its mood and subject (its "moral bewilderment and confusion") approximate *Philaster*'s;[26] indeed, the problem of piercing false appearance plagues all Beaumont and Fletcher's heroes. Yet while the Philaster of 1.1 seems meant to recall Shakespeare's prince in both character and situation, Beaumont and Fletcher start their modifications early. Structurally, Philaster is less prominent, as well as less active. Nor is he the play's moral voice, the dominant consciousness through which its vision is established. Although titular hero, he remains a victim of events. His importance lies in his private, emotional relationships, and state concerns are handed over, after 1.1 to the court lords for interpretation and to the citizens for active intervention.

Altering the initial situation provides the conditions for a non-tragic resolution and establishes romantic love as *Philaster*'s primary theme. The King of Calabria has usurped Sicily in the minority of its rightful prince and, to ensure that Philaster is stripped of all hope, the king plans to marry his daughter Arathusa to the visiting Spanish prince, Pharamond. Tyrant king and dispossessed heir roles provoked tension and confrontation in 1.1, but Philaster has no murdered father to avenge, and the usurper is also true king of a country to which he can return. *Philaster*'s king remains a flat, uninteresting (and unnamed) character, swinging between ranting tyranny and remorse for past deeds, but the guilty conscience and genuine concern for his daughter partially prepare us for his final conversion and acceptance of Philaster as son-in-law and king. Philaster shares Hamlet's moody indecisiveness but little else, and his vacillation between opposed commitments lacks wider political or metaphysical implications. Only tongue-tied love for the usurper's daughter keeps Philaster from more than verbal assertion of his right to Sicily. Pharamond's prominence, too, helps shift the emphasis away from political concerns, for this rival proves unsuitable not only as foreigner but also as comic braggart and sensualist.

The play in fact briefly becomes romantic comedy when the plucky Arathusa takes matters in hand. She woos the bashful Philaster, and he gives her his beloved new page, Bellario, to act as go-between; learning of Pharamond's assignation with one of the court ladies, Megra, Arathusa devises a plot to discredit her father's choice of husbands. Yet the scene of Arathusa's comic triumph, 2.4, also plunges the play back toward tragic complications. Caught with Pharamond, the vicious Megra tries to extenuate her guilt by accusing Arathusa of the same sexual misconduct with Bellario. In a slandered-beloved plot the challenge is Philaster's, and this test demands not clever intrigue but a lover's faith. Neither king nor courtiers believe Arathusa's innocence, and her affection for the servant, as well as Bellario's loyalty to his master's mistress, lead to bold defenses of each other whose language seems to confirm their guilt before the lover who judges them.

A naif in love as well as politics, Philaster understands himself and the nature of passion as little as he understands women. In the wooing scene he had been uneasy with Arathusa's forthright declaration of love, for "how this passion should proceed from you, / So violently, would amaze a man, / That would be jealous" (1.2.94–96). Apparently betrayed by the two people he loves most, Philaster's torment is assured when the courtier Dion falsely swears, "I tooke them: I my selfe" (3.1.111). This misguided attempt to turn Philaster against the princess and spur him to political revolt instead throws Philaster into hysterical despair and removes even his will to live. Chaos is come again, and for two acts the dramatists move Arathusa, Bellario, and Philaster from court to forest and through every possible emotionally charged encounter. Confronted with Bellario's "smooth . . . brow" and unchanged appearance, Philaster wavers. Seeing that "the face you [gods] let him weare / When he was innocent, is still the same, / Not blasted," Philaster "cannot now / Thinke he is guilty" (3.1.150–55). Impaled on apparent contradictions, Philaster both forgives and banishes his page. His lady "A meere confusion . . . That love cannot distinguish," Philaster flings at Arathusa any "right I have / To this poore Kingdome" and seeks only a wasteland in which to curse all women "Till my last houre" (3.2.105–27). Later he asks Arathusa to kill him; when she refuses, he tells her to say her prayers and then turns his sword on her. Prevented from completing this Othello-like "peece of Justice" (4.5.71) by a Country Fellow, the wounded Philaster flees, only to come upon the sleeping Bellario and stab him, too.

Through escalating violence and despair events seem to have reached an impasse, and the three wounded principals are found by the courtiers and dragged off to prison. In fact, at the beginning of act 5 the personal crisis has been resolved: both Arathusa and Bellario proved their loyalty by trying to protect Philaster even after he had wounded them. In prison each asks and bestows forgiveness. Arathusa and Philaster are wed, and Bellario dressed as Hymen blessing the marriage, precedes them into the king's presence. Private resolutions do not engender public ones, however: the king remains unmoved. Philaster's execution is prevented only by an armed rising of the citizens, who capture Pharamond and hold him hostage. Political revolt and fear tap the king's conscience. He reinstates Philaster as prince and offers both Arathusa and his own repentance.

The play threatens to double back on itself when this harmony is shattered: the banished Megra repeats her earlier charge. Arathusa seems to have been returned to the end of act 2; the king repeats his earlier credulity and anger. Philaster has new reason to despair and threaten suicide, since he has innocently granted the king's request for a "favour" that proves to be the torture of Bellario. The surprise resolution of this last crisis turns on a deployment of *Twelfth Night*'s act 5 recognition scene that also recycles the faithful Urania of *Cupid's Revenge*. Bellario disproves Megra's charge by revealing that "he" is a "she," Dion's own daughter Euphrasia. We were told in 1.2 of her existence, away on a mysterious pilgrimage; in fact, out of love for Philaster she disguised herself to serve him and, in his service, help court his beloved. Ever-forgiving Arathusa accepts, even urges, Bellario-Euphrasia's continued devotion to Philaster, and the play ends with lovers reconciled and parents reunited with children.

One obvious feature of *Philaster*'s structuring of events is its constant alternation of generic models. The play does not simply start as tragedy and then proceed to work out a comic resolution. Rather, the "middle mood" of Beaumont and Fletcher's tragicomedy is attained by the play's seeming to head in one direction, as in act 2's development as Arathusa's romantic intrigue-comedy, until stopped by a plot twist that implies a wholly different outcome.[27] And this oscillation is not simply between plot "signals"; it is established by the mingling of kinds of scenes, by the calculated movement between highly rhetorical verse and earthy prose, and by the play's shifting perspectives on its own action.

Dion and his two friends in 1.1 provide exposition, bawdy jokes, and sarcastic political commentary. They reappear frequently with similar contributions. More prominent and more skillfully integrated into the plot than the threesome in *Cupid's Revenge*, their cynical realism creates one of the perspectives that in *Philaster* coexists with the idealized love of Philaster, Arathusa, and Bellario. Like the lords in *Cupid's Revenge*, those in *Philaster* give us the sense of an often shrewd court—their opening "characters" of the king and court ladies prove accurate—but also in moral terms a rather tawdry one. They are at home in the Pharamond-Megra world of acts 1 and 2. Dion's lie to Philaster disturbs both in its social and political immorality and in Dion's easy rationalization ("tis without question so"—3.1.27). Although the lords are apparently ready to second Philaster if he will rebel, and Dion actually stands up to the absolutist king in 4.4 by reminding him of both human and divine limits on secular power, they are too close to the time-servers of *Cupid's Revenge* to establish themselves as fully reliable moral spokesmen. They misjudge both Arathusa and Philaster. They continually mock the vulgar citizens, but most of their own criticism is safely delivered in asides. It is the despised shopkeepers who save Philaster, and the self-righteous courtiers' real attitude seems best indicated by Dion's cautious remark that "I feare not for my selfe, and yet I feare too: / Well, we shall see, we shall see: no more" (1.1.117–18).

This juxtaposition of perspectives is fundamental to the play. The choric lords merge with and provide commentary asides to court scenes; they are also given scenes of their own which offer direct contrast to the intense passion and psychological torment of the young lovers. Ostensibly marking the change of locale to the woods, 4.1's bawdy prose shocks after the despairing, highly wrought verse of Arathusa's interview with Bellario and of Arathusa's prayer to Diana for a death that will "have my story written in my wounds" (3.2.173). Other scenes introduce new, unexpected characters, like the Woodmen awed by Megra's heroic sexual capacity and interested only in "tumbling" errant court wenches (4.2.20–30). The rustic yokel who intervenes to save Arathusa from Philaster's "justice" in 4.5 offers yet another view. The two sequences of rising passion involving Philaster, Arathusa, and Bellario are thus cut across by the voices of a world that finds the lovers' exquisite sensibilities unintelligible. Again in act 5, the citizens' scene removes us from the impassioned court. We are offered the verbal humor of a Captain addressing his shopkeeper "troops" in their own language and the farcical collapse of Pharamond's braggadocio rhetoric as the citizens threaten to cut off different parts of his anatomy for their own particular uses.

Philaster thus presents a diverse array of voices and perspectives—court, country, city—that together make up its world. In terms of plot and structure, the frame is political and social. Contemporary allusions suggest a nod at Jacobean realities of power, in the king's passion for hunting and for political absolutism, though the court background is developed in theatrically familiar terms of Italianate corruption.[28] Still, linguistically, in the lords' and Woodmen's racy prose, as well as in the play's very London shopkeepers and cynical depiction of the court, there are enough ties to suggest that despite the conventionality of the portrait, this is *Philaster*'s realistic pole.

In this world the lovers must negotiate their existence, yet they do not speak or act in its terms. That their interrelations, and later their laments, belong to a different realm, that of pastoral romance, is clear as early as Philaster's lyric description of his first meeting Bellario at a forest well (1.2.111–39). Interestingly, if in one sense *Philaster* is structured by surprise contrasts and juxtapositions, both between scenes and within them, in another Beaumont and Fletcher have kept their worlds separate, in effect have folded one within the other. For this they have chosen their setting well. Unlike the mythical realm of *Cupid's Revenge*, *Philaster*'s Sicily evokes an at least pseudohistorical world of real conflict between Spain and Italy as well as the idyllic pastoral Sicily of Theocritus, from whose spring Arathusa takes her name. Just as the play's action takes place in both court and forest, its world "is not entirely the world of pastoral romance, nor is it a true reflection of the world of actuality."[29] Traditionally, pastoral provides a landscape for the tribulations of the heart, and in acts 3 and 4 *Philaster* moves beyond the "contemporary" world into this timeless inner realm.

Physically, the locale does not shift until act 4, when the two landscapes coexist: a real wood, inhabited by Woodmen and country rustics, to which the court has come for sport, and a symbolic one in which the lovers wander disconsolately, oblivious of their surroundings. Yet we also witness the destruction of the lovers' private world, the way in which mistrust annihilates identity. This reversal the court initiates, and for it Beaumont and Fletcher introduce a different type of dramatic construction. In plot terms, the play stops. Development is now thematic and emotional, on the pattern Fletcher had explored in *The Faithful Shepherdess*. Bellario assumes equal prominence with Arathusa and Philaster, and dramatic "events" become the shifting conjunctions that mark their spiral toward isolation and despair. Two long sequences unfold this tragic mental progress; though each has its own emotional crescendo, they also create a sustained movement toward the final eruption of psychic pain into physical violence.

The first sequence, act 3, establishes the way in which Megra's defensive falsehood works its havoc. The situation's pathos is increased by having each of the principals hear the accusation, secondhand, from someone already convinced of its truth. Dion asserts, as common knowledge, that Arathusa is "knowne a whore" (3.1.63). Philaster's frenzied rejection—"It is impossible . . . it cannot be" (3.1.92, 97)—suggests the extent to which this young idealist has reconstructed his lost political identity entirely around his beloved. If the charges be true, then it is "truth / That woman-kind is false" (3.1.90–91). The failure of such a fundamental bond shakes Philaster's sense of himself as well as his world. Dion's confirmatory lie produces immediate despair: Philaster wishes either to be killed or to be made bestial and so insensible to betrayal.

Beaumont and Fletcher dramatize not the gradual deterioration of a psychologically complex Philaster, but the way his sudden transformation affects his relations with Bellario and Arathusa. Bellario interrupts Philaster's soliloquy, and their first interview builds to the page's helpless denials and offer, as proof of innocence, to die on Philaster's threatening sword. Caught between the convincing appearance of virtue and his "knowledge" that Bellario's protests must be false, Philaster exhibits the schizophrenic behavior this newly contradictory world seems to demand. Such "honest lookes" require that "A love from me to thee / Is firme, what e're thou doest," yet at the same time Philaster cannot endure Bellario's presence: "something is done . . . that will make me mad, / If I behold thee" (3.1.274–81). Bellario and Philaster go their separate ways, and we watch Arathusa's father, with his talk of what the "common people speake," explode her childhood faith that things are what they seem (3.2.32). The king's accusations are succeeded by Philaster's, and in the scene's last interview the bewildered Arathusa in turn reproves a now thoroughly distracted Bellario for plotting against her with Philaster. Each departs seeking solitude and death.

With all the misunderstandings established, and Philaster apparently locked in an endless circle of suspicion, anger, and self-flagellation, act 4's forest provides the despairing lovers with neatly choreographed "chance" meetings that culminate in a triple interview and the theatrical stabbings of 4.5 and 4.6. Philaster's rage

at Arathusa's betrayal prompts him to execute "Justice" on her, but
he is in fact as suicidal as the others. Unable to bear the world into
which they have been thrust, each begs death at the hands of the
beloved, and this propensity for self-sacrifice changes the whole tone
of what had seemed to be climactic confrontations. As in the other
collaborations, the impulse to obliteration is not projected, but
internalized. All reach an abnormally heightened state: if Philaster,
claiming a "temperate . . . heart," has a pulse that "keepes mad-
mans time," the same diagnosis must apply to Arathusa's and Bellario's death-directed submission (4.5.46, 55).

The passionate heart of *Philaster* lies in this despairing self-aban-
don, an inner world of all coherence gone reflected in Philaster's
shifts between anger and passivity and in all three lovers' desire for
oblivion. The emotional and rhetorical patterning that leads to
physical action is carefully executed. That emotional pitch is also
calculatedly "placed," both by the treatment of the lovers themselves
and by the structural alternation and contrast that refuses them the
isolation they seek. *Philaster*'s two worlds run parallel courses until
the courtiers stumble on the wounded Arathusa in 4.5 and then on
Bellario and Philaster in 4.6, but we have heard the voices of that
crass outer world, intermittently, all along, and they enforce a more
detached view of what to the romantic young lovers is a private
tragedy. The response appropriate to the new, mingled drama stems
not merely from the substitution of superficial wounds for the intended ritual murder—the danger not the death—but from the
way the playwrights set off, "italicize," the lovers' behavior.[30] Just
as Philaster's oscillation, now within a few lines, works against the
dignity and incremental power of an heroic surrender to ungovernable jealousy, so the coarse humor and pragmatic emphasis of the
intervening scenes undermine tragedy's sense of relentless fatality.

Perhaps most revealing of Beaumont and Fletcher's care to maintain this double view is their treatment of the emotional and rhetorical climax of the lovers' interaction. A willing Arathusa, on the
point of receiving "peace in death" from Philaster, is interrupted
not by a shepherd but by the Country Fellow's comic turn. Critics
focus on the Country Fellow for good reasons. Such a radical juxtaposition of styles and perspectives can hardly be accidental. The
wandering yokel's initial soliloquy brings to the scene of strained,
ultimately suicidal, passion a whole world of normal, stolid but
good-natured folk who "hunt" only the occasional "gay sights" to

round out a satisfying life. However disputed its effect, the Country Fellow's entrance changes our relation to events, and when Arathusa turns on him, not for help but to berate him as "ill-bred" for intruding, her surprising description of the "tragedy" he has disturbed —"our private sports, our recreations" (4.5.89–90)—ensures our sudden disengagement. The Country Fellow offers both linguistic contrast and the common sense that "sees" literally: "I know not your rethoricke, but I can lay it on if you touch the woman" (4.5.96–97). The sudden dose of comic realism explodes our unequivocal acceptance of the action as, for dramatic purposes, both plausible and affecting.

The play balances delicately between two opposed views of its story. The central misapprehension, with its attendant emotional crises, is both all important to its sufferers, capable of overturning their world and annihilating the will to live, and also unreal, incomprehensible to normal countrymen and courtiers alike. To the play's audience, which knows Arathusa's innocence, it is a mistake become nightmare through Philaster's disoriented imagination, the product of a mind spinning helplessly in a void it has itself created. Neither view cancels the other. The play makes us participate in both.

This balance is, by and large, maintained, and from it arises that peculiar aesthetic distance and structure of feeling we associate with Beaumont and Fletcher tragicomedy. The rustic humorist need not return (though the comic citizens do). The shift in perspective releases us from Philaster's claustrophobic hysteria and reminds us of our status as spectators. Through it the play confesses its own artifice as well as Philaster's emotional distortions. Sharing the authors' awareness of their characters' limitations, we find the distance from action appropriate to nontragic experience. We can accept Philaster as romantic "hero" in a new sense, for we are not asked wholly to adopt the young lovers' valuation of themselves or their predicament. The lavish praise showered on Philaster, which as tragic protagonist he could not fulfill, can assume its proper function: comedy's guarantee that this extravagantly emotional young man, so apparently committed to misguided extremism in the pursuit of virtue, will prove salvageable as both husband and ruler.

After the Country Fellow, we watch more impartially Philaster's disintegration as he confronts Bellario. In immediate terms, Philaster's frantic behavior—the attempt to evade capture, the stabbing and repentance, the creeping in and out of bushes—provides unexpected theatrical excitement, even comedy at his expense, while also tracing the possible progress of an abnormality the play has acknowledged. At the same time, self-destruction offers the opportunity for re-creation. Philaster discovers the grounds for belief in his lovers' loyalty, and through their faith he finds himself. He can now move out of his fantasy realm, the nightmare wood in which all the lovers have wandered. The play's two worlds remeet on the comic note of Philaster's and Bellario's wonderfully hyperbolic tussle over the honor of taking blame for Arathusa's wounds, a verbal contest that involves fabricating publicly acceptable explanations—a servant's revenge, a prince's ambition—quite foreign to the "real," in some sense much more serious, psychological dislocations we have witnessed.

It is this sense of dislocation that characterizes both the form and effect of the Beaumont-Fletcher collaborations. Until the final *coup de théâtre* the genres as well as the plot seem hopelessly deadlocked, with romantic comedy unable to rescue, or absorb, the political-social world. Private and public realms remain separate, the individual and his needs apparently at odds with the universe in which he must act. We have, of course, been assured from the beginning that the gods are just and that in some unforeseen manner things will work out, but the dramatists have withheld clarification. With the romance discovery of Bellario's identity all comes right, but the particular generic blend that is *Philaster*'s formal solution is also, to modern critics, the root of its failure. Pressures set up by the initial *Hamlet* allusions and an apparent trajectory toward death threaten to subvert the final demand that we accept another genre's openness to compromise and manipulated endings. Not only does the action seem suddenly arbitrary rather than inevitable, but the cost in richness or depth of characterization is also high. Yet neither psychological depth and complexity, nor the gradual anatomizing of one heroic character's response to the discovery of evil and betrayal, engage *Philaster* as goal or dramatic method. Beaumont and Fletcher have their own interests, and the concern with emotional design, within scenes or sequences of scenes, provides more than purely rhetorical or aesthetic effects. Their focus is the pattern of experience illustrated by their characters' plights, not the characters themselves. Diffusion of interest among Arathusa, Bellario, and Philaster helps discourage tragic intimacy or empathy; repetition of experience serves not just to recycle effective scenes but to define a world in which such replication is inevitable.

That world is one in which appearance and reality remain indistinguishable. Despite the courtiers' apparent knowledge in 1.1 of court ladies, Pharamond, the king and Philaster, Dion introduces a potentially tragic ambience when he remarks on the difficulty of seeing through to truth and on man's ability to hide his nature: "Every man . . . has not a soule of Christall, for all men to reade their actions through: mens hearts and faces are so farre asunder, that they hold no intelligence" (1.1.248–52). In such an atmosphere Dion (quite mistakenly) distrusts the citizens' loyalty and constancy, and Philaster has learned (it turns out, ineffectually) that "Our eares may be corrupted: Tis an age / We dare not trust our wills to" (1.1.316–17). While the king may extol Arathusa's silent modesty as more expressive than the "offer'd language" of those "whose eye / Speakes common loves," his own hypocrisy later destroys this faith (1.1.101–3). Skepticism about the possibility of virtue is reenforced when the known guilty, Pharamond and Megra, can look repentant, "like a mortefied member," or so "modestly" that no man can "see in her face, but that shee's honest" (4.1.19–26). Not surprisingly, belief in Megra's accusation is immediate and widespread.

If its characters struggle to "read" each other in vain, *Philaster* also calls in question their ability to interpret the nature of their world. Assertions of faith in a benevolent Providence are there, to be sure. Arathusa announces that in wooing Philaster she is merely the gods' instrument to restore his kingdom, for they "make the passions of a feeble maide, / The way unto [their] Justice" (1.2.33–34). The king's guilty conscience shows his belief in a righteous heaven, and he readily interprets political setbacks as the "just" reward for "the sinne / I have committed" (2.4.62–63; cf. 4.4.52, 72). Both Philaster and Arathusa at least begin assuming that innocence is its own protection (1.2.91–92; 3.2.8–9). Perplexed by a reality that suggests otherwise, Philaster tries to maintain his faith: Bellario, for instance, could not so convincingly swear his innocence if he were lying, since "if it were not true, / The gods would not endure him" (3.1.267–68). Yet this is a world in which both eyes and ears can be abused, and innocence proves no guard because it cannot be established. The calumniated Arathusa rightly asks, "What way have I deserv'd this?" She may pray for a "breast

/ Transparent as pure Christall, that the world . . . may see the foulest thought / My heart holds," but in a fallen world she cannot make her truth known (3.2.130–33). At the end, discovering his page's sex, Philaster offers blessings on "you powers that favour Innocence," yet in context his response is comic, not authoritative (5.5.128). Irony also hedges the king's final words, the coda that purports to sum up the play's moral: "Let Princes learne / By this to rule the passions of their blood, / For what Heaven wils can never be withstood" (5.5.216–18).

The nature, if not the power, of that "Heaven" is in some doubt. More ambiguous than *Cupid's Revenge,* this play lacks the flat contradiction of an onstage malevolent representative of the powers that be. Yet *Philaster*'s dominant impression, too, is of its characters' helplessness, before each other and before the inscrutable workings of their universe. Action is pointless where the individual cannot hope to control his life and even one's sense of self is determined by others. Self-assertion repeatedly collapses back into the overriding sense of impotence, just as Philaster's claim to his political rights yields to assuring the king that "I am dead sir, y'are my Fate: It was not I / Said I was wrong'd . . . My weake starres leade me too; all my weake fortunes" (1.1.261–63). Philaster, Arathusa, and Bellario establish a new identity through love but soon find apparently inexplicable betrayal. Doubly accused, Bellario enters a world beyond rational explanation—indeed, the world of *Cupid's Revenge:* "Oh what god, / Angry with men, hath sent this strange disease / Into the noblest minds?" Only "time," which may prove merciful though men do not, has the power to "Reveale the truth" (3.2.146–48, 159). When Arathusa cries, "Where may a maiden live securely free / Keeping her honour faire?" she can answer her own question: "Not with the living" (3.2.36–37). Death becomes a release from suffering "we all persue," where life is "a game, / That must be lost" (3.1.257–58).

In such a world all are potential victims or initiators of mistrust. The long, frequently lovely arias of bewilderment and desertion may float free of a naturalistic mooring in individual character or situation, yet they create more than simply a distinctively Beaumont-Fletcher sentimentalism. They voice the condition in which all the characters act and have their being. Retreat to the forest, desire for oblivion, blind confidence in a moral universe—these seem humanity's only alternatives, for heaven's "justice" remains "secret"

(1.2.103). "Nature" may have "her ends" and know "she does well," but she "loves not to be questioned" (1.2.23–25). Men will never understand her workings and can only hope that what they wish, even try to bring about, is what unalterable "Desteny" has "decreed" (2.3.26–29).

In *Philaster* Destiny has, of course, ordained a fortunate issue and so may be said to validate belief in its ultimate benevolence. Yet *Philaster* refuses to stress the hopefulness of its conclusion. Amid the joyful reconciliations it reminds us of a world resistant to happy endings and, in the final focus on Bellario, it retains a tragicomic mood. Action is suspended for Bellario's lengthy account of her history, from the father's praise that predisposed her heart to the moment she met Philaster "by the Fount / Where first you tooke me up" (5.5.151–84). In one sense, such a conclusion sustains the play's return to romantic idealism: we end with a lyric description of love, emphasizing selfless dedication, and with Arathusa's serene confidence in welcoming Bellario into the marital arrangement. Yet romantic comedy's heroine is Arathusa, not Bellario, and it is not simply the stage action that has been interrupted. Comedy's drive toward union, regeneration, and society's future is balked in this figure of static pathos and sublimated desire. In Bellario's equivocal final "identity" we are recalled to Beaumont and Fletcher's central preoccupation with feelings of abandonment, with helpless immobility and the annihilation of self. The skewed comic conclusion fits the play's attenuation of romance possibilities even as it provides the properly wonderful conversions and recognitions.[31]

We do not share the characters' final untroubled joy, and Beaumont and Fletcher further distance us from their resolution by insisting on its arbitrariness. What has been condemned as a major flaw is, successful or not, part of its design. A potentially tragic world of moral ambiguity, human weakness, and loss has been saved, but by frankly artful means. The citizens are brought on, with at least some preparation, as a political deus ex machina; the Bellario "solution" is plucked from the realm of romance marvels and transposed intact to *Philaster*'s un-golden world. The conventional, patterned exchange of information between Dion and his daughter openly places this "recognition" in a long tradition of such scenes. It satisfies theatrical and generic criteria, yet is simultaneously admitted to be no real resolution at all. We are conscious not of the providential nature of a world that will itself work out comedy's ending, but of the artists who control this portrait by manipulating their fiction.

Encouraging our detachment suits Beaumont and Fletcher's dramatic method throughout: this play asks us to participate in its self-conscious, sophisticated double view of itself. With Philaster's question to Bellario, whose answer is the improbable history of her love and vow of silence, we are invited to acknowledge and appreciate the artistry—and artificiality—of the whole tangled web of deceit, despair, and restoration we have witnessed: "tell me why / Thou didst conceale thy sex . . . All these Jealousies / Had flowne to nothing, if thou hadst discovered, / What now we know" (5.5.146–51). A disciple of Beaumont and Fletcher and one of their astutest critics, James Shirley recognized this combination of detachment and involvement as among their distinguishing characteristics. In his epistle to the 1647 folio, Shirley offers the reader "passions raised to that excellent pitch and by such insinuating degrees that you shall not chuse but consent, & go along with them, finding your self at last grown insensibly the very same person you read, and then stand admiring the subtile Trackes of your engagement."[32]

Chapter Five
The Maid's Tragedy
Date, Sources, Contemporary Issues, Genre

Probably Beaumont and Fletcher's next collaboration for the King's Men, *The Maid's Tragedy* may have been first presented during the winter season of 1610–11.[1] Unpublished until 1619, it was presumably extant by 31 October 1611, when Sir George Buc licensed for acting a titleless play that he designated "This second Maydens tragedy (for it hath no name inscribed)."[2] The play's first certain mention lies in the court records of performances for the wedding celebrations during the winter of 1612–13, where it is joined by *Philaster* and *A King and No King*.[3] *The Maid's Tragedy* is, by general agreement, largely Beaumont's in execution, though Fletcher's scenes are all key ones.[4]

"That anomaly among Elizabethan tragedies," *The Maid's Tragedy* boasts an original plot.[5] The lack of an historical source for the central action does not preclude minor borrowings and influences, both literary and dramatic; indeed, given previous practice, we might expect such appropriation. Memories of Sidney's *Arcadia*, so extensively mined for *Cupid's Revenge*, may have helped shape the manner of Aspatia's death: killed by the man she loves in a duel she has provoked while disguised as her own brother. In book 3, chapter 16 of the "New" *Arcadia*, Sidney's Parthenia disguises herself as a stranger-knight and in a tourney wins death at the hands of the man who had earlier killed her husband. The importance of the friendship between Melantius and Amintor may also derive ultimately from the dramatists' admiration for Sidney, though in immediate terms they draw on their portrait of Leucippus and Ismenus in *Cupid's Revenge*.[6] In developing this relationship they again press Shakespeare into service, for the quarrel between Melantius and Amintor (3.1) is modeled on that between Brutus and Cassius in *Julius Caesar*.[7] *Hamlet* remains a potent influence, from cribbed lines on the divinity that hedges kings, to character borrowings (touches of Calianax from Polonius, and of Melantius from Horatio and

Laertes), to particularly theatrical scenes of confrontation (Melantius's menacing conversion of his sister and Hamlet's of his mother).[8] An additional possible dramatic source, for Aspatia's visual description of her grief in terms of mythological parallels (2.2), is the "painter scene" of the 1602 additions to Thomas Kyd's *Spanish Tragedy*.[9]

The most obvious "source," in more general terms, is *Philaster*. Beaumont and Fletcher's predilection for recycling material—their own as well as others'—appears in the hopeless but devoted love of Aspatia and Bellario-Euphrasia, in the lyric pathos with which both voice their despair, and in their resort to male disguise to gain their ends. Amintor recalls Philaster in his oscillation of response and highly rhetorical speeches, in the apparently irreconcilable demands made by his situation, and in his suicidal reaction to it. A minor thread of *Philaster*'s largely romantic tapestry, the challenge to royal absolutism reappears as a major subject of *The Maid's Tragedy*. Indeed, although its sensational plot, distant locale, and timeless "romance" events and chronology would seem to brand *The Maid's Tragedy* as escapist entertainment, it may not have seemed so to its contemporary audience. The king's pursuit of private pleasure at his subjects' expense opens questions of royal privilege, and the conflict of personal rights and duties with public obligations, debated within the play, is not without relevance to issues fundamental to James's struggle with Parliament over the Great Contract in 1609 and 1610.[10]

In suddenly pitting private and public codes against each other, the play also throws into question the meaning of "honor," since deciding what constitutes an honorable response to the king's act determines the main characters' behavior. Among the many shifts from the medieval to the modern world evident in the Renaissance, the concept of honor was slowly losing its feudal and chivalric emphasis on the reputation accorded high birth and brave (usually military) deeds. Gradually, it was becoming equated with "honorableness of character," as an innate virtue and as a code prescribing behavior, although in the seventeenth century both emphases still shared an uneasy coexistence.[11] The question of honor occupied both public and private stages. In plays of differing genres, Shakespeare had anatomized the points of conflict in this variously defined ideal— in *Henry IV*, part 1, and *Julius Caesar*, in *Troilus and Cressida* and *All's Well That Ends Well*. Yet one of his most recent tragedies,

Coriolanus (1607–9), seems most immediately relevant to *The Maid's Tragedy*, in part because it offered a partial model for the Rhodian general Melantius, and in part because it so clearly explores some of the same political and social problems.[12] Less complex in probing the idea of honor and the individual's relation to the state, though perhaps as bleak in its final vision, *The Maid's Tragedy* participates in this debate.

Reexamining the concept of honor, and with it the meaning of heroism and nobility, produced in *Coriolanus*—or, in a private theater example, Chapman's Byron plays (1608, Blackfriars)—"tragedy" of an unusual kind. Dramatists of the next generation, Beaumont and Fletcher create further dislocations in the form as well as the effect of their contribution. The ambiguous title suggests one departure: *The Maid's Tragedy* lacks a single protagonist or focus. The "maid" appears to be Aspatia, deserted on virtually the eve of her marriage to Amintor because the king has ordered Amintor to marry Evadne, the king's mistress, to provide a socially acceptable "father" for the fruits of his liaison. Yet having appeared briefly in acts 1 and 2 and been allotted one scene in which to lament her plight, Aspatia disappears from the play; she reenters only at the end, disguised, to goad Amintor to a duel and die on his sword. The play is "not centrally the tragedy of Aspatia, but it is not purely and centrally anyone else's either."[13] Its focus seems rather to be the whole state of affairs created by the king's two preplay deeds: the seduction of a willing Evadne and the command that Amintor substitute Evadne for his intended bride. The "tragic" situation is a tawdry one, its effect apparently private and limited, and this sense of diminished scope is exacerbated by other developments. The king lacks regal stature and remains an unnamed tyrant, as coarse and petty as his chamber grooms. Enmeshed in circumstances, the other principal characters seem restricted to the point where "their responses must lack the amplitude of gesture that we associate with the tragic hero."[14]

To the action's progress Aspatia is largely irrelevant, except as another casualty, for it revolves around the discovery of and response to this situation by Amintor, by his best friend and Evadne's brother, Melantius, and finally by Evadne herself when, converted at sword point, on Melantius's orders she murders the king who whored her. A tried-and-true genre, revenge tragedy, this play refuses to provide in clear form what we most expect, a revenger. No one of the four principals dominates the play. Amintor is prevented from acting by his belief in the divine rights of kings; the motive force behind the revenge, Melantius convinces his sister to commit the deed. As Evadne kills the king she makes clear that she acts for them all, one sword thrust for each victim, yet the completed revenge is not the play's climactic action. At the end, *The Maid's Tragedy* returns to the private reverberations of its central action. In the neatly executed triple suicide of Aspatia, Amintor, and Evadne—and attempted suicide of Melantius—the play ends with a tableau of psychological devastation and, despite a nod toward political stability in the new and wiser king, of the utter inadequacy of revenge as personal resolution.

The Maid's Tragedy

The Maid's Tragedy is structured in almost musical terms: an overture adumbrating both themes and mood; two long movements, broken around a partial resolution, in which each scene prepares for the next; and a final coda. Within these sequences of rising tension, emotional heightening is developed on the model of *Philaster*'s acts 3 and 4 with a series of rhetorically, even physically, choreographed confrontations. In *The Maid's Tragedy*, of course, generic demands make circumstances press more heavily on the characters, and they are offered no timeless pastoral landscape in which to bewail their woes or resolve their dilemma. With the exception of the forsaken Aspatia's elegiac lament (2.2), a lyric interlude within the play's first sequence of action, the principals argue in the court's terms. They are bound to their society by circumstance but also by belief; no separate world or personal realm of values exists, and even Aspatia is forced from her static isolation to seek death in the courtly dance of honor.

The Maid's Tragedy differs from earlier work in other ways. Despite the concealment of Bellario's sex in *Philaster* or our special knowledge of Cupid in *Cupid's Revenge*, neither play experiments so interestingly with the audience's relation to dramatic action or character, though *The Knight of the Burning Pestle* suggests this concern is not new. For its entire first act, *The Maid's Tragedy* refrains from telling us the facts—about Evadne, about the king, about the wedding it celebrates. Not until the surprise revelations in 2.1 do we learn, with Amintor, the information that gives the preceding action and its speeches a new, ironic significance. In 3.1 we then savor the double meanings in Amintor's answers to the king, the grotesque edge in the ignorant courtiers' jokes about wedding-night delights and loss of maidenheads; we remain in a privileged position for the first third of this sequence's culminating scene, the interview in which Amintor finally confesses the truth to Melantius (3.2). Again in 4.2, we know the real situation that the king and court misread.

In act 1 apparent exposition thus lulls us into taking appearance as reality. With the courtiers, we simply accept the immediate action: the marriage preparations, the happy bridegroom's reunion with his best friend and brother-to-be, the gorgeous pageantry of the masque that occupies most of 1.2. The deception is more than just a dramatic trick, though it certainly provides the *coup de théâtre* of 2.1. In *Philaster* we were first told, then shown, that in its world both eyes and ears could be deceived; *The Maid's Tragedy* forces us to experience this discovery, to participate in the emotions of characters within the fiction.

Initially, like Amintor and the court, we brush aside or ignore evidence that the times in Rhodes are out of joint. The cynical lords who open 1.1 establish a familiar background. Less prominent or smutty than the gentlemen-commentators of *Cupid's Revenge* and *Philaster,* they yet sketch a milieu content with trivial pursuits. They enjoy the peace Melantius buys "with blood abroad," look forward to the evening's dancing, and prefer young ladies who "in their wanton blood, / Tell mirthfull tales . . . that fill the roome / With laughter" (1.1.14, 98–100); they are echoed in a coarser idiom by the grooms of the king's chamber who contemplate having "a snap" at Evadne "one of these nights as she goes from him" (5.1.115–16). A man out of tune with "soft and silken warres," Melantius is a soldier whose "daunce [is] with armes"; though he has a mistress, he neither trusts nor idealizes her: her heart "is stone, no better" (1.1.41–43, 149). A believer in the efficacy of deeds, he answers Lysippus's florid welcome with his own scarred limbs, that "spoke my love and truth unto my friends, / More then my tongue ere could," and asserts a fiercely independent standard of value: "where I finde worth / I love the keeper, till he let it goe, / And then I follow it" (1.1.21–25). Virtue is not tied to birth; it must be earned, and it can be lost.

This is a court wholly determined by its king, who rearranges his subjects' lives by royal fiat. As Lysippus tells Melantius, "The

breath of Kings is like the breath of gods, / My brother wisht thee
here, and thou art here" (1.1.15–16). The king's word has created
the present marriage—so suddenly that Melantius must be told of
the switch in brides—and summoned up the festivities with which
it will be celebrated. His word is all-powerful, but signs of its ill
effects are already apparent. Loyalty to the king's "strict command"
has prevented Diphilus's duty to his brother Melantius, who sent
for Diphilus to join him on the battlefield. In forbidding Amintor's
intended marriage, the king has forced Amintor to break his promise, dishonored Aspatia's father Calianax, and produced the mourn-
ing Aspatia herself, who wanders the court with "an infectious
griefe" (1.1.94). Indeed, in retaining his office as chamberlain (as
well as holder of the strategically important fort), Calianax sees that
he has become unnatural in his role as father; now he does "service
for him that hath forsaken her [Aspatia]" (1.2.19). The court is
already an unruly place, with those outside pushing and shoving to
get into the presence chamber; Calianax's scurrilous insults to Melantius further lower the scene's tone. As Melantius turns away from
the cowardly Calianax in disgust, he speaks more truly than he
knows: "This *Rhodes* I see is nought / But a place priviledg'd to
doe men wrong" (1.2.83–84).

Finally, though its songs reaffirm social ideals and offer a foil to
the corrupt realities of 2.1's actual wedding night, in mythological
and symbolic form the masque portrays a world in which those
realities find their natural place.[15] Despite Strato's conviction that
masques are nothing but empty hyperbole, lies that conventionally
"commend" both king and wedding couple because "tied to rules
/ Of flatterie," the Masque of Night figures forth the anarchic
passions unleashed by the king's lust (1.1.8–11). Egotism and ambition are the Queen of Night's distinguishing traits: she resents
sharing dominion and delights that "in the quenching sea / The
Sun is drownd, and with him fell the day" (1.2.112–13). During
the masque we learn that Boreas, the rebellious North Wind, has
broken his chains and escaped. No more than the human king he
supposedly flatters can Neptune order reality to obey his words; he
calls for "Musique to lay a storme," but when the song ends we
learn that the "sea goes hie, / *Boreas* hath rais'd a storme" and,
unless he is suppressed, "ere day / Many a tall ship will be cast
away" (1.2.240, 249–52). Envy and aggression operate everywhere.
At the masque's end, just before Cinthia offers the mandatory royal

compliment, Night is still cursing the approaching day, hoping "to see / Another wild fire in his axeltree, / And all fall drencht" (1.2.267–69).[16]

The masque serves its courtly, ceremonial function, to be sure. It rehearses the conventional assumptions—"pre-nuptial chastity, bridal bliss and royal integrity"[17]—while its darker implications and failure to resolve its own tensions go unremarked. Yet even before Evadne's revelations, the play hints that the assumptions themselves are a kind of self-flattering masque, played by society to its own applause. As the women prepare Evadne for bed, Dula is contrasted with Aspatia. Dula's bawdy jokes, her eagerness to take Evadne's place, acknowledge the hypocrisy of the publicly celebrated sex roles: women can cast false modesty aside "When we'are alone" (2.1.12). Aspatia may be society's chaste and true ideal, but she has been rejected, left to sing the funeral song of her own virtues. Her faith was answered by Amintor's falsehood; if once into her "credulous eares, he powred the sweetest words / That art or love could frame," he readily accepted the king's ban and looked instead "to loose my lusty youth" in Evadne's arms (2.1.52–53; 1.1.138). Dula, Evadne, and the court ladies and lords are at home in a world far different from the masque's ideal vision. To them Aspatia's song seems merely "strange"; Evadne calls for Dula's answering ditty, one that praises physical pleasure, variety, and a heart that hourly "prompt[s] mine eie / On some other man to flie" (2.1.80, 85–86).

Amintor is the figure in whom these sets of values meet, and his inability to navigate their contradictions, or his own divided feelings, destroys him. A naive youth whose "promise" has yet to be "perform'd" (1.1.57–58), he has accepted uncritically his society's public self-portrait. He sees himself and his relationships, as friend and lover, in terms of these bright romance ideals. His share in the less attractive passions enacted behind this civilized facade is unacknowledged, though Beaumont and Fletcher remind us by showing Amintor's speedy rationalization of his guilt ("I onely breake a promise, / And twas the King that forst me") and immediately renewed desire for Evadne, "the luster of whose eie, / Can blot away the sad remembrance / Of all these things" (2.1.135–36, 138–40). The loss of innocence he so eagerly anticipates will be intellectual and moral, not sexual.

Evadne explodes the myths by which Amintor has lived. She

turns his Petrarchan self-image back on him in mockery and, when he assumes her words merely cloak a modest desire to put off the moment of surrender, her own disbelief matches his: "A maidenhead *Amintor* / At my yeares?" (2.1.193–94). Each revelation widens the abyss before him: she is not a virgin; she will be his bride in name only; in denying him she is being true to her lover; she is the king's mistress. Amintor's identity has been reduced to words now drained of significance—"husband" to Evadne and "father" of the king's bastards. So, in the newly inverted language, "sinne" may become "honorable" (2.1.316–18). For seventy-five lines Amintor denies what he hears. Evadne is either raving mad or playing some grotesque game, and he keeps asserting that she must be what he has been taught women are: "this cannot be / Thy naturall temper . . . I doe rage in vaine, / She can but jest . . . thy heart cannot be hard" (2.1.194–95, 227–28, 266). Clearly, Evadne's truths threaten the fabric of Amintor's world. Their conversation must be a "dreame," a nightmare from which he can "awake," because if women share "the hot and rising blood" of sexuality, then love and marriage are lies and men may as well indiscriminately serve their bestial lust "as other creatures doe" (2.1.207, 287, 224–25). Content and ceremony, inner and outer, must coincide or the whole social and linguistic order crumbles. Evadne cannot be false to him, since her beauty remains unblemished; the identity of her lover is an impossibility: "Tis not the King" (2.1.304).

In splitting his own two bodies and allowing the private man's lust to subvert the royal figure's responsibilities, the king has forced his subjects to reevaluate not merely their own duty to him but the whole system of values and beliefs he theoretically embodies. A woman of passion and ambition, Evadne freely embraces the world discovered beneath society's platitudes. A Hobbesian reality of aggression, power, and lust offers her scope, the chance to shape her fortunes in a way denied her by the traditional order. Accepting the loss of absolute meanings, the reduction of all values to negotiable social currency, she shocks even her seducer. When the fatuous king assumes her devotion, she coolly corrects his mistake: "I love with my ambition, / Not with my eies" (3.1.175–76). She must live within the patriarchal social and political system and preserve its appearances, but she no longer subscribes to its ideals. In himself, as a man, the king is nothing; his value rests solely in arbitrary, externally conferred significance. She "would never love / A man of lower place," but should his "fortune" change, she "would bend to him / That won your throne" (3.1.171–75). In this parody of her brother's dedication to "worth," "love" and personal loyalty go the way of "husband," "father," "bride," and "marriage."

Evadne's cynical pragmatism emphasizes and clarifies Amintor's opposite reaction to the unmasking of courtly appearances. He discovers not freedom but chaos. Having believed the social myths and defined himself in their terms, he finds his identity suddenly turned inside out. Even his reputation for honor has only qualified him for dishonor. The old absolutes, the code words he accepted, cannot help him; indeed, their internal contradictions are exposed. "Duty," "honor," and "right" suddenly become problematic, perhaps as useless in defining conduct as the other terms Evadne has just mocked. Like Philaster, or Leucippus in *Cupid's Revenge,* Amintor becomes lost in the gap separating appearance and reality, precept and practice, and the resulting spiral of despair, self-loathing, and self-justification is familiar. Placed in a grotesquely untenable position by Evadne's revelations, Amintor can see "no meane, no moderate course to runne" (2.1.246). The appeal to heavenly justice—"Why does not heaven speake in thunder to us?" (2.1.249)—yields no answer. Baffled, he asks Evadne to kill him. As he says later, she has brought him to a "dull calamitie," a "strange misbeleefe of all the world, / And all things that are in it" (4.1.211–13).

Left by heaven and Evadne to salvage his identity, Amintor at first simply reaffirms the system in which he had found his self-image. Language fails to conjure reality back into the old mold, however: neither asserting what must be true nor denying Evadne works. When he must accept her naming the king, he finds another way to reclaim both order and self-respect. If by his response Amintor can rescue "King" from the apparently universal devaluation of verbal coinage and instead maintain its sanctity, he can avoid the dishonor of either accepting the sham marriage or committing murder. Evadne's seduction has for her demythologized the concept of kingship;[18] to Amintor she has "nam'd a word" so "sacred" that it "wipes away / All thoughts revengefull" (2.1.306–7). With such fancy logical footwork Amintor can honorably maintain loyalty to the office, the king's annointed body, even while its living representative dishonors him. Responsibility passes to the gods, who will "Speake to him when they please, till when let us / Suffer, and waite" (2.1.310–11).

That Amintor's assertion of the divine right of kings comes in the accents of Rosencrantz and Guildenstern is no accident. Amintor, too, seeks to be absolved of the need for choice or accountability. He retreats to social meanings but must accept them in the newly devalued sense Evadne has exposed: "reputation / Thou art a word, no more" (2.1.333–34). "Honor" splits from its personal significance and becomes a matter of opinion. Because the eyes and ears can be so easily deceived, it also becomes another meaningless verbal counter: "me thinkes I am not wrong'd, / Nor is it ought, if from the censuring world / I can but hide it" (2.1.331–33). He dons the mask of happy bridegroom and joins Evadne in the cynical game of hood-winking the court.

Amintor's rhetoric is as extreme as his situation, but he is not wholly unbelievable. Beaumont and Fletcher suggest the psychological pressures that his choice of passive suffering attempts to satisfy. Both with Evadne in 2.1 and in 3.1 with the king, the logical contortions by which Amintor tries to maintain his sense of himself as a man of honor are both comic and pitiably understandable. The "adolescent intensities" are grounded in an adolescent reluctance to enter the complicated, disappointing, often mystifying adult world of compromise, deceit, and rebellious sexuality.[19] Ultimately the role of victim proves as intolerable for Amintor as for Aspatia, but initially it appears to separate him from what he finds most threatening. Any action against the king would betray the noble purity of Amintor's self-image and admit not merely that, like Calianax, he has been "made an asse, / A Court stale" but that his desire for Evadne led him to choose this fate and, in the process, betray both Aspatia and his own ideal of romantic love (2.2.95–96). If the king "Has not my will in keeping," however, he must commit regicide now and accept retroactively his guilt in deserting her (2.1.131). Amintor for much of the play retreats from examining his society's values, but also himself.

To challenge the king's absolute privilege, to sit in judgment on what the king "may" do by virtue of his position and what he "may not" do because immoral (the terms are Calianax's, 2.2.81), leads to questioning the whole received cosmic order. This challenge is not Amintor's. Briefly, he contemplates a world that hints total moral anarchy: if Evadne's breath can still be "sweete as Aprill," then "ile be guilty too, / If these be the effects" (3.1.39–40). With a "sudden gaze" he peers at Melantius, mistrusting "those noble lookes" because, on the principle he has just learned, "by the course / Of nature thou shouldst be as quickly chang'd / As are the windes, dissembling as the Sea" (3.1.45, 49, 57–59). The prospect is unbearable, and Amintor returns to traditional dogma. The cost of stabilizing his world is high. The king remains inviolate, hedged by the "Divinitie" of his sacred office (3.1.237–41). To justify his gods as upholders of truth and constancy, Amintor, like Leucippus in *Cupid's Revenge,* internalizes the guilt for what has happened; he must accept one of the responsibilities he had tried so tortuously to avoid. When Evadne and the king force on him the ultimate indignity and demand he be their pander, Amintor explains his fate as proper punishment: "The faithlesse sin I made / To faire Aspatia is not yet reveng'd, / It followes me" (3.1.218–20).

With Amintor's choice of passivity, the king's plan seems to have worked and passions reached an equilibrium. Yet the morning-after masquerade does not convince Melantius. The first sequence of action leads finally to the friends' confrontation and the possibility that one word, one ideal, remains that can withstand the ravages of courtly egoism. Melantius's friendship is, he declares, a love both selfless and absolute: he desires only to "cut through thy foes / Unto thy quiet, till I place thy heart / As peaceable as spotlesse innocence" (3.2.116–18). When Amintor confesses the truth, Melantius's initial disbelief, anger, and challenge to a duel melt before this supreme value: "The name of friend, is more then familie, / Or all the world besides" (3.2.168–69). By the end of this passionate interview Amintor believes he has found his resting point, the one person in whom words, "noble lookes," and essential nature coincide. Leaning on his friend, Amintor feels "a kinde of ease": "o wretched I, thy love *Melantius,* / Why I have nothing else" (3.2.253, 258–59).

This value, too, will dissolve under pressure, decomposing before our eyes until the "name of friend" has become merely another hollow word. The seeds of that dissolution are apparent even in 3.2. When Melantius declares he "will never cease / My vengeance till I finde thy heart at peace," he assumes the identity of their causes and that the same act will restore honor and "peace" to both (3.2.201–2). With a good deal of logical casuistry that slides between various,

incompatible meanings of "honor," Amintor explains why this is
not so: Melantius must not avenge his family honor because this
act would dishonor Amintor, branding him a coward, a cuckold,
and a fool for having respected the king's divinity. Confusingly,
Amintor allows "honor" to mean different things to each of them;
Melantius accepts the distinction without seeing its full implications, and he repeats this failure with the cognate "honest." "Honest," used to describe Amintor by both the king and Melantius,
means loyalty to the king's sacred office; when Melantius uses it of
himself, it designates loyalty to private, family values: "my honestie
/ Shall steele my sword" (3.2.191–92). Melantius has grounded
friendship in truth-telling and loyalty; it is his highest value and
the bond by which he demanded to know Amintor's grief. Yet he
now dissembles (and again in 4.2), assuring Amintor as "my friend"
that he will not place "the braverie of our house" above Amintor's
honor (3.2.245–48). Ambiguously, he promises to "doe what worth
shall bid me, and no more" (3.2.251).

Melantius's is the third response to the situation created by the
king, and he finds an authority by which the king stands judged
and condemned: an older, more barbaric code than the one Amintor
tries to uphold by maintaining loyalty to the principle of kingship.
Dishonored as brother and as soldier by the king for whom he fought,
Melantius trusts his instincts to dictate proper action: "I hope my
cause is just, I know my blood / Tels me it is, and I will credit
it" (3.2.288–89). The family blood stained by the king and Melantius's own anger merge to annihilate the sacred name. He gives
no thought to the heavenly "curse" Amintor fears. Melantius's gods
sanction revenge, though on earth man must supply the "thunder"
they have withheld (4.1.80). As agent of these gods, Melantius
threatens his sister with death—"This sword shall be thy lover"—
until she confesses and repents; when she has, he assumes her own
"brave anger" will direct her "To kill this base King" (4.1.98,144).
Regicide is not sinful; indeed, "al the gods require it, / They are
dishonored in him" (4.1.145–46). Melantius destroys his sister by
bringing her back within the fold of the system in which her actions
as free agent condemn her as whore, then stripping that system of
its "modern" accretions, such as the inviolability of the royal pa-
triarch. The family pragmatism is now Melantius's: he will make
Evadne his instrument and circumvent punishment by blackmailing
Calianax into yielding up the fort.

The contrast—and incompatibility—with his friend's ethic is clear. Amintor's gods secure the king's safety; they are also moral in explicitly Christian terms. When Evadne convinces Amintor of her change of heart, he forgives her and calls "repentance, the best sacrifice" (4.1.241). In his eyes, their unnatural relationship has found its resolution: "may each sin thou hast, / Finde a new mercy, rise, I am at peace" (4.1.258–59). Melantius's heavenly powers require blood, not penitence, and converting his sister is merely a step toward preparing that sacrifice, not an end in itself. The "peace" he promised Amintor he destroys.

By addressing the contradictions revenge tragedy often skirts o seeks to minimize, and by altering the conventional plot, Beaumon and Fletcher expose fissures in their own society's beliefs. The choose to explore some of the most basic questions this genre raise the nature of the universe that has allowed the wrong that must l avenged, and its relation to the human nature of those who try establish, or restore, the moral and social order. If *The Mai. Tragedy* can be seen as an examination of the problem posed by i own first act—the relation of the court to the natural world re resented in the masque—then it is a deeply disturbing one. Tl play itself is no more reassuring about the traditional pieties tha its ending is of the established political hierarchy.

The revenge action, a grotesque inversion of 2.1 in which the sword-as-lover replaces abstinence, is hedged with deflating ironies. The dramatists split the heroic avenger into reason and passion, planner and actor, and they add a long scene (4.2) in which Melantius brazenly outfaces the always-comic Calianax and deceives the king while, in the king's very presence, co-opting Calianax's aid. Never very regal, the king becomes the butt of our laughter, both here and in 5.1, as he confidently misinterprets his situation. In a court he has taught the effectiveness of impudent deception, he refuses to believe Melantius's innocent looks could harbor treasonous intent. Certain of his sacred invulnerability, he denies Evadne's assertions that she is going to kill him, but he discovers that the breath of kings no longer has the power to command reality. She will both "speake" and do what he commands her not to. The smutty jokes of his waiting servants reaffirm the king's fundamental humanness: "how quickly he had done with her, I see Kings can doe no more that way then other mortall people" (5.1.117–18).[20]

With Evadne, the king meets his reduction to the private sphere.

The woman who declared her loyalty to his "place" is no more: "I am not she" (5.1.64). Deeds, not rank, determine value for Evadne now: to his assertion that "I am thy King," she answers "Thou art my shame . . . thou foule man" (5.1.96, 99). In a grotesquely literal way, Evadne will force appearance and reality again to coincide. She will write the king's sins upon his body—one stab for each of those he wronged—so that finally his evil can be "read" by the court. Amintor had been baffled at the disparity between Evadne's moral nature and her beauty, his inability to "finde one blemish in thy face / Where falsehood should abide" (2.1.188–89). With the king's body she carries out Melantius's threat to kill her and leave her naked, "That on thy branded flesh the world may reade / Thy blacke shame and my justice" (4.1.108–9).

Having debased civilized society's rituals and language, the king suffers the fate of having left his subjects only blood in which to articulate their suffering. Yet Evadne's act cannot retrieve the "world of vertue" she deserted or reanimate the language and ceremonies she violated (5.1.78). Instead, it writes upon her a new identity as murderess. Bloody, still holding the knife, she claims Amintor as husband. Certain she has killed her sins and "cal [led] backe" the wrongs done Amintor, she demands, "am I not faire? / Lookes not *Evadne* beautious with these rites now?" (5.3.110, 118–19). For Amintor, Evadne has compounded her sins: "stain'd with a Kings bloud," her "colour now" is "Blacke" (5.3.148, 135). In the final working out of 2.1's perverted marriage night, Evadne dies for Amintor—not the sexual consummation once refused him, but the suicide by which "*Amintor* thou shalt love me now againe" (5.3.169).

To Melantius falls the public justification of regicide and, because he holds the fort, the terms under which order will be restored. The language that will declare the "innocence of this act" and "bring our banisht honours home" is a soldier's: the threat of physical force (5.1.142; 5.2.3). On the new king Melantius imposes his own idea of "honor" and with it a subject's right to choose his loyalties: "Whilst he was good, I cald him King, and serv'd him" (5.2.40). Political anarchy has been avoided, and the play ends on Lysippus's cautious assertion that he has learned "To rule with temper" (5.3.293). Melantius, too, has denied the "breath of Kings," yet he and his code have not restored communal meanings. That kings earn their subjects' loyalty by royal deeds sounds like a recipe for stable political order; that each subject should judge "worth" and "honor," and act on his personal evaluation, does not. A disturbing egotism underlies Melantius's assertion of the primacy of acting "like my selfe": "Thus I have flung him off with my allegeance, / And stand here mine owne justice to revenge / What I have suffred in him" (5.2.48–51). The corrosion of language and ceremony by a corrupt political order has led to dangerous individualism, to a self-authoring, self-validating use of language that cuts the individual off from his community. If Rhodes refuses to accept his interpretation, Melantius is fully prepared to "unbuild / This goodly towne" (5.2.58–59).[21]

That Lysippus acquiesces as much from prudence as conviction further qualifies our acceptance of Melantius as the play's "answer" to the issues it raises. More important, *The Maid's Tragedy* does not end with his defense and a restored—albeit no longer divinely sanctioned—state. Instead, we are returned to the private realm. Here confusion and despair reign, and Melantius's "honor" has pushed his sister beyond the bounds of sanity and doubled his friend's torment. To Amintor, Evadne's news "keepes night here / And throwes an unknowne Wildernesse about me" (5.3.149–50). The bright new political day has not dispelled the Masque of Night.

The events that so plainly demonstrate the triumph of justice to Melantius, that allow Lysippus to reaffirm the traditional cosmic order, drive Aspatia and Amintor to question the existence of either justice or order. Holding the Aspatia he has killed by mistake, Amintor is agonizingly torn between received belief—"out of justice we must challenge nothing"—and the hard fact that "No comfort comes, the gods denie me too" (5.3.236, 240). He can make neither rational nor moral sense of what has happened and chooses death as release. For Aspatia, loss is certain but wholly arbitrary; she never even discovers the reason for the switch in brides. Yet she explains her actions in terms of the play's concern with absolutes. She will provoke Amintor to kill her because her life indicts the gods: "she that can endure the miserie / That I have on me, and be patient too, / May live and laugh at all that you can doe." Hence, "It is more honour for you that I die" (5.3.5–8). Only her death can preserve the gods' goodness, since her very existence—as pure victim—calls in doubt their morality. Aspatia's logic is that of Gloucester in *King Lear*.[22]

In the masque, Cinthia answered Night's wish to "hold our places and out-shine the day" by asserting that "we may not breake / The

gods decrees" (1.2.135–38). The play refuses to show that these
"decrees" extend beyond the rules of physics. The ideals by which
men seek to restrain egotism and violence lose their grounding in
a natural moral order even as humanity's share in the unruly forces
beyond the court is insisted upon. The conscienceless king is both
monstrous in terms of the human order he has perverted—stripping
of meaning its rituals of affirmation, even the language by which
men communicate—and frighteningly "natural." Fittingly, Evadne
describes him as both "a shameless villaine" and "A thing out of
the overcharge of nature" (5.1.90–91). Like a "thicke cloud," a
"plague," or Boreas in the masque, the king is a kind of natural
eruption within the social and political body of the urges it attempts
to hold in check. As passion bursting its confines, the rebellious
North Wind is also associated with Melantius's unrestrained anger,
an equal but opposite force generated by a universe founded on
opposition and conflict (4.1.72–74). Between them, they lodge
"night" and the "unknowne Wildernesse" securely within the court
(5.3.149–50).

Facing the possibility that humanity exists in an indifferent or
malicious world—that its institutions and values bear no higher
sanction, are perhaps in a fundamental way unnatural—devastates
each of the principal characters. Even Melantius, in 5.2 so confident
that pursuing his idea of "worth" and "honor" would restore an
order temporarily perverted by one man, in the end finds the honor
he regained as hollow as Aspatia finds the gods'. Following one
absolute, the egoism of personal honor, he has betrayed another,
the friendship that claims Amintor as "Sister, Father, Brother, Sonne,
/ All that I had" (5.3.266–67). If the gods demand revenge, as
Melantius insisted in 4.1, they have ensured that action in this
world will be self-defeating, as flawed as the mortals who initiate
it. The play ends anticlimactically, with the successful general
stunned, confused, and himself suicidal. Around him Lysippus and
the court blandly assert traditional values whose disintegration we
have witnessed.

More centrally than *Philaster* or *Cupid's Revenge, The Maid's Tragedy*
focuses on the moral and philosophic question of the nature of the
universe in which man dwells and its relation to the civilizing arts
by which he tries to shape his life. This emphasis derives in part
from the prominence accorded the Masque of Night. At the same
time, the masque introduces us early to the dramatists' concern with

the nature and function of art in its narrower sense, and the play's two great displays of artistic creation suggest a self-conscious awareness of both the power and limits of their craft.

The Masque of Night establishes themes, imagery, and mood; it can also be seen as an analogue for the play itself, one whose unusual placement helps us both to "read" *The Maid's Tragedy* and to understand its status as theatrical art. Elaborate, physically gorgeous, the marriage masque epitomizes courtly artifice while celebrating the rite most centrally concerned with union and harmony in both public and private spheres. Significantly, despite Stratos's conviction that such entertainment is by nature mendacious, the masque in its way tells the truth. Even the masquers' hymeneal songs reflect the court's association of sex with violence and aggression (especially the second song). The mythological frame also adumbrates a close relationship between the cosmic powers and the human society they have come to honor. Cinthia complains that, drunken and lazy, "poets when they rage / Turne gods to men, and make an houre an age" (1.2.160–61), but she is wrong on two counts. In a literal sense these gods are men, since acted by members of the court within the fiction and by the King's Men in the theater. In the masque's metaphoric mirror of the court, Night ("Queene of shaddowes") and Boreas also represent—perhaps authorize—Evadne and the king. Men both are and are not like the gods; the masque is both a fiction, the highly structured artifice of civilized man, and a suggestive allegory of the world beyond human control.

Beaumont and Fletcher's delight in altering the audience's perspective, in moving us through different relations to character and action, is evident throughout *The Maid's Tragedy* and affects each of the major confrontations. Having allowed us in act 1 to accept the court at face value and the masque as mere superficial pageantry, then shocked us in 2.1, the dramatists set up a potential model for their own play. We can simply enjoy *The Maid's Tragedy* as entertainment: the artistry of its structured surprises and reversals; the intellectually titillating dramatization of the sexual puns of Petrarchan love poetry;[23] the sensational events and extreme, highly rhetorized emotion. Certainly, these elements help sever obvious links to the audience's "real" world, and the whole is rounded off with the excitement of a thoroughly villainous king's murder and the neatly choreographed demise of almost all the main characters. In its way, this is the court's response. The spectacle carried on in

its midst is of course not entertainment, but it is distanced, both
an apparently unnatural aberration that has worked itself out and a
sequence of events—safely over—narrated and interpreted by
Melantius. The new king can call the tableau of dead bodies "strange"
and then reassert the traditional pieties; Diphilus can term his brother's attempted suicide "unmanly" (5.3.249, 279).

We are permitted to join the court again, to walk away. We may
also have learned from the masque that the poet's highly wrought
fiction can in its own way explore fundamental questions, can through
its very artifice make humanly tolerable the contemplation of ex-
periences that challenge our sense of ourselves. Having learned of
events with the principal characters, we have, at a remove, felt their
significance. Unlike the court, we have passed through the emotional
sequence at the play's heart, the psychic pain resulting from immediate loss but also the challenge to a whole order of belief. To
understand *The Maid's Tragedy* at its most disturbing, the level at
which it works out the masque's implications about the universe in
which the masquers sing and dance their measures, is to understand
why the play does not conclude with Evadne's revenge, why the
final tableau of suicides is not "strange" at all.

The second example of human artistry appears in the scene of
Aspatia and her waiting-women. Extraneous to the plot, an interlude
marking time between Evadne's wedding-night revelations and the
couple's morning-after appearance at court, in placement and content 2.2 is central both to the play's mood and to its concern with
art. Isolated by Amintor's desertion, Aspatia floats timelessly, obsessed with betrayal and death. Lysippus's initial "character" associated her both with the natural world—where with a pastoral
sorrow that recalls *Philaster*'s Bellario she can see a "bancke / Stucke
full of flowers" only as a proper burying ground for lovers—and
with the power of storytelling, for her songs "of the silent death /
Of some forsaken virgin" stifle the court ladies' mirth and "send
them weeping one by one away" (1.1.89–90, 101–4). In 2.2 Aspatia's "infectious griefe" infects the play. She counsels her women,
"Goe learne to love first, learne to lose your selves, . . . Beleeve
all faithfull, and be miserable" (2.2.5–10). Her sorrow doubles
Amintor's and in its elegiac, generalizing quality projects over the
play what proves to be an apt lament for them all. Even Evadne's
clear-eyed barter of sex for position dissolves into a realization of
self-betrayal, and her most haunting lines echo Aspatia's sense in

2.2 of helpless abandonment: "Gods where have I beene all this time, how friended, / That I should lose my selfe thus desperately, / And none for pittie shew me how I wandred?" (4.1.177–79). In all its varieties, love entails self-destruction. The final suicides simply literalize what has been implicit throughout.

Aspatia places men squarely in the hostile, deceitful nature sketched in the masque. Rather than believe "that beast" man, "beleeve the sea / Weepes for the ruin'd marchant when he rores, . . . rather the sunne / Comes but to kisse the fruit in wealthy Autumme, / When all falles blasted" (2.2.27, 17–22). Aspatia expands this theme with a list of mythic betrayals reaching back to Oenones, left by Paris for Helen, and to Dido's tearful sight of Aeneas's departing ship. Finally, in her handmaid's embroidery Aspatia finds her own analogue: she emblematizes herself as "sorrowes monument," the living image of a psychological "desolation" that her women will eternize with their needles (2.2.72, 75). Her own lineaments copied for Ariadne's, Aspatia transforms herself into art, the "miserable life of this poore picture" (2.2.76). Amintor's breach of faith becomes merely one modern instance, and Aspatia's evocation of his predecessors further challenges conventional assumptions about fidelity in love.

As artist and moralist Aspatia remains unsatisfied, for the ancient tales record no punishment. With her handmaids, Aspatia can exercise the "breath of Kings": she can revenge herself on the life that has condemned her to Ariadne's fate. Although the "story" recounts Theseus's free escape from Naxos, in this reworking she orders that he "shall not goe so"; instead, she adds a quicksand, a deceptive "smiling water" and a "feare" done "to the life" (2.2.52–56). In the art she can control she recasts the legend "wrong'd by wanton Poets" to satisfy a human need for justice (2.2.57). But in fact the poets have not lied, either here or in the masque or in *The Maid's Tragedy*. Aspatia's psychological annihilation, her sense of being lost in a wild desert, is true, and she is one in a long line of forsaken women. Rhodes, as Naxos, is a vulnerable isle at the mercy of Boreas.

Metaphorically, Aspatia's embroidery is the art of Beaumont and Fletcher's tragicomedies, at the last moment snatching poetic justice from the jaws of a world that by nature seems indifferent to it. Within the fiction, reality can be commanded to answer human necessities and present us with what "should ha been so" (2.2.49).

In a truly tragic world, Aspatia's art cannot coerce nature's; the dramatists refuse to intervene, as they do at the end of *Philaster* and *A King and No King*. Aspatia's question to her ladies about the story of Theseus and Ariadne both echoes Amintor's to Evadne in 2.1 and looks ahead to the reason why in 5.3 she reenters to seek her death: "could the Gods know this, / And not of all their number raise a storme? / But they are all as ill" (2.2.49–51).

Without implying undue claims for its greatness, *The Maid's Tragedy* might usefully be seen as Beaumont's *King Lear*—and perhaps Fletcher's, though his own tragedies suggest he renounced his share in its vision. Despite the fact that he and Shakespeare were writing now for the same company, Beaumont represents the next generation in more than age. In terms of the passing of an era, the important difference between the plays is not one of quality. The principal characters of *The Maid's Tragedy* are thrust into glimpsing Lear's world, where ideals of honor, love, friendship, and justice have no force and men betray themselves as readily as the world betrays their hopes. Yet *The Maid's Tragedy* not only lacks a central protagonist; it also reduces its four main figures in stature, both socially and in their capacity for greatness of soul, and it surrounds them with a trivializing court and with the humour antics of figures like Calianax.

With such diminished characters, *The Maid's Tragedy* proposes a relation between man and his world that no one within it can bear to contemplate. The Elizabethan humanists' belief in humanity's inherent nobility and potential for self-transcendence has no place in this world, and therefore no representative. Significantly, the play's psychological dynamic is not generated by a king who discovers that he is also a man and then pushes on into the wilderness to face what this might mean, but by the king's subjects discovering that their king is nothing but a man. Indeed, as representative figure he is one in whom the liberating effects of power have revealed man's kinship with beasts. Beaumont and Fletcher offer no ideology, value, or character to bridge the gap between things as they are and as we would have them be. *The Maid's Tragedy* may address some of the same issues as Shakespeare's play, but it is in this respect a version without either Cordelia or King Lear.

Chapter Six
The Legacy: Tragicomedy and Comedy

A King and No King: Date, Sources, Partnership

A King and No King was entered in the Stationers' Register 7 August 1618 and published, as "Acted at the Globe, by his Majesties Servants," in 1619. Unusually in this study, external evidence exists to bring us closer to the play's first appearance. Sir Henry Herbert records that it was "allowed to be acted in 1611" by Sir George Buc, and the King's Men performed it at court on 26 December 1611 and again during the winter season of 1612–13.[1] Six more editions before its printing in the second folio (1679) attest to the play's popularity.[2]

Although no single original for its plot is known, behind A King and No King lies a heterogeneous collection of possible and likely sources of inspiration. The heroic, military, and vaguely historical setting, some of the characters' names, and suggestions for the play's central incident can be traced to Xenophon's Cyropaedia, that classical life of the perfect warrior-ruler so beloved of Renaissance defenders of poetry from Sidney to Milton. The play's title character—Arbaces, King of Iberia—does not appear in Xenophon, but an Assyrian commander Gobryas does (bk. 4, chap. 6), and he lends his name to Gobrius, Arbaces's true father. Tigranes, the defeated Armenian king in Beaumont and Fletcher, is in the Cyropaedia a philosophically minded prince of Armenia who becomes a loyal follower of Cyrus (bk. 3, passim); he also appears in the chapter that presents the captive lady Panthaea and again mentions Gobryas (bk. 5, chap. 1).

In A King and No King Panthea becomes the young Iberian princess Panthaea, supposed sister of Arbaces, with whom both he and Tigranes fall in love. Beyond Panthaea's name, the Cyropaedia suggests situational and thematic parallels. In a joking discussion of beauty's power to distract, Araspes, a young man who boasts of his ability to resist passion, argues that "love is a voluntary matter," unlike thirst or hunger; as proof, Araspes claims that "a brother does not fall in love with a sister . . . for fear and law are sufficient to prevent love." Cyrus laughs at such certainty in man's rational control, calling love rather a "distemper" to which men become slaves, and Araspes is driven to admit this may be true for "weak and unhappy men" who wrongly blame love for their own failings (bk. 5, chap. 1).[3] Araspes's naiveté is soon demonstrated. Given the beautiful Panthea to guard, he promptly falls hopelessly in love and even threatens to force her submission (bk. 6, chap. 1).[4] In *A King and No King,* both Arbaces and Tigranes repeat, with variations, Araspes's attitude and fall.

Other classical texts may have contributed in minor matters. Suggestions for Bessus, Beaumont and Fletcher's cowardly captain, as well as for Arbaces probably derive from the *Bibliotheca historica* of Diodorus Siculus. There a Median prince Arbaces captures Sardanapalus; he is accompanied by the Babylonian captain Belesus who later tries to withhold some of the captured treasure but, surprisingly, receives forgiveness rather than beheading (bk. 2, chaps. 23–28). Mardonius, Beaumont and Fletcher's sturdy soldier and honest adviser, may have been taken from Herodotus (bk. 6, chap. 43; bk. 7, chap. 51), where he is a Persian commander influential with Xerxes and son of another Gobryas, or from Plutarch's "Life of Aristides," where he commands an army under Xerxes. In Plutarch's "Life of Lucullus" another Tigranes of Armenia appears, but this one in character seems closer to Beaumont and Fletcher's Arbaces: an insolent, overbearing monarch who demands flattery from his men and is described as "king of kings."[5] More generally, Plutarch's habit of summing up the faults as well as the virtues of his subjects may have influenced Mardonius's often startlingly contradictory verbal portraits of Arbaces in *A King and No King.*

The main plot of *A King and No King* evolves from adding to Xenophon's Panthea episode the rival suitor Tigranes and an apparently unnatural attraction between Panthaea and Arbaces. The suggestion for an incestuous love may derive from Araspes's confident assertion to Cyrus that such things do not happen, but a number of more modern works could have inspired the romance variation employed in *A King and No King,* where incest is averted by the timely discovery of true identity. The old Spanish tale of

Abencerraje and Jarifa found its way into Montemayor's enormously popular *Diana,* and Perez's continuation of Montemayor had already been used for *Philaster.* In the *Diana,* book 4, a supposed brother and sister tentatively declare a sinful passion but soon discover they are not related and can marry.[6] The first story of Juan de Timoneda's *El Patrañuelo* (1567) and Alonso de la Vega's play based on it, *Tolomea,* tell of an "incestuous" union that has produced a child before the penitent parents learn from the governess who switched babies that they are not siblings. Closer to home, a subplot brother and sister in John Lyly's *Mother Bombie* (Q2 1598) resist their illicit passion but finally discover they are changelings and their love "natural." The prevention of real incest, again by the revelation of true identity, appears in Claude Fauchet's account of King Thierry in *Lez Antiquitez Gauloises et Francoises* (vol. 1, bk. 5, chaps. 2–5), a recent French history followed rather closely for *The Tragedy of Thierry and Theodoret.*[7]

Finally, *A King and No King*'s explanation of its sensational temptation seems to derive from Masuccio of Salerno's fifteenth-century collection of tales, *Il Novellino* (pt. 5, "novel" 42). In the last act we learn that Arbaces is really his counselor Gobrius's son, given at birth to Arane, Queen of Iberia, who feared that her elderly husband would produce no successor. Princess Panthaea was later born legitimately to the king and queen, and in the interests of this true heir Arane has tried repeatedly to have her "son" killed. Gobrius, equally ambitious for his child, hopes that when Arbaces sees Panthaea after many years apart they will fall in love; thus, when the truth is revealed, Arbaces will retain his position by marriage. In Masuccio's story a more culpable Queen of Poland, in love with a courtier-knight, promises to do away with the child with which she is pregnant so that the next child, conceived in adultery, will inherit the kingdom. She exchanges the duly-born legitimate heir for the son of the wife of a visiting Hungarian knight and then kills the surrogate prince. Believing her own son has also died, she bears her lover a daughter. By a bizarre sequence of events, the true prince of Poland not only lives but is exchanged again, now for the Queen of Hungary's son; when he grows up he is unwittingly betrothed to his half-sister. Truth will out, incest is avoided, and the King of Hungary finally marries his daughter to his erstwhile "son," thus producing the paradox of regaining as son-in-law the King of Poland he lost as blood heir. The Queen's bargain as well as the paradoxical final situation bear obvious relevance to *A King and No King* and, perhaps, to its riddling title.[8]

In execution *A King and No King* is considered largely Beaumont's.[9] As with *The Maid's Tragedy*, however, some evidence implies that Fletcher participated more fully than scene distribution would indicate. Much of his contribution lies in the comic prose scenes of acts 4 and 5 in which the cowardly braggart Bessus tries to salvage his lost "honor" but ends up, with his new friends the Sword-men, being physically beaten by the disgusted courtiers on whom they try out their casuistical defense. To Fletcher also falls, however, a major scene of sequential confrontations among the play's principal figures (4.2): between Tigranes and Spaconia, the Armenian lady to whom he was betrothed before Arbaces proposed the match with Panthaea; between them and Arbaces, now incensed that Tigranes may have won Panthaea's heart; finally, between Arbaces and his soldier-confidant Mardonius. More than a knowledge of plot and character is suggested in Robert Herrick's commendatory poem for the 1647 folio. In "Upon Master Fletchers Incomparable Playes," Herrick praises the "high designe / Of *King and no King* (and the rare Plot thine)."[10] Herrick may refer in general terms to the play's originality, but he may also have had grounds for a more precise attribution of the story's outline to Fletcher. Before being sent to Cambridge, from 1608 to 1613 Herrick was his uncle's apprentice in London and may have seen the play's first performance; later, as a "Son of Ben" and part of Jonson's circle, Herrick in all likelihood knew Fletcher personally.[11]

Whatever Fletcher's share in its planning, many critics have felt that, of the joint plays, *A King and No King* "in spirit comes closest to the Fletcherian definition of tragi-comedy"; in it "the pattern" of Beaumont and Fletcher tragicomedy, which Fletcher was to carry on, "is finally established."[12] *A King and No King* looks more squarely toward later English practice in both tragicomedy and heroic drama than the more typically Jacobean, indeed Shakespearean, *Philaster* and *The Maid's Tragedy*, both of which were popular through the Restoration but also suffered alteration.[13] Even as the partnership dissolved, it created the form for which it became most famous.

A King and No King

Despite its links with the other collaborations, *A King and No King* works out a generic mixture in which the balance that marked

Philaster shifts toward the comic emphasis Fletcher seemed to find more congenial. The dramatic world of *A King and No King* is less dense and fully realized, its characters flatter, and, in part because the central situation is so extreme, more wholly a product of their rhetoric. *Philaster* allowed each of its component genres its due, and this respect for the action's tragic potential created a kind of equipoise between a recognizable world of human suffering and the enforced aesthetic distance that asked us also to enjoy the dramatic skill with which its problems were developed and, finally, given a happy issue.[14] In *A King and No King* we remain largely detached from the dramatized action. Teasing hints of a solution, like Gobrius's in 2.1, make us more consistently aware of the playwrights' art and the self-conscious intricacy of their plotting.

Instead of satiric and romance perspectives creating a multifaceted view of character and event, as they do in *Philaster,* in *A King and No King* they clash in ways that more nearly cancel each other out. The result is a different kind of comedy, one that includes kings and the possibility of disastrous action but finally negates both the threat and the issues it introduced. For its main plot at least, as Eugene Waith observes, *A King and No King*'s "most radical departure from the familiar forms is in the abandonment of the meanings of tragedy and of comedy, though many of their techniques and some of their effects are retained."[15]

This frustration of affective engagement stems from a more persistent use of techniques that undermine the protagonist's stature and, frequently, distance us from the play's action even in scenes that develop his plight. The decision to employ elements of a morality-play structure—Arbaces poised between good and bad angels—provides two foil characters who help determine our attitude toward the king.[16] The secondary plot in which Tigranes, too, falls in love with Panthaea offers a third. Each functions differently within the dramatic structure, but each in some way diminishes Arbaces. That *A King and No King* also asks us to pity Arbaces, and to accept as a given the good qualities we are told he possesses, results in Arbaces becoming a kind of void—or question mark—at the center of a play that appears to focus on him as its hero.[17]

The story of the cowardly Bessus forms one strand of *A King and No King,* and much of it is developed in separate scenes. Yet the morality-play structure also weds Bessus firmly to the main plot's characterization of Arbaces: as "bad angel," Bessus represents one side of his king's potential and balances Mardonius's "good angel" advice. Indeed, these two opposites open the play and establish its tone. For eighty lines of comic prose Mardonius exposes as empty words Bessus's claim to a reputation for valor, and Mardonius also prepares us here for his king's contradictory and volatile nature, flatly stating that Arbaces is "vain-glorious, and humble, and angrie, and patient, and merrie, and dull, . . . in extreamities in an houre" (1.1.82–83). Arbaces enters with his prisoner Tigranes and proceeds to act out the qualities attributed to him, though the emphasis is decidedly on "vain-glory." Lest we miss the point, Tigranes tells him he brags intolerably and, when Arbaces continues his self-deification while denying "ostentation," Mardonius's mocking asides further cue our response. Although Arbaces actually is a valorous conqueror and intends Tigranes's marriage to Panthaea as an honor, the parallels with Bessus, who remains onstage, are enforced. Arbaces becomes the scene's comic butt, an anti-Cyrus who lacks dignity and demands flattery even when he asks for "truth." That Arbaces's failure to exhibit truly regal qualities contributes to the play's teasing preparation for his nonroyal birth does not cancel the effect of choosing, for so much of the play, to make that failure demeaning.

Bessus remains a prominent figure. Although the comedy of his efforts to save his reputation does not involve Arbaces, analogies between these plots qualify the seriousness with which we take the play's development of its "tragic" action. In 4.3 the Sword-men's attempt verbally to redefine reality—Bessus's demonstrated cowardice as "honor"—provides a farcical version of Arbaces's astonishing response to his sudden desire for his sister: "It cannot be . . . Shee is no kinne to me, nor shall shee be; / If shee were any, I create her none" (3.1.148, 161–62). As Bessus says in 3.2, though in context referring to Bacurius, the way to counter unpleasant facts is with "impudence: Therefore will I outsweare him" (3.2.142–43).

Bessus reenters the main plot in 3.3, again as foil to both Mardonius and Arbaces. Devoted unto death to his king, Mardonius reserves the right to decline dishonorable service. Asked to procure Panthaea, Mardonius refuses to act in "so base a businesse" and leads Arbaces to admit "It was a motion misbeseeming man" (3.3.82, 92). Arbaces's conscience wracks him with the knowledge that what he desires is "a sinne that needs must damne us both" (3.3.78), but it cannot control his passion. When Bessus arrives, Arbaces sees his chance. He dismisses the censorious Mardonius—"I can spare you now" (3.3.132)—and redirects his request. Bessus's cheerful amorality and gross reductionism shock Arbaces as well as the audience: "O you would have a bout with her? Ile do't, Ile do't Ifaith . . . and when this is dispatcht, if you have a minde to your Mother tell me, and you shall see Ile set it hard" (3.3.147–48, 167–69).

As with the analogously structured scene in *Philaster,* the Country Fellow's intrusion in 4.5, the contrast works in complex ways. Yet the Country Fellow had introduced a normal, everyday world's interpretation of events and thus provided a needed corrective to the distraught lovers' extravagant rhetoric and behavior. Bessus brings laughter to a scene of strained emotion, but it is not normative. He mocks the whole idea of human morality and threatens to make irrelevant the play's larger concern with what differentiates men from beasts. And because Bessus has in vulgar terms merely restated his king's request, Arbaces's self-righteous indignation must seem comically hypocritical: the vocabulary with which he tries to transfer his guilt doubles back to describe himself. The conscienceless Bessus, innocently wondering what all the pother is about, in one way of course emphasizes his king's superiority, for "conscience" is precisely the cause of Arbaces's despair and self-loathing. Yet given Arbaces's demonstrated inability to temper his passions, his own assumption that he will yield to forcing his sister, the scene also suggests that the major difference between them is one of vocabulary.

The "low" comedy thus works by obtruding upon the story of Arbaces's passion, as well as through analogies established by juxtaposition. Frequently, it is used to bracket major scenes of emotional confrontation (3.1; 4.4; 5.4). Indeed, this technique appears in little within the completely extraneous 2.2, where several anonymous citizens gather to watch Arbaces's triumphal homecoming procession. They open the scene with comic bickering and, after Arbaces's public address, close it by commenting hilariously on the grandiose speech they have misheard and, hence, misinterpreted.

Distancing of characters as well as issues extends beyond the deployment of farcical city comedy. Interest is even more widely distributed than in *Philaster* and, although Arbaces obviously extends the Leucippus-Philaster-Amintor line of young men baffled and tormented by life's contradictions, he lacks Philaster's comparative centrality and, however narrowly conceived, complexity and growth.[18] All the joint plays employ external characterization, yet

with Arbaces it remains the dominant mode. After introducing him,
Mardonius continues to define and interpret his king. At the end
of 1.1, Mardonius lists to Arbaces both his virtues and "the qualities
that doe eclipse your vertues" (1.1.335). Later Mardonius again
explains to the king his "childish follies" and tells him the remedy:
to be "temperate" (4.2.173, 188). Dramatic technique seems to
have retreated to the overdetermined, directive analyses of *Cupid's
Revenge.*

Mardonius contributes to another distinguishing feature of *A King
and No King,* one that inhibits empathy and a sense of impending
tragedy. The scenes of Arbaces's terrible passion are marked by an
extraordinarily heavy use of asides. In 3.1, while Arbaces tries to
deny his kinship and redefine "facts," Mardonius's comments point
up his prince's folly and undercut the tragic grandeur of his passion:
"What, is he mad? . . . O this is fine . . . This is better and
better" (3.1.113, 169, 307). This humorous, disjunctive effect also
marks the treatment of Tigranes's equally abrupt attraction to Panthaea, itself a comic reversal: Tigranes now desires the princess he
had been ordered against his will to marry; suddenly he is denied
her by the brother who wants her for himself. Both Tigranes and
Arbaces describe to us their feelings, not merely as they fall in love
but throughout the scene, and Spaconia's asides inject yet another
viewpoint, that of a silent captive who can only watch helplessly as
her lover deserts her. The overpowering strength of passion, certainly
no new theme in Beaumont and Fletcher, is underscored by Arbaces's
and Tigranes's private revelations. Yet 3.1's setting is public, its
stage densely populated, and the welter of separate commentary
repeatedly shifts our perspective and keeps us at a greater distance
from the characters' plights than in either *Philaster* or *The Maid's
Tragedy.*

Later, 4.2 returns to the pattern of 1.1, with Mardonius's in-
terpretive asides directing our response. Surprisingly, he does not
emphasize the situation's horror: the private man's incestuous im-
pulses; the violations of public responsibility in the tyrannic im-
prisoning of Tigranes and Spaconia and unjust treatment of honest
Bacurius. Rather, Mardonius's running commentary, after virtually
every speech, mocks Arbaces and debases him to the level of a child
(or a Bessus) who simply needs physical correction: "If he had beene
well beaten, he had beene temperate: I shal never see him hansome

againe, till he have a Horse-mans staffe poak't through his shoulders, or an arme broke with a Bullet" (4.2.120–23).

Arbaces and Panthaea are allotted only one scene alone together to garner our sympathy, 4.4. Here they discover their apparently unnatural passion is mutual, and this scene offers the play's full statement of its more general subject—the opposition between humanity and the natural world, reason and passion. It also builds to a titillating flirtation with incest when they rationalize as "lawful" sibling behavior both hand-holding and kissing. Yet Beaumont and Fletcher do not retain this pitch or focus. Arbaces and Panthaea do not reappear until the play's finale, and 4.4 is framed by scenes of Bessus comedy. Moreover, our attention is soon shifted to the father-daughter confrontation between Ligones and Spaconia, and to the final reconciliation of Tigranes with both.

Tigranes's prominence furthers this dispersion of focus, since to the play's thematic concerns he is as important as Arbaces. Unlike Mardonius, a static commentator who tells us how to view Arbaces, Tigranes is a dramatically conceived foil. His sudden love for Panthaea provides plot complications as well as a doubling and universalizing of Arbaces's apparently unnatural desire. The two kings become variations on passion's arbitrary power and its ability to warp even the best human intentions; both men have every reason to wish themselves immune to Panthaea's beauty. Gobrius's revelation that Arbaces is his son, not Panthaea's brother, retroactively cancels the horror and turns a threat to the social fabric itself into "straightforward" romantic comedy of love at first sight. Tigranes from the start represents the more realistic and typical situation of falling in love with a beautiful woman while already betrothed to another. Through him Beaumont and Fletcher reexamine in a wider context the problem of love's faith and its testing by irrational passion that was central to *Philaster* and to the Aspatia-Amintor relationship in *The Maid's Tragedy*.

A King and No King establishes at the outset its primary virtue: constancy, in temper as well as in love. Arbaces conspicuously lacks this virtue even before he sees Panthaea, as Mardonius's commentary in 1.1 makes clear. In the next scene, Spaconia reminds a despondent Tigranes that firmness of mind and self-control liberate man from his physical circumstances. Captured Tigranes need not be a "slave" because Arbaces "won but halfe of thee, / Thy bodie"; Tigranes's "minde may be as free" as his conqueror's, for Arbaces's "will never did combate thine, / And take it prisoner" (1.2.18–21). It is on this ideal of human freedom in spirit and commitment that Tigranes founds his promise to remain faithful to Spaconia despite Arbaces's boastful confidence that any sister of his "can doe as much / In peace, as I in Warre; sheele conquer too" (1.1.188–89).

Although the main plot mutes the issue, *A King and No King* thus sets up its conflict in terms that relate it to the earlier collaborations. Passion proves to be destructive of one's sense of self as well as of others, and its apparently amoral force challenges conventional assumptions about civilized man and about humanity's relation to both the gods and the natural world. Despite the ideal of self-command outlined by Spaconia and by Mardonius's criticism of Arbaces's erratic behavior, distrust of the realities of human nature is disquietingly frequent. Spaconia's love forces her beyond the bounds of modesty in asking Panthaea to refuse Tigranes as proposed husband. She also acknowledges her request unreasonable, since she doubts it is "in the power / Of you to doe what I would have you grant" (2.1.262–63); honor among women must crumble before sexual attraction. Later, Ligones assumes that if his daughter and Tigranes are together, Spaconia must be the Armenian king's whore, and in 5.4 Gobrius's account of past events suggests an equal cynicism about human virtue. Mardonius and Bacurius are loyal, truthtelling counselors, yet they can neither cure nor moderate Arbaces's folly.

The kings who yield so quickly to desire seem to bear out this darker view. By the end of 3.1 Arbaces has acknowledged Panthaea as his sister but allows himself to "wade in sinne, / And foolishly intice my selfe along" by kissing her (3.1.301–2). He collapses into fatalistic acceptance of his passion and assumes, despite self-loathing, that he must eventually yield to its demands: "How wilt thou vex me when this deede is done / Conscience, that art afraid to let me name it" (3.3.16–17). Like other Beaumont-Fletcher protagonists, Arbaces accepts what happens, however strange, because he shares their sense of impotence. Briefly, he wonders at the lack of coherent meaning in events: "Why should you that have made me stand in war / Like fate it selfe . . . Decree such an unworthy end of me, / And all my glories?" (3.1.320–23). "Logic" is restored by reinterpreting the enigmatic as "this punishment upon my pride" or, more vaguely, the "unpardonable" and "hastie errors of my youth" that "draw a sinne / Helplesse upon me" (4.4.79; 5.4.62–64). The gods stand justified, and so does Arbaces's passivity. His "loathed Fate may turne about," but he cannot effect that turn himself (3.3.111). The "destinies" have "Their fix't decrees," beyond men's power of alteration (5.4.56–57).

Bewildered, Arbaces is thrust into a world of moral anarchy. Desire is repeatedly seen as a disease or sickness whose implications are metaphysical: the only "cure" he envisions is a satisfaction of appetite that would "Orethrow Divinity, all morall Lawes, / And leave mankinde as unconfinde as beasts" (3.1.193–95). Arbaces can defend his lust only by adopting the arguments of a fashionably shocking philosophic primitivism, which proposed man's natural and proper condition as the state of nature existing in a Golden Age before the artificial impositions of Law and Custom.[19] He thus laments the "curious rules" that fetter "Accursed" rational man's action, for "Who ever saw the Bull / Fearfully leave the Heifer that he likt, / Because they had one Dam?" (4.4.131–38). Spaconia employed the same figure for indiscriminate sexuality in berating Tigranes, though her usage brands such a retreat impossible as well as grotesque: "The Princesse . . . will sooner / Be wonne to marrie with a Bull, and safer, / Then such a beast as thou art" (4.2.67– 69).

Physical appetite links humanity with a lawless nature beyond domestication. Spaconia's images for Tigranes's betrayal associate it with an "unconstant," hostile world familiar from earlier plays. Tigranes's "faith" is fickle as the wind or the "raging overflowes, / That no banke can command"; his inability to order his affections mirrors man's helplessness before nature's turbulent energies, for he is like the "beaten Marriner" futilely attempting with his whistle to "Calme the loude murmurs of the troubled maine" (4.2.48–55). Yielding to forbidden desire, Arbaces tells Panthaea that without his "reason," the "onely difference betwixt man, and beast," he feels himself as horrifyingly "farre without a bound, / As the wild Ocean that obeyes the winds; / Each suddaine passion throwes me as it lists" (4.4.64–69).

Initially, as their asides in 3.1 make clear, Tigranes parallels Arbaces and seems to confirm the frightening rapidity of this descent into nature. Seeing Panthaea, Tigranes provides an immediate rationalization: "There can no falshood come of loving her; / Though I have given my faith, shee is a thing / Both to be lov'd and serv'd beyond my faith" (3.1.94–96). Despite Spaconia's presence and his sense of being "about to sinne," Tigranes finds "I cannot / Stifle my passion longer" (3.1.153, 209–10). While Arbaces asks Mardonius and then Bessus to procure him Panthaea, however, Tigranes next appears struggling for self-mastery. He is given the dignity of a long soliloquy—no Mardonius asides or Bessus foolery—and the maturity of a man who finally pins himself to his responsibilities and so recovers his identity and self-respect. Tigranes begins by condemning his folly, since he arranged for Spaconia's presence at court. Yet thoughts of the two ladies soon turn from tactical mistakes in the pursuit of Panthaea to consideration of Spaconia's virtues and the wrong he has done this woman who gave up her freedom, even her name, for him: she "so much lov'd thee that in honestie / And honour thou art bound to meete her vertues" (4.2.18–19). He finds he has betrayed not only Spaconia but himself. Shame at his "inconstancie," the "unmanly, beastly, sudden doting / Upon a new face," rekindles his original devotion and frees him from bondage to transitory desire (4.2.28–29).

As the gulf widens between the two responses to infatuation, the play's repeated use of the paradoxes of freedom and bondage helps clarify the fundamental issue of human nature such passion raises.[20] Spaconia had reminded Tigranes that he could remain essentially free by refusing to yield his mind and will to the man who had defeated him in battle. He discovers for himself that liberation from another kind of subjection comes with exercising the particularly human ideals of respect for virtue and goodness, and of behavior in accord with the honor due oneself and others. To be a pipe for passion's winds is to give oneself over to the body's compulsions and the natural physical world to which that body ties us. Though victor in war, Arbaces is passions' subject. The sight of Panthaea merely adds lust, jealousy, and wild despair to pride and vaingloriousness.

In some ways *A King and No King* is bleaker—or perhaps more cynical—than *Philaster,* since with its romance resolution the play seems to self-destruct. Gobrius's revelation negates the central dilemma on which dramatic suspense had been built and, apparently, Arbaces's need for maturity and self-control. Accepting events as both "Fate" and, however inexplicable, "just," Arbaces had turned back on the gods the moral responsibility for his behavior with Panthaea: "If you above love not such sinnes as these, / Circle my heart with thoughts as cold as snow" (4.4.6–7). His passions became more inflamed in Panthaea's presence, of course, but since they are not in fact brother and sister, the main plot's denouement might be said to reassure us of gods who authorize human morality and abhor "such sinnes as these." Certainly when Arbaces asks Arane to "tell me who I am," he means it in the most literal, genealogical sense (5.4.150). He is saved in spite of himself—ultimately by the playwrights' craft, within the story by their surrogate puppeteer Gobrius, whose ambition for his son placed Arbaces on the royal throne, preserved him from Arane's murderous stratagems, and predisposed his affection for Panthaea with "witching letters" (5.4.85). Gobrius admits to being "the cause"; in effecting his plot, as for any tragicomic playwright, timing is all: "Now it is ripe. . . . Now is the time" (5.4.97, 65, 108).[21]

Gobrius and his ending offer reassurance. We can rejoice with the lovers and laugh at Arbaces's final transformation into Sir Epicure Mammon, busily inventing an impossibly fabulous triumphal return to Armenia for Tigranes and Spaconia. We are allowed to look back on the whole as entertainment, to be enjoyed and admired for the brilliant artifice of its construction. Beaumont and Fletcher's play is more complex and ambiguous than Gobrius's, however, and they leave a few disturbing reminders that, beyond his purview or control, there are problems to which the facts of Arbaces's birth are irrelevant. *A King and No King* places less emphasis than the tragedies on an actively hostile world of natural egotism and aggression, yet even in a tragicomedy so tilted toward final happiness for all, there lingers a sense of precariousness surrounding the human community and its values.

Bessus remains an accepted part of the unchanged Iberian court, despite having been called a "monster" fit only for deserts remote from human habitation (3.3.179–83). Arbaces may have wished that "conscience" and "kinship," like "brother" and "sister," could be reduced to "meere sounds," social fictions, but he was at least haunted by a sense of sin (4.4.113). Bessus throughout demonstrates that "conscience" is not innate. His farcical refusal to accept "honor" as more than a word to be redefined to his own uses becomes grotesquely threatening when applied to "sister" or "mother." Having a human form does not ensure one's participation in the bonds— and boundaries—by which society defines itself. Nor is moral value inscribed on the created world: Arbaces proposing incest and Bessus eagerly agreeing each look physically unchanged. Arbaces can only "see" Bessus as evil by superimposing an allegorical portrait of the devil and hellmouth on the figure who cheerfully resists his description: "I feele no such thing, but tis no matter how I looke, Ile doe your businesse" (3.3.159–67).

The difficulties raised by Bessus's amorality can be muffled, but for them Gobrius's revelation provides no cure. Bessus remains a comic figure, and thoroughgoing cowardice tempers any active threat he poses, but he is not the play's only hedge against the apparent moral frivolity of its main plot. Even within act 5's redefined, theoretically wholesome and romantic terms, Arbaces's attraction to Panthaea disturbs in its force and violence. Compulsive and destructive rather than ennobling, this "love" sees no alternative to legal possession but rape. The comic scene of anonymous citizens (2.2) extends the impression of widespread—almost random—sexuality and aggressiveness constantly pulling against the social fabric.

If, as the play implies beneath its juggling surface, morality is created by men acting as moral beings, then Tigranes provides one of Beaumont and Fletcher's most positive depictions. His betrayal of love's faith is real, yet he is the one to call his attraction to Panthaea "unmanly" and to recognize the difficulty in practicing his ideal of human conduct. From *Cupid's Revenge* on, Beaumont and Fletcher's protagonists' most prized quality is their "innocence": the word rings through the plays as characters either assert this virtue or wish desperately to regain it when they feel they have erred. A kind of prelapsarian condition associated with the gods' protection, it is what Arbaces seeks when he prays that his tears may wash him back to "childlike innocence," and he ties the possibility of exercising "constancie" to the recovery of this state of grace (1.1.457–63).[22] "Innocent" is just what these young men are not, however, and though they in varying degrees resist recognizing it, the plays dramatize their passage into fallen adulthood and a morally ambiguous world where it is not at all clear that the gods protect or favor innocence.

Arbaces's demand to know who he is is superficial, Tigranes's self-discovery is not. In confessing "I know I have / The passions of a man"—passions that may again endanger the fidelity he wills—Tigranes acknowledges a complex, precarious human condition (5.2.88–89). He recognizes the force, and hence the threat, of irrational, egotistic desire—not merely male sexual desire but all the "wilde passions" we have seen sway humanity and annihilate constancy to oneself or others (5.4.128). Despite the weak verse, Tigranes's recipe for maintaining "a new strong constancie" reveals that he has learned from experience: should another such temptation as Panthaea "hold my eyes / More firmely then is fit; Ile thinke of thee, / And runne away from it" (5.2.91–93). Knowing oneself at this level offers at least the possibility of self-control; it accepts the wary vigilance necessary for the human maintenance of human values. Ironically, Bessus's Falstaffian motto—where cowardice "shewed discretion, the best part of valour" (4.3.60)—may be the best wisdom for a world beyond the dramatists' fifth-act ministrations.

This discussion may seem to have hypostatized a play more substantial than a cursory reading—or, perhaps, production—would justify. Certainly, this is the Beaumont-Fletcher play most antipathetic to modern sensibilities. Nor, of course, did the play's seventeenth-century popularity rest on the implications of the imagery or the Tigranes-Spaconia by-plot. Arbaces and Philaster, Amintor and Evadne, were the figures who captured the contemporary imagination. Their sensational dilemmas, heightened rhetoric, and impassioned "heroic" absolutism—as well as the playwrights' skill in fashioning the emotionally charged turns and counterturns of a constantly exciting plot—were what received the tribute of praise, stage revival, and imitation. These features Beaumont certainly helped create, and Fletcher continued to make them the cornerstone of his practice. Yet with a play that to such a degree looks ahead, and that appears to be Beaumont's last significant contribution to the stage, it has seemed worth looking for connections to his earlier work. Such links, in the moral as well as verbal texture, clearly exist, albeit pushed to the margins of *A King and No King*. They receive even sharper definition if we compare this play with Fletcher's next, independent, tragicomedy. *The Honest Man's Fortune* (1613) offers no troubling ambiguities in any of its plots.

Collaborative Comedy

Under James I and on through the Restoration, the most consistently popular plays in the "Beaumont and Fletcher" canon were the major joint plays already discussed and comedies by Fletcher, alone or with Beaumont's participation. Although after *The Knight of the Burning Pestle* Beaumont seems to have confined his dramatic writing to collaboration, even before 1613 Fletcher also wrote independently—comedy as well as tragedy, for both public and private stages. As collaborators, too, they maintained an affiliation with the Blackfriars boys (after January 1610, officially the Children of the Queen's Revels). While writing tragicomedy and tragedy for the King's Men, they composed two comedies—*The Coxcomb* (?1609) and *The Scornful Lady* (?1610)—for their old troupe.[23]

The Coxcomb

Of the two plays, *The Coxcomb* is the more clearly Jacobean, a rollicking farce that demonstrates its origin in the satiric intrigue-comedy, often mixed with courtship themes, typical of the private theaters. It reflects more than any of the other collaborations the comic gifts Beaumont displayed in *The Woman Hater* and *The Knight of the Burning Pestle:* exuberant, good-natured parody of both literary conventions and contemporary plays; a contagious delight in human eccentricity and its rhetorical expansion into happy, unself-conscious absurdity. At the same time, *The Coxcomb* well illustrates both young men's versatility; together they continued to experiment, however much Fletcher later stuck to repeating successful formulas. They had jointly attempted tragedy with *Cupid's Revenge;* despite individual failures in comedy and tragicomedy—*The Knight* and *The Faithful Shepherdess*—they returned to these genres with new ideas. Interestingly, *The Coxcomb* treats in an ironic mode some of the serious concerns that provide *Philaster's* "tragic" pole.

The Coxcomb offers two largely distinct stories, yoked by personal acquaintance and chance so that they begin and end in the same physical locale (a city house, a country house). The main plot may derive from Cervantes's "The Curious Impertinent," an inset narrative in part 1 of *Don Quixote,* although if so it is an ingenious variation. In this test of friendship and marital fidelity, a husband (Antonio) and his friend (Mercury) return from a three-year European tour to a party given by Antonio's wife. Mercury becomes infatuated as soon as he sees the beautiful, witty Maria and, torn between his obligations as friend and guest and his wish to seduce her, Mercury tries to flee temptation. Antonio, however, turns out to be a humour character obsessed with an extravagant ideal of heroic friendship, and he vows that what is his is Mercury's. When Mercury refuses the offer of free access to Maria, Antonio goes into disguise to procure his wife for his unsuspecting friend.

Disguises and stratagems keep Antonio a farcical type-figure, the man who with great care and self-approbation contrives what other husbands seek at all costs to prevent. Through him Beaumont and Fletcher parody the kind of romance concerns they elsewhere employ seriously. Here, the usual situation of opposed love and friendship is transposed from competitive courtship, and the "beloved" being passed from one male to another is a wife. Antonio's feverish desire to stand with Pylades and Orestes, Damon and Pythias, becomes ever more ludicrous as his tawdry shifts brand him a self-deluded, would-be wittol. The demeaning disguise as Irish foot-post earns him a beating from his own servants and is itself mocked as a convention. Maria repeatedly sees through her husband's pretense, and finally, in exasperation, gets her revenge by following his urgings. In another twist of convention, Antonio's humour remains unexploded. He never learns of his "success"; when finally forced to drop his disguise to prove he is alive, he rapturously praises his wife as a model of marital chastity and apologizes to Mercury for having failed as friend.

The main plot thus ends with an intelligent, insulted woman's revenge. Having chosen to place a misinterpreted ideal above his responsibilities as husband, Antonio remains a fool, though a likeable one whose wild dreams of glory offer some of the rhetorical gusto of Lazarillo's pursuit of his fish head in *The Woman Hater.* The play's refusal to judge Maria harshly, its defiance of the traditional sexual double standard, recalls *The Woman Hater's* apparent approval, at least until its last scene, of Oriana's plucky independence. In *The Coxcomb,* the final husband-wife reconciliation remains unidealized. Antonio continues in delusion, about his male supremacy as well as his wife's fidelity; in any real-world terms, this marriage would obviously depend on the wifely common sense he does not even recognize.

The play's second plot, most of it Beaumont's, lightheartedly chronicles the tribulations of young love in the misadventures of Viola and Richardo. For reasons unknown, Viola's father opposes their marriage, and she leaves home the night of Maria's party intending to meet Richardo at midnight and run away with him. Initially a gentry version of the Jasper-Luce flight in "The London Merchant" plot of *The Knight of the Burning Pestle,* the stories soon diverge, for Richardo is anything but a sensible, resourceful apprentice. Viola has committed herself and her trust, but Richardo fails the first test of how "faithfully" he will love her (1.1.17). He and his more cynical companions arrive early at the rendezvous and decide to pass the time in a nearby tavern. Predictably, they become gloriously drunk and lecherous; when they finally meet up with Viola they mistake her for a prostitute, fight over her, quarrel with the Watch, and send the timorous Viola fleeing into the night. Unable to gain shelter at her friend Maria's, since Antonio believes she is a robber faking distress, Viola begins the comic trials of her escape to the countryside. Naively believing in others' goodwill, she is first mugged for her clothes and threatened in the lowest billingsgate by a Tinker and his Trull, then propositioned by a country gentleman, Valerio, and left on her own when she refuses to become his mistress. Rescued finally by two good-hearted milkmaids, Nan and Madge, Viola becomes a fellow servant to their mistress, who turns out to be Mercury's mother. It is to her house that all, including an incompetent local Justice of the Peace investigating Antonio's "murder," will repair in act 5.

Here Beaumont's talent for burlesque and parody takes flight. Viola's wanderings afford a series of comic vignettes, and these linguistic sketches create a range of characters who share the homey reality of George and Nell in *The Knight of the Burning Pestle*. The country Justice ("a shallow one" in the *dramatis personae* of the 1679 folio) adapts Shakespeare's Shallow from *Henry IV,* part 2, but the parody is rather good-natured tribute than satiric attack. Indeed, such satiric focus as *The Coxcomb* displays is wide-angled and forgiving. Degrees of folly proliferate everywhere, in both town and country; even the young lovers become subjects for our amusement. As the naive, idealistic, betrayed maiden, Viola has our sympathy, but she is not the symbol of victimage for which this figure is used in *The Maid's Tragedy* or *A King and No King*.[24] Removed from her proper romance genre, Viola is transported to a real world peopled by thieves and milkmaids as well as rural gentry, one in which common sense and hard work are given their due value. Viola's inability to perform the simplest tasks leads to one of the play's funniest scenes: in 4.7 Mercury's mother and her steward learn with mounting exasperation that Viola has broken a favored glass and then spilled the mincemeat. Viola is of course out of place as a servant, but a world of competent, no-nonsense gentlewomen like

Maria and Mercury's mother (a "stirring woman" fond of a good story), who manage large households with ease, makes its own comment on the conventions of maidenly helplessness appropriate only in literary genres.

Richardo receives analogous treatment, one that inverts the pattern of romance tragicomedy. In *Philaster,* the high-minded young lovers are qualified by the cynical, pragmatic court and by the "normal" response of the Country Fellow; yet despite these other perspectives, Philaster, Bellario, and Arathusa remain the play's ideals, those who promise a brighter political as well as personal future. In *The Coxcomb,* Richardo's rhetoric and behavior—drunken carousing, extravagant repentance—more consistently make him a figure of fun, a composite dramatic creation whose marriage to Viola will not, and should not, bear closer inspection. Both as gallant turned lover and as penitent, Richardo suffers from juxtaposition with the country folk's common sense. The milkmaids think that courting is "fine sport," but they also know how much young men are to be trusted, and Nan's advice to Viola goes beyond comic self-revelation: "keepe the men out, they will mar all that you make else, I know that by myselfe" (4.3.82; 3.3.171–72).

Richardo's self-flagellation is put in its place by the country gentleman as well as the servants. Valerio's is a normal, accommodating, practical virtue. He fears his wife's wrath if he takes the beauteous Viola home; he wants Viola, but will not force her. When Richardo later enlists Valerio's aid, Valerio pities the lover and, over protests that they must dash to Viola's rescue, kindly offers him bed, food, and drink (the latter producing an hilariously guilty response in itself). They finally come upon Viola and the milkmaids, and Valerio's commonsensical replies cut through Richardo's escalating hyperbole. Richardo calls them both villains and suggests that their wickedness in deserting Viola should be carried abroad to corrupt whole continents, but Valerio refuses this pilgrimage of evil, since "I am honester, / Then you know how to bee" (5.2.50–51). He describes Richardo as "finely mad" and not fit for converse until "soberer" (5.2.74–76). Richardo is indeed again drunk, though now with self-abasement. His behavior with Viola—standing or kneeling at a distance lest he infect her—also receives Nell's and Madge's sarcastic evaluation, since the lady swoons and he does nothing but talk: "And you bee a man com hither, and helpe a woman. . . . Th'art a prating Asse, ther's no goodnesse in thee"

(5.2.83, 91). Fortunately for these two inept young lovers, Viola's father suddenly reverses his opposition to their marriage.

Although usually said to be unrelated, except mechanically, *The Coxcomb*'s plots bear some thematic connections. Between them they treat of faithfulness and constancy in both romantic love and marriage. What we see of marriage, and the tests to which this bond is subject, slyly comments on the reunited Viola and Richardo. It also contributes to the play's generally detached, ironic tone, for while *The Coxcomb* is less cynical than some of its kind—Chapman's *The Widow's Tears,* for instance—its view of human nature is certainly realistic and pragmatic. When Viola wonders how Valerio fell "in love with such a creature" as he describes his wife to be— ugly, old, jealous—he freely admits it was hidden avarice and open flattery that forged his marriage (3.3.49). He answers cautiously Viola's request for a definition of love, since he is trying to seduce her, but his counsel of happy ignorance is not inappropriate: "Why, love faire maid is an extream desire, / That's not to be examin'd but fulfil'd," for "knowing what love is, / Would make thee sixe and forty" (3.3.14–15, 25–26). When Viola rejects his advances and, by now having some small experience of the world, asks if any honest men exist, Valerio's reply fits *The Coxcomb*'s fallible, though largely good-hearted, cast of characters: "More honest then my selfe / Good sooth I doe not know" (3.3.103–4).

Mercury and Maria complete the portrait sketched by Valerio. Maria is not the libidinous wife of Restoration comedy, seeking young lovers behind her husband's back. Rather, adultery is her exasperated counterplot against the silly man who violates his duty to protect her from assault and treats her as a possession, to be exchanged for his undying fame. Mercury may share the wit and sexual desire of later gentlemen rakes, but he does not live by their libertine code. He recognizes social institutions and bonds, and his self-respect depends on adhering to them. Seeing Maria, he wishes he "were a knave," or that there were "any waies to bee dishonest and save my selfe" (1.2.83, 100–1); there are not, and he tries to flee temptation. When he does capitulate, he believes Antonio dead and has offered to marry Maria before consummation. After, far from gloating over his conquest, Mercury's soliloquy reveals disillusionment and self-disgust: "Now what am I the better for enjoying / This woman that I lov'd so? . . . Why should a man that has discourse and reason" seek his own "shame"? (4.8.1–10).

Maria's evaluation appears to be the play's. A strict, conventional morality is not enforced, but neither is amorality. She describes Mercury as "the honestest man that ever was entic'd," and herself as "the honestest woman without blushing, / That ever lay with another man" (4.8.55–60). Despite Valerio and Richardo's cynical companions, for the principal characters love and marriage remain the goal and standard by which behavior is judged, even by those who are "entic'd" into temporarily violating them. At the same time, *The Coxcomb* offers a realistic rather than romantic perspective on humanity's inability consistently to honor its own ideals.

The Scornful Lady

The Scornful Lady proved to be one of the most popular works in the "Beaumont and Fletcher" canon. The only play commanded by Charles I for the Christmas season of 1641–42, it was performed steadily until the mid-eighteenth century.[25] Although it is in execution apparently almost wholly Fletcher's, Beaumont's contributions suggest he had a hand in the planning, at least for the main plot. To him belongs 1.1, introducing most of the principal characters and establishing the willful Lady's teasing persecution of her devoted suitor. Beaumont is also credited with this embattled courtship's resolution (5.2): after numerous failures, the Elder Loveless finally hits on a stratagem that tricks his Lady into marrying him. With characteristic allusiveness, Beaumont in the winning deception also offers a friendly nod to Jonson's *Epicoene*, recently performed by the same troupe.

The Scornful Lady's two plots—"cozening" farce and aristocratic romantic comedy—are familially related. The subplot belongs to the wastrel young brother who is given charge of the house when Elder Loveless sets off for the year of European travel ordered by the Lady as punishment for having publicly boasted of her favors. Young Loveless is a witty, carefree, shameless gallant, and his escapades provide satiric city comedy of the inverted "Prodigal Son" variety employed (albeit more inventively) in *The Knight of the Burning Pestle*. The subplot brims with stock types, from the usurer Moorecraft, who courts a wealthy widow at the same time that he seeks to oppress Young Loveless, to the prodigal's drinking companions (Captain, Poet, Tobacco-man, and Traveler). Although Young Loveless suffers no qualms about spending his own, and now his brother's, estate, he proves to be an intelligent exploiter of what chance offers, and he manages to maneuver Moorecraft out of both the debt and the widow. The surprise here is not the prodigal's outwitting of the usurer but his successful defense of his companions to his new wife and the spontaneous conversion of Moorecraft, who turns gallant and starts giving his money away.[26]

Until its final scenes, the main plot plays more boldly with its conventional subject, courtship and marriage. In the Lady and her witty skirmishes with her suitor, Beaumont and Fletcher created a heroine who remained a model for Caroline and Restoration dramatists.[27] Mistress of her house and wealth, without brothers or father to check her independence, the Lady demands that she be wooed on her own terms. In anger she dispatches Loveless to France, despite the fact that, though she will not admit it, she fully intends to wed him. The Lady's reluctance to commit herself, to love or the subservient role of wife, is highlighted by the opposite behavior of her Waiting Gentlewoman, Abigail, a lusty old maid now too unattractive to interest anyone but the stock comic figure, Sir Roger the Curate. Several funny scenes and a good deal of bawdy humor revolve around Abigail's chasing of the appalled Welford, a new suitor to the Lady who provides plot complications but also a means to the final resolution.

Since constancy, devotion, and apologies have gotten him nowhere, Elder Loveless turns to craft. First, he returns in disguise to report his own death by drowning and to berate the Lady for having thrown away a worthy man. Like Maria in *The Coxcomb,* the Lady sees through the trick, and she punishes him by vowing to marry Welford immediately; when Loveless reveals himself, she sends him off again on his travels. Pretending to have fallen out of love, he next appears to rail at her. He succeeds in piquing her pride, but when she tests his resolve by fainting, Loveless melts, recants, and must endure the scornful laughter of the Lady, her sister, and Abigail. Truly angry as well as desperate, Loveless in his last stratagem uses the Lady's pride and jealousy against her and forces her to admit how much she fears losing him. As though on his way to be married, he returns in the evening with Welford disguised as the modest, humble woman who has replaced the Lady in his affections. Apparently cornered, the Lady can retain Loveless only by agreeing to substitute herself as bride. They depart for a priest; the disguised Welford is invited to share the bed of the Lady's sister. The next morning brings everyone together—including Young Loveless and his bride; the newly married Abigail and Sir Roger; the newly gallant Moorecraft. The Lady is furious ("Lord, that I were unmaried againe"—5.4.82–83), but she has been wedded and bedded, and she cannot retreat to her old pose. Her sister and Welford are sent off to make legal the union they have in deed already established.

Managing four marriages out of so much discord is part of the play's appeal and, despite the up-to-date satiric elements and bawdiness, its playful reworking of the kind of witty, exuberant Elizabethan romantic comedy perfected by Shakespeare. In its way, *The Scornful Lady* stands in the line of *Love's Labors Lost, Much Ado about Nothing,* and Shakespeare's mature romantic comedies as much as with Marston's *The Dutch Courtesan* and *The Fawn,* or Chapman's *The Widow's Tears. The Scornful Lady* even suggests an old-fashioned evaluative gradation in its couples: Abigail, who has settled for a good-natured fool; Young Loveless, unreformed but in possession of the widow; the Lady's sister and Welford (whose good qualities we must assume, though he did not care which sister he married); the Lady and a truly constant, devoted Elder Loveless. The play is not pure romantic comedy, of course. Life is here a battle of wits, and Welford's motto fits them all: "catch that catch may" (1.1.257). Only one union is truly a love-match, and a prickly one at that; in quantitative terms, economics weighs more heavily than romance.

The Scornful Lady thus manages to exploit as well as mock older conventions. It again demonstrates Beaumont and Fletcher's talent for turning staple elements to uses that later generations found "modern" and stageable when other early plays seemed dated. Forced onto his wits by his Lady's whims, Loveless often sounds like a Restoration rake: he angrily lists to her her faults; he declares that marriage means "I should give away my freedome, and venture a perpetuall bondage" (1.1.140–41). Yet although he savors his final triumph, "constancy and obedience" have been his watchwords and marriage his purpose (1.1.76). He straddles two worlds: the romantic hero of conventional comedy, he is forced to woo his woman in a new way. In wit and independence the Lady appears even more forward-looking, yet she, too, transposes an older convention. Beneath her emancipated behavior lies a humour character, and the play sets out to cure her of her folly. Ordering Loveless to serve a year abroad is willful and capricious, not a needed test of his maturity. Its reduction to "Travell, or know me not" humorously echoes the widow's stubborn insistence that her second husband be a knight: " 'tis this Sir, No knight, no widow" (3.1.271; 2.3.140). When it appears the Lady has lost her man, Abigail's comment reminds us of how comically self-defeating her mistress's behavior has been: "this is still your way, to love being absent, and when hee's with you, laugh at him and abuse him. There is another way if you could hit on't" (4.1.379–81).

More complex than a humours fool, the Lady recognizes her own problem. In her soliloquy just before Loveless's success she discovers that self-knowledge is not enough: love cannot tame her frowardness. She knows that reason cannot account for "why I stoppe my selfe / From mine own wish; and stoppe the man I love / From his; and every houre repent again, / Yet still goe on" (5.2.4–7). She admits "a strange pevishnes / And anger, not to have the power to doe / Thinges unexpected, carryes me away / To mine owne ruine" (5.2.13–16). Her independence, but also her reputation for it, is all important, even when it defeats her own desires: "I had rather dye / Sometimes then not disgrace in publike him / Whom people thinke I love" (5.2.16–18). She answers herself, at least in private, with a very conventional moral: "Men, you must answer this, that dare obey / Such thinges as wee command" (5.2.20–21). To the extent that the Lady's proud behavior is presented as merely a form of destructive self-love, Loveless's trick saves her from herself. She needs his constancy and strength of purpose to stabilize her world of compulsive opposition and flux.

Yet under its surface gaiety, multiple marriages, and the Lady's deliverance from her obsession with singularity, *The Scornful Lady* is finally more hard-edged and aggressive than *The Coxcomb* — features that, along with its witty raillery, presumably helped endear it to its Restoration audiences. The earlier comedy struck a kind of balance, a theatrical mutual commentary, between its romantic subplot and realistic, satiric main plot. Viola and Richardo are "placed" by the environment in which they try to act, but they also remind us of the appeal of young love and its naive idealism. The main plot's final pragmatic accommodation to adult folly is saved from cynicism by the inclusion of the reunited, adoring young lovers as well as by Maria's forgiving wit.

In *The Scornful Lady,* the area for maneuvering between the sexes appears more a battleground, the available roles and social arrangements more severely limited. It lacks the complexity of perspective offered by a calculated juxtaposition of kinds of plots and by such characters as Maria, Mercury, Mercury's mother, even Valerio. Despite the main plot's inclusion of love as a motive, in *The Scornful Lady* each side struggles for dominance and personal satisfaction. Two of the marriages are opportunistic, and the subplot appears to champion the wily Young Loveless's determination that marriage will not interfere with his pleasures. Abigail may have satisfied her desperate desire for a man, but she has to accept her humiliation and apologize to Sir Roger. Together, Welford and Loveless join forces to defeat the new, emancipated woman, and they succeed. The Lady both is and is not "saved" by Loveless's trick. Intelligent and independent as well as victim of her own pride, she needs a new kind of marriage as well as a new kind of wooing, but the play stops short in this respect. In its resolution *The Scornful Lady* offers no challenge to the traditional social structure, and the Lady had every reason to be skittish about marriage. Both Welford and Loveless preen themselves on their sexual prowess and success in having duped her ("you are cozend meerely. / I have cast beyond your wit"—5.4.6–7). The extended ribald exchanges at her expense add to the finale's high spirits but also reveal the Lady's new subjection as wife.[28]

Chapter Seven

Conclusion

Seventeenth-Century Dominance

Beaumont's early reputation as poet and dramatist, however surprising on the strength of such a limited oeuvre, has been illustrated in chapter 1. More widespread recognition arrived with the immediate success of his collaborations with Fletcher. As early as 1612, in the epistle to *The White Devil* that lists the playwrights in whose light he wishes to be read, John Webster mentions "Master Beaumont, and Master Fletcher" after Chapman and Jonson but before the "copious industry" of Shakespeare, Dekker, and Heywood.[1] Although Beaumont retired from playwriting while still in his twenties, his renown persisted for nearly a hundred years.

In part, of course, this stature was a fiction, the consequence of his own early commercial success. Like Shakespeare with those plays now relegated to the "Shakespeare Apocrypha," Beaumont was fathered with works in which he had no hand, many written after his death, because his name was considered a selling point. Hence Beaumont continued to be associated with Fletcher in print, as half-parent of both the 1647 and 1679 folio collections. Yet despite his limited contribution, even to the second folio, in significant ways Beaumont did live on as a theatrical presence after 1613. Fletcher may be rightly called the single most important English influence on Caroline and even early Restoration dramatists,[2] but it was with Beaumont that he had worked out the formulas he continued to develop until his death in 1625. While every vigorous generation of writers seeks both to establish itself and renew an ever-fosilizing inheritance, they had been the ones to create the new forms—especially in comedy and romantic tragicomedy—that prevailed. Moreover, while Fletcher and Fletcher-Massinger plays, the bulk of the "Beaumont and Fletcher" canon, outweighed in number Beaumont's share in later revivals, the original Beaumont-Fletcher collaborations almost all enjoyed sustained popularity into the eighteenth century. Even Beaumont's *The Woman Hater* (perhaps understandably) and *The Knight of the Burning Pestle* (less explicably) were swept back onto the stage in the general demand for "their" works.

For many Caroline writers, as the commendatory verses to the 1647 folio attest, "Beaumont and Fletcher" proved awesome and inhibiting predecessors. They had created and defined *the* forms; they could only be imitated reverentially, not surpassed.[3] In fact, Queen Henrietta Maria's passion for D'Urfé and the cult of platonic love, as well as changing standards of taste (toward the sentimental) and decorum (in language), meant that the "Beaumont and Fletcher" heritage was indeed altered, its satiric edge blunted and its wit bowdlerized.[4] Yet so potent was the magic of their names that the 1647 encomiasts recognized no advances in their own work.

With the Restoration came writers both more gifted in themselves and farther removed from Beaumont and Fletcher, dramatists soon ready to strike out and establish their own modes. Yet for two reasons "Beaumont and Fletcher" continued to dominate the early Restoration stage and to figure prominently in discussions of the status of English drama. In practical terms, their corpus offered a body of proven successes to theaters that reopened in 1660 desperate for material but as yet without their own repertoire of new plays. More significant, to a greater degree than any other Jacobean dramatists available for revival, Beaumont and Fletcher's innovations provided models for the kinds of plays Restoration dramatists proceeded to develop in their own way. According to Dryden in 1668, and corroborated by records of performances, "Their plays are now the most pleasant and frequent entertainments of the stage; two of theirs being acted through the year for one of Shakespeare's or Johnson's [sic]." Dryden goes on to explain the basis of this commanding popularity: "a certain gaiety in their comedies, and pathos in their more serious plays, which suits generally with all men's humours. Shakespeare's language is likewise a little obsolete, and Ben Johnson's wit comes short of theirs."[5] Although Restoration playwrights ultimately created their own distinctive types, Beaumont and Fletcher's comedy and tragicomedy helped shape the new drama with which they shared a stage—both the comedy of manners, for which *The Scornful Lady* and later Fletcherian comedies offered precedent, and the heroic drama that became the Restoration's favored "serious plays."

In fusing their private and public theater heritages, Beaumont and Fletcher had adapted the clever, independent heroine associated

with Shakespearean romantic comedy by integrating her courtship
with two features of satiric city comedy: its portrait of contemporary
life and manners, and the intrigue plotting that governed its dramatic structure. Elements of this mixture are evident in Beaumont's
The Woman Hater, although there the witty exchanges take place
between Oriana and Gondarino, not Oriana and the man she will
marry. In *The Scornful Lady* especially, they reassigned some of city
comedy's urbane, often scurrilous, wit from sarcastic asides or speeches
on standard satiric topics to the barbed interaction of the romantic
couple whose courtship is now the play's primary focus. The heroine
of this, and numerous later Fletcherian comedies, preserved and
passed on the "dramatic irony of the inner conflict between wit and
emotion that her duel with her suitor usually involved"; they also
put her in an upper-class milieu more appealing to the restricted
audience of Restoration comedy and "treated her assumed recal-
citrance to passion as a strategy . . . made necessary by the double
standard of sexual morality."[6]

   In other ways, too, Beaumont and Fletcher provided some of the
materials, though not the final combination or emphasis, of later
comedy. The "studied restraint and ironic self-consciousness of the
Restoration hero" appears in Valore in *The Woman Hater,* although
he is not the romantic protagonist.[7] To be à la mode as a lover their
hero needed to be upgraded in decorous behavior and language,
made less fond of tricks and disguises, and given a distinct, libertine
philosophy. Beaumont and Fletcher are still of their own time, in
the line of Lyly and Shakespeare, in the openness and multifacet-
edness of their comic portrayal of love. They also show a healthy
Jacobean interest in presenting the whole spectrum of society, not
just in comedy but in tragedy and tragicomedy as well. The bril-
liance of Restoration manners comedy at its best leaves "Beaumont
and Fletcher" behind in the sweepstakes for verbal wit and fine
discriminations among its representatives of fashion and form. They
provided a needed lesson in dramatic skills, however, for at its worst,
and in early plays by even the most distinguished playwrights,
Restoration comedy is not only narrower in scope but also theatrically less adept in virtually every way.

   On Restoration serious drama the French influence was stronger
than on comedy, both in dramatic theory and in its popular romance
sources. Yet Beaumont and Fletcher's romantic tragicomedy offered
stageworthy English precedents for combining exalted characters, a

heightened and emotionally charged rhetoric, pseudohistorical exotic settings, plots built around a series of strong scenes, and the happy ending.[8] In 1664 Richard Flecknoe gave credit to *"Beaumont and Fletcher* [who] first writ in the Heroick way, upon whom *Suckling* and others endeavoured to refine agen; one saying wittily of his *Aglaura* [1637] that 'twas full of fine flowers, but they seem'd rather stuck then growing there."[9] They had also made fashionable the later drama's content: Dryden argued "that an heroic play ought to be an imitation, in little, of an heroic poem; and, consequently, that Love and Valour ought to be the subject of it."[10] Interestingly, as the heroic play established itself and its conventions, Beaumont and Fletcher's "serious plays" were increasingly found wanting, and adaptations in the later Restoration revise their originals to align them with the new dramatic criteria. In general, the revisions take the high standards of heroic conduct for granted and heighten the characters' nobility until they become patterns of flawless virtue; they also bolster the quantity and grandiloquence of the speeches (sometimes adding rhyme). Rigorous patriotism and royalist sentiments are imposed, along with the dramatic unities where possible, and the happy endings made happier still by additional marriages.[11]

Decline and Fall

Literary history tells us what was not immediately apparent in the seventeenth century: Beaumont and Fletcher were poets not for all time, but for their own. Cracks in the universal acclaim appeared even before the plays fell out of favor in the second half of the eighteenth century. If in the later Restoration adaptations were deemed necessary for commercial success, critical estimation ran a parallel course. Despite Dryden's early enthusiasm in the "Essay of Dramatic Poesy," ten years later what praise he can muster for *A King and No King,* after Rymer's attack on its language and plotting, is defensive. Shakespeare's star is rising, and Fletcher's characters seem "poor and narrow" by comparison; Shakespeare now deserves imitation, for Fletcher was but his "copyer."[12]

Admired in the Restoration, part of the "conversation of gentlemen" praised by Dryden, the comedies' witty obscenity proved to the later eighteenth century indecent and to the nineteenth century positively immoral. Despite murmurs of praise for lyric passages, excerpted and considered as pure poetry, and for some of the comedies, the nineteenth century firmly affixed the seal of aesthetic and moral decadence that has continued to mark most discussion of Beaumont and Fletcher.[13] Romantic ideals of organic form and richly three-dimensional characterization condemned Beaumont and Fletcher in both respects to "artificiality," a term now applied with a solely pejorative meaning; prurience of language and situation rounded out a nearly wholesale condemnation. Coleridge consolidated the attack on their dramaturgy and helped set the *ad hominem* tone of subsequent criticism when he also called them "servile jure divino Royalists" and "high-flying, passive obedience Tories."[14]

Exactly the qualities valued in the seventeenth century had fallen, perhaps permanently, out of favor. The ironies of literary history come full circle with T. S. Eliot in the twentieth century: the image with which Flecknoe in 1664 dismissed Beaumont and Fletcher's inept Caroline imitator returns to haunt the originals and to complete Coleridge's attack. Eliot finds that on close inspection of their verse, "the blossoms of Beaumont and Fletcher's imagination draw no sustenance from the soil, but are cut and slightly withered flowers stuck into sand."[15] The usual modern assessment had taken its definitive shape: spiritual emptiness, superficiality, sensationalism, and the cynical pandering to a coterie audience already debauched by James's court.[16]

Francis Beaumont

An ironist and chronicler of the unexpected fate of human intentions, Beaumont might have wryly appreciated the "success" to which his brief fling with commercial popularity condemned him. Having tried apparently with some determination to keep his name from permanent association with his stage compositions, he ended up in posterity's eyes as joint author of all fifty-odd plays in the "Beaumont and Fletcher" canon and, of course, joint recipient of that collection's fate. So firmly did the first folios wed their names that despite occasional disclaimers, or analyses of "Fletcher's" dramaturgy, subsequent critics have generally discussed both men as a unit and the influence of the plays, good or bad, as one for which they bore equal responsibility.

Yet the whirligig of time has been kinder to Beaumont than to his more prolific colleague. Fletcher remains an important figure historically, but the universal acclaim he shared with Beaumont has disappeared into the abyss separating seventeenth- and twentieth-century taste. To modern eyes, Beaumont wrote one minor masterpiece, *The Knight of the Burning Pestle.* Sophisticated and accomplished, strikingly modern in its exploration of metadramatic issues, this initial failure today ensures Beaumont's stature and is his most highly valued work. The double reversal in Beaumont's reputation combines with studies in attribution to stimulate interest in the younger dramatist and allow him an individual status, slightly apart from the "Beaumont and Fletcher" phenomenon. The two playwrights are not always tarred with quite the same brush, and some distinctions thread their way through even largely negative studies of the collaborations.

Contemporaries credited Beaumont with the firmer sense of dramatic construction, and modern critics are inclined to agree. Praise of Fletcher now largely confines itself to his gift for light comedy; Beaumont's cast of mind is seen as the more serious, his the potentially tragic sense of life that gives the collaborative plays weight. Indeed, those who scour the Beaumont trail—Macaulay in the nineteenth century, Gayley and Finkelpearl in the twentieth—tend to become eager partisans, certain of Beaumont's superiority as man and playwright. As the foregoing analyses suggest, the present author, too, finds much of interest in the plays themselves, beyond their historical usefulness as indexes of shifting theatrical tastes or, more vaguely, the moral fiber of the time.

Beaumont remains a frustratingly elusive figure, however. On the basis of *Salmacis and Hermaphroditus* and *The Woman Hater* we can fairly say that, despite occasional lapses in clarity of purpose or technique, this was a young man of promising talent; when we include *The Knight,* of rare originality. Yet two dissimilar comedies and some scattered poems do not make for confident pronouncements, especially when the major collaborations were in new forms of tragedy and tragicomedy. The same difficulties that complicate questions of attribution—insufficient exempla of Beaumont's individual work—plague any attempt to pin down the dramatist's ideas or specific contribution. Certain concerns—philosophic as well as dramatic—seem to link the plays in which Beaumont had a hand and to disappear in Fletcher's later work. Such negative evidence tantalizes but must remain inconclusive. Beaumont's stature today, both as independent dramatist and as collaborator, rests finally on the fact that, out of the 1679 folio's massive collection, the plays most frequently reprinted and discussed are either all or in part his: *The Knight, Philaster, The Maid's Tragedy,* and *A King and No King.*

Notes and References

In quotations from original texts and from modern old-spelling editions, *i* /*j*, *u* /*v*, and *vv* /*w* have been normalized. All quotations from the plays by Beaumont, alone or in collaboration with Fletcher, will be taken from the old-spelling Cambridge edition under the general editorial direction of Fredson Bowers, *The Dramatic Works in the Beaumont and Fletcher Canon*, 6 vols. to date (Cambridge: Cambridge University Press, 1966–), hereafter cited as *Dramatic Works*. Cyrus Hoy's seven articles, numbered separately under the general title "The Shares of Fletcher and his Collaborators in the Beaumont and Fletcher Canon," *Studies in Bibliography* 8–9, 11–15 (1956–62), will be short-titled as "Shares" with the appropriate roman numeral and abbreviated volume reference.

Chapter One

1. *The Works of Francis Beaumont and John Fletcher,* ed. Arnold Glover and A. R. Waller, 1:xxii, xxxv (roman for italic font); see also Sir John Berkenhead's tribute, xli–xliv.

2. *Aubrey's Brief Lives,* ed. Oliver Lawson Dick (London: Secker & Warburg, 1950), 21. In *The Works of Beaumont and Fletcher,* 11 vols. (London: Edward Moxon, 1843–46), 1:xxxvi, Alexander Dyce suggests that Hales may have "overcharged the picture of our poets' domestic establishment" for the credulous Aubrey; Dyce wryly notes that Beaumont's "marriage must have left Fletcher in undisturbed possession both of the lady and the wardrobe."

3. The most comprehensive attempt to differentiate authors is Cyrus Hoy's in "Shares." The representative editor's comment on the closeness and efficiency of the collaboration is Andrew Gurr's in his Revels edition of *Philaster* (London: Methuen, 1969), xxiv. Only from his later collaborators does Fletcher's style differ sufficiently to make distribution of shares relatively secure; though it will record the possible division of labor, the present study will treat these works as fully joint efforts.

4. *The Poems of Sir Aston Cokayne,* ed. Richard Morton (Hamilton, Ontario: Cromlech Press, 1977), 137–38, 219.

5. See especially Philip J. Finkelpearl's "Beaumont, Fletcher, and 'Beaumont & Fletcher,'" *English Literary Renaissance* 1 (Spring 1971):144–64.

6. The standard critical biography is Charles Mills Gayley's *Beaumont, the Dramatist* (1914; reprint, New York: Russell & Russell, 1969), though later studies supplement and correct some of Gayley's facts.

7. Anthony Wood, *Athenae Oxonienses,* ed. Philip Bliss, 4 vols. (London, 1813), 2:437.

8. The certificate is reprinted in Dyce, *Works,* 1:xxii, n.l.

9. Philip J. Finkelpearl, *John Marston of the Middle Temple: An Elizabethan Dramatist in His Social Setting* (Cambridge: Harvard University Press, 1969), 23–31; quoted passages from 73, 25. See also Wilfred R. Prest, *The Inns of Court under Elizabeth I and the Early Stuarts, 1590–1640* (London: Longman, 1972), 153–68.

10. In *A Chronicle of the Kings of England* (London, 1653) Sir Richard Baker describes Donne in the 1590s as "a great visiter of Ladyes, a great frequenter of Playes" (617). In the mid-1620s Edward Heath of the Inner Temple attended 49 plays (Prest, *Inns of Court,* 155).

11. *Ben Jonson,* ed. C. H. Herford and Percy and Evelyn Simpson, 11 vols. (Oxford: Clarendon Press, 1925–52), 3:421.

12. Quoted from Bernard H. Newdigate, *Michael Drayton and his Circle* (Oxford: Basil Blackwell, 1941), 192.

13. Much of this paragraph is indebted to Mark Eccles, "A Biographical Dictionary of Elizabethan Authors," *Huntington Library Quarterly* 5 (April 1942):294–300.

14. *Poems Lyrick and Pastorall,* Spenser Society, n.s. 4 (1891; reprint, New York: Burt Franklin, 1967), 88.

15. In *Elegies upon Sundry Occasions* (1627), Drayton refers to them as "My deare companions whom I freely chose / My bosome friends" (*Poems of Michael Drayton,* ed. John Buxton, 2 vols. [London: Routledge & Kegan Paul, 1953], 1:155).

16. E. K. Chambers, *The Elizabethan Stage,* 4 vols. (1923; reprint, Oxford: Clarendon Press, 1951), 2:50–54.

17. Herford and Simpson, *Ben Jonson,* 1:133. As the editors note, Drummond "must have misreported here" and meant Beaumont rather than Fletcher (1:155, n. 55).

18. Letters from both Chapman and Jonson at the time of incarceration suggest that Marston did not share their fate; see R. W. Van Fossen's edition of *Eastward Ho* (Manchester: Manchester University Press, 1979), 4–6.

19. As leading actor and by now seventeen, Field was doubtless considered partially responsible; he probably also figures among the "sundry" committed to prison the following year for Day's *Ile of Guls* and again in 1608 for Chapman's Byron plays. See Roberta Florence Brinkley, *Nathan Field, The Actor-Playwright* (1928; reprint, Hamden, Conn.: Archon Books, 1973), 26–27.

20. In *Bartholomew Fair* Jonson has Cokes ask the puppet-master

"which is your *Burbage* now? . . . Your best *Actor*. Your *Field?*" (Herford and Simpson, *Ben Jonson,* 6:119–20). See also 1:137 and, for Chapman's verses for *A Woman is a Weather-cocke* (Q 1612), *The Plays of Nathan Field,* ed. William Peery (Austin: University of Texas Press, 1950), 70.

21. *Four Plays in One,* first printed in the 1647 folio, is of unknown date or theatrical auspices. Its last two "Triumphs" are universally assigned to Fletcher; for the first two and the Induction there is less agreement, but Gayley thinks all are by Field (*Beaumont, the Dramatist,* 301–5), and in "Shares (IV)," *SB* 12 (1959), Hoy agrees (95–97).

22. Herford and Simpson, *Ben Jonson,* 1:30–31. Another dedicatee, Sir William Skipwith, was a friend of Francis's brother. At Skipwith's death in 1610, John Beaumont commemorated him in an affectionate elegy (Eccles, "A Biographical Dictionary," 296).

23. Herford and Simpson, *Ben Jonson,* 11:324. "Upon the Silent Woman" was perhaps written for a now lost quarto of 1609 or, more probably, 1612; see Jonson's editors' commentary, 5:142–48.

24. Ibid., 11:325.

25. Ibid., 1:136, 8:44.

26. *John Dryden 'Of Dramatic Poesy' and Other Critical Essays,* ed. George Watson, 2 vols. (London: J. M. Dent, 1962), 1:68.

27. Glover and Waller, *Works,* 1:xli–xliv, xxxviii–xxxix. This estimate is furthered by Aubrey's assertion, on the authority of Earle, that Beaumont's "maine Businesse was to lop the overflowings of Mr. Fletcher's luxuriant Fancy and flowing Witt" (*Brief Lives,* 21).

28. Eccles, "A Biographical Dictionary," 295–96, and Gayley, *Beaumont, the Dramatist,* 46–61.

29. Wallace Notestein, *The House of Commons, 1604–1610* (New Haven: Yale University Press, 1971), 14, 410, 507, n. 4. See also Linda Levy Peck, *Northampton: Patronage and Policy at the Court of James I* (London: George Allen & Unwin, 1982), 206.

30. *The Sermons of John Donne,* ed. George R. Potter and Evelyn Simpson, 10 vols. (Berkeley: University of California Press, 1953–62), 7:408. Fellow Middle Templar with Donne, friend of Jonson, and a man of both literary and political interests, John Hoskins admits that "I have used and outworn six several styles since I was first Fellow of New College, and am yet able to bear the fashion of [the] writing company." See *Directions for Speech and Style* (ca. 1599), ed. Hoyt H. Hudson (Princeton: Princeton University Press, 1935), 39.

31. Graham Parry, *The Golden Age restor'd: The Culture of the Stuart Court, 1603–42* (New York: St. Martin's Press, 1981), 64–94, and Roy Strong, *The Cult of Elizabeth: Elizabethan Portraiture and Pageantry* (London: Thames & Hudson, 1977), 187–91.

32. G. E. Bentley, *The Profession of Dramatist in Shakespeare's Time, 1590–1642* (Princeton: Princeton University Press, 1971), 26–27.

33. Finkelpearl, *John Marston of the Middle Temple*, 84.

34. Richard Helgerson, *Self-Crowned Laureates: Spenser, Jonson, Milton and the Literary System* (Berkeley: University of California Press, 1983), 146.

35. Glover and Waller, *Works*, 1:xiv.

36. Both men wrote poems to her, and Jonson refers to Beaumont's elegy in his conversations with Drummond (Herford and Simpson, *Ben Jonson*, 1:163).

37. Bentley, *Profession of Dramatist*, 35.

38. In "The Role of the Court," *Criticism* 24 (Spring 1982):153, Finkelpearl argues that the kind of aid from the earl of Huntingdon to Fletcher suggested by an epistle from Massinger to the earl of Pembroke would make most sense in the early 1600s.

39. On poetry's traditional function within a literary system "dedicated to an amateur conception of letters," see J. W. Saunders, *The Profession of English Letters* (London: Routledge & Kegan Paul, 1964), 36–43, and "The Stigma of Print: A Note on the Social Bases of Tudor Poetry," *Essays in Criticism* 1 (April 1951):139–64.

40. Virgil B. Heltzel, "The Dedication of Tudor and Stuart Plays," in *Studies in English Language and Literature*, ed. Siegfried Korninger (Stuttgart: Wilhelm Braumüller, 1957), 75–78.

41. See Stephen Orgel, "The Royal Theatre and the Role of King," in *Patronage in the Renaissance*, ed. Guy Fitch Lytle and Stephen Orgel (Princeton: Princeton University Press, 1981), 272, and Patricia Thomson's "The Literature of Patronage, 1580–1630," *Essays in Criticism* 2 (July 1952):280, and "The Patronage of Letters under Elizabeth and James I," *English* 7 (Autumn 1949):278–82.

42. See Herford and Simpson, *Ben Jonson*, 11:13–14.

43. Even this may grant Beaumont too much publicity. *The Masque of the Inner Temple and Gray's Inn* was performed 20 February 1613 and presumably published immediately. The original title page assigns the masque to "Francis Beamont, Gent.," but the attribution line has been canceled in most extant copies. As Fredson Bowers observes, no evidence exists to link Beaumont with "the cancellation of the original title, but some direct connection would seem to be reasonably plausible" (*Dramatic Works*, 1:113). For a possible exception—2 poems to the countess of Rutland that may have been published by Beaumont—see Dyce, *Works*, 11:505.

44. Dyce reprints Sir Henry Beaumont's will, proved 3 February 1605/6 and witnessed by Francis, in *Works*, 1:xxviii.

45. Charles Lamb, *Specimens of English Dramatic Poets* (London: Henry G. Bohn, 1854), 298, n. 1.

46. Herford and Simpson, *Ben Jonson*, 11:319–20.

47. Thomas Fuller, *The Worthies of England* (1662), ed. John Freeman

(London: George Allen & Unwin, 1952), 590–91. Such encounters may, however, be more literary tradition than fact.

Chapter Two

1. George Walton Williams summarizes the problems surrounding *Love's Cure* and estimates that the 1647 text shows "vestigal remains" of an original Beaumont-Fletcher play written probably between 1602 and 1606 (*Dramatic Works*, 3:6). R. Warwick Bond discusses the historical materials dealing with the seige and the possibility that the main plot of a Beaumont-Fletcher work already offered some of the elements Massinger found elaborated in *La fuerza de la costumbre* ("On Six Plays in *Beaumont and Fletcher*, 1679," *Review of English Studies* 11 [July 1935]:257–75, esp. 266–67). See also E. H. C. Oliphant, *The Plays of Beaumont and Fletcher* (New Haven: Yale University Press, 1927), 418–32, and "Three Beaumont and Fletcher Plays," *Review of English Studies* 12 (April 1936):197–202.

2. Both Chapman plays reached print in 1606 but probably date from the last years of Elizabeth's reign; see John Hazel Smith's edition of *The Gentleman Usher* (Lincoln: University of Nebraska Press, 1970), xiv–xv.

3. Cyrus Hoy, "Shares (VI)," *SB* 14 (1961):48–56. Hoy regards the play as a Beaumont-Fletcher collaboration in which acts 1, 4, and 5 have been rewritten by Massinger.

4. Hoy thinks that "in its original state" *The Woman Hater* was "almost certainly a product of Beaumont's sole authorship," but that its printed form shows Fletcher's hand in five scenes; see "Shares (III)," *SB* 11 (1958):85, 98–99. See also Albert W. Upton, "The Authorship of *The Woman Hater*," *Philological Quarterly* 9 (January 1930):33–42, and George Walton Williams, ed., *Dramatic Works*, 1:150–54. Hoy assigns Fletcher 3.1.1–153, 4.2, and 5.2,4 (in Williams's edition); Williams adds 3.2 and, more tentatively, suggests Fletcher's presence in 3.3 and 5.1. The Children of Paul's last recorded performance was in July 1606.

5. William W. Appleton, *Beaumont and Fletcher* (London: George Allen & Unwin, 1956), 11.

6. This description of "tragie-comedie" is not Beaumont's; it first appears in the prefatory letter to the quarto of Fletcher's *Faithful Shepherdess*, ca. 1609–10 (discussed in chap. 4).

7. Although a few sixteenth-century English plays had been designated tragicomedies, and Tasso's *Aminta* and Guarini's *Il Pastor Fido* were available in London by 1591 (the "Dymock" English translation of Guarini in 1602), "tragicomedy" had not yet established itself as an accepted, clearly understood generic label. John Marston's *The Malcontent* was entered in the Stationers' Register 5 July 1604 as "An Enterlude called

the Malecontent, Tragicomedia"; yet in the dedication and prefatory letter
Marston refers to "this Comedy." In " 'Tragical-Comical-Historical-Pas-
toral': Elizabethan Dramatic Nomenclature," *Bulletin of the John Rylands
Library* 43 (September 1960), Allardyce Nicoll cites Beaumont's prologue
as one example of "play" used broadly to mean a dramatic narrative for
which there existed no defining term (86–87). For the slow recognition
of "tragicomedy" as a label for a particular kind of mixed genre, see Frank
Humphrey Ristine, *English Tragicomedy: Its Origin and History* (1910; reprint, New York: Russell & Russell, 1963), 91–110.

   8. Under the title of the Italian translation, which altered the characters' names, Juan de Flores's Spanish romance *Grisel y Mirabella* enjoyed
a wide European popularity. By 1606 at least four versions of *Aurelio e
Isabella,* in polyglot form, had probably appeared in England. In addition,
a loose adaptation, the anonymous *A Paire of Turtle Doves,* was published
in 1606. See Barbara Matulka, *The Novels of Juan de Flores and Their European
Diffusion,* Comparative Literature Series (New York: Institute of French
Studies, 1931), 176–77, 212, and Dale B. J. Randall, *The Golden Tapestry:
A Critical Survey of Non-chivalric Spanish Fiction in English Translation (1543–
1657)* (Durham, N.C.: Duke University Press, 1963), 51, n. 40. If
Beaumont knew this story, he transposed the original outcome to a comic
key.

   9. For Giovio and the fashion of collecting portraits, see Roy Strong,
The English Icon: Elizabethan & Jacobean Portraiture (London: Routledge &
Kegan Paul, 1969), 46. After Machiavelli and Guicciardini, Giovio (Paulus
Jovius for his Latin works) was probably the best known sixteenth-century
Italian historian; see Federico Chabod, *Scritti sul Rinascimento,* Biblioteca
di cultura storica 94 (Turin: Einaudi, 1967), 241–67; Ettore Rota's chapter
in *Letteratura italiana,* 11 vols. (Milan: Marzorati, 1956–64), 6:927–48;
and Benedetto Croce, *Poeti e scrittori del pieno e del tardo rinascimento,* 3 vols.
(1945; 2d ed., Bari: Gius. Laterza & Figli, 1958), 2:27–55. *De Piscibus
romanis* was also frequently bound with a work likely to pique English
curiosity, Giovio's *Descriptio Britanniae, Scotiae, Hyberniae, et Orchadum.* In
whatever form, it seems to have been read well into the seventeenth
century: in Pierre Bayle's *Dictionaire historique et critique* (first ed., 1696),
the entry on Augustin Chigi includes in a footnote the Tamisius story.
The source of Beaumont's subplot was discovered via Bayle by an anonymous contributor to the *Athenaeum* 2 (November 1807):484.

   10. This second issue also assigns *The Woman Hater* to Beaumont as
well as "John Fletcher Gent." (*Dramatic Works,* 1:148).

   11. *The Shakespere Allusion-Book: A Collection of Allusions to Shakespere
from 1591 to 1700,* rev. 1909 by John Munro, 2 vols. (reprint, Oxford:
Oxford University Press, 1932), 1:179, 194. Literary allusion has been
given a topical, satiric bent. Reaction to the increasing use of "intelligencers" in the months after 5 November 1605 was strong; for political

allusions in the nearly contemporary *Volpone*, see Richard Dutton, *Ben Jonson: To the First Folio* (Cambridge: Cambridge University Press, 1983), 144–52.

12. Albert W. Upton argues for specific satiric thrusts at James I and at Philip Herbert and James Hay in "Allusions to James I and His Court in Marston's *Fawn* and Beaumont's *Woman Hater*," *PMLA* 44 (December 1929):1048–65, esp. 1053–65. See also Finkelpearl, "Beaumont, Fletcher, and 'Beaumont & Fletcher,' " 149–50.

13. Michael Hattaway, ed., *The Knight of the Burning Pestle* (London: Ernest Benn, 1969), ix.

14. Appleton sees Oriana as the morally ambiguous "comic *Venus predatorix* of Restoration comedy": she "remains *virgo intacta*," yet her behavior suggests a less than pure imagination (*Beaumont and Fletcher*, 13). For S. T. Coleridge's even harsher judgment, see *Coleridge on the Seventeenth Century*, ed. Roberta Florence Brinkley (Durham, N.C.: Duke University Press, 1955), 659.

15. Oriana's "modern" attitude might suggest that Beaumont had been reading Montaigne on the evils of Custom. Oriana's remarks could also derive from dramatic sources: in Marston's *Dutch Courtesan* (Q 1605), 3.1, Crispinella complains in Montaigne's terms of social hypocrisy and the artificial kind of modesty imposed on marriageable young women.

Chapter Three

1. Dating limits for *The Captain* are cited from Chambers, *Elizabethan Stage*, 3:226, and for *Beggars' Bush* from Fredson Bowers, ed., *Dramatic Works*, 3:227–28. Beaumont's participation in these plays is uncertain or extremely limited; they will not be included in the present study. On *The Captain*, see Hoy, "Shares (VI)," *SB* 14 (1961):45–46, 65, and L. A. Beaurline, ed., *Dramatic Works*, 1:545. *Beggars' Bush* is a still more clouded case: in *The Jacobean and Caroline Stage*, 7 vols. (Oxford: Clarendon Press, 1941–68), 3:316, G. E. Bentley will admit only to its not being new at its first recorded performance in 1622. As with a number of these collaborations, dating depends largely on a conviction of Beaumont's presence in addition to Fletcher's and Massinger's. In "Shares (III)," *SB* 11 (1958):87–89,100, Hoy insists on Beaumont's hand in acts 2 and 5; Bowers accepts Hoy's conclusion, noting that this would make Beaumont's scenes probably the "last dramatic writing before his retirement" (*Dramatic Works*, 3:228). While the King's Men performed *Beggars' Bush* in 1622, this may not have been its original company; a number of plays later associated with them had come via the Queen's Revels children and then the Lady Elizabeth's men.

Other plays in which Hoy finds traces of Beaumont seem too doubtful to be more than noted. The case for Beaumont in *The Noble Gentleman* seems convincingly refuted by L. A. Beaurline (*Dramatic Works*, 3:115–18). Also editor of *Love's Pilgrimage*, Beaurline tentatively accepts Hoy's claims for Beaumont's part in that play (*Dramatic Works*, 2:569–73), but says it was probably revised after Fletcher's death; internal allusions suggest original composition in 1615 or early 1616, and this would require altering the usual assumption of Beaumont's retirement ca. 1613. Perhaps to be included with *The Captain* and *Beggars' Bush*, as plays to which Beaumont contributed in a very minor way (at least in the surviving text), is *The Tragedy of Thierry and Theodoret* (Q1 1621), but date and authorship remain in doubt. Most critics see some hand besides Fletcher's and Massinger's, though conjectures range widely. See Hoy, "Shares (III)," 97–98, 105; Robert K. Turner, *Dramatic Works*, 3:365–66; Oliphant, *The Plays of Beaumont and Fletcher*, 276–82; Gayley, *Beaumont, the Dramatist*, 387–88.

2. About *The Coxcomb* and *The Scornful Lady* there is universal agreement on Beaumont's collaboration. Beaumont's share in *The Coxcomb* suggests almost equal partnership with Fletcher: in "Shares (III)," 89–90, 101, Hoy assigns Beaumont 1.4; 2.4; 4.1, 3, 7, and all of act 5. In *The Scornful Lady* Hoy gives Beaumont three scenes: 1.1, 2.1, 5.2 (96, 105). Dating these plays remains conjectural, but *The Coxcomb*, on the basis of allusions and its probable partial source in the "Curious Impertinent" episode from Cervantes's *Don Quixote* (1605; separate French translation 1608), appears to have been composed in 1608–9. The year 1609 is favored by Gayley (*Beaumont, the Dramatist*, 335), Oliphant (*The Plays of Beaumont and Fletcher*, 267), and Michael Shapiro in *Children of the Revels: The Boy Companies of Shakespeare's Time and Their Plays* (New York: Columbia University Press, 1967), 265. It may have been played at Blackfriars, for Chambers thinks the children continued using this theater through the winter of 1608–9, or at Whitefriars, where they moved in autumn 1609 (*Elizabethan Stage*, 2:55); its first recorded performance is by this troupe, since January 1610 called the Children of the Queen's Revels, at court on 2 or 3 November 1612 (ibid., 3:223). *The Scornful Lady* is the first play entered in the Stationers' Register as by both Beaumont and Fletcher, 19 March 1616; the Q1 title page says it was acted by the Queen's Revels children, although by the 1620s it, like *The Coxcomb*, had passed to the King's Men. Despite Gayley's claim for 1613 (*Beaumont, the Dramatist*, 371–73), Baldwin Maxwell argues persuasively from allusions both literary and political for early 1610, at least for the play's first version (*Studies in Beaumont, Fletcher, and Massinger* [Chapel Hill: University of North Carolina Press, 1939], 17–28).

3. On *The Knight* as Beaumont's alone, see Hoy, "Shares (III)," 91–92, and *Dramatic Works*, 1:3. Among the plays by various authors entered in the Stationers' Register (29 June 1660) by Humphrey Moseley appears "*The History of Madon, King of Brittain*, by F. Beamont," but nothing more is known of the play.

4. Thomas Dekker, *The Guls Horne-booke* (London, 1609); in the quarto, pages 28 and 32 (mistakenly set as 30).

5. Quoted from Gayton's note on chap. 21 of book 4 in *Pleasant Notes upon Don Quixot* (London, 1654), 271.

6. "To the worthy Author M. *John Fletcher*," ll. 1–6, in *Dramatic Works*, 3:492.

7. Anon, Q 1606. Chambers argues for performance ca. 1602–6, by the boys of Paul's (*Elizabethan Stage*, 4:53–54). Baldwin Maxwell suggests correspondences between *Wily Beguiled* and *The Knight*'s inner play (*Studies in Beaumont, Fletcher, and Massinger*, 14–16).

8. See Thelma N. Greenfield, *The Induction in Elizabethan Drama* (Eugene: University of Oregon Press, 1969), 113–14, and Steven C. Young, *The Frame Structure in Tudor and Stuart Drama*, Elizabethan and Renaissance Studies, no. 6 (Salzburg: Institut für Englische Sprache und Literatur, 1974), 152.

9. See Mary Patchell's *The "Palmerin" Romances in Elizabethan Prose Fiction* (New York: Columbia University Press, 1947), "Stories for Amusement and Edification," in *Middle-Class Culture in Elizabethan England*, by Louis B. Wright (Chapel Hill: University of North Carolina Press, 1935), esp. 375–93, and John J. O'Connor, *Amadis de Gaule and its Influence on Elizabethan Literature* (New Brunswick: Rutgers University Press, 1970). On dramatized chivalric romance, see C. R. Baskerville, "Some Evidence for Early Romantic Plays in England," *Modern Philology* 14 (August and December 1916):229–51, 467–512.

10. Wright reprints a 1575 letter about the library of a prosperous Coventry mason, Captain Cox, whose collection of 52 books included thirteen separately listed chivalric tales (*Middle-Class Culture*, 84–85). See also David Cressy, *Literacy and the Social Order: Reading and Writing in Tudor and Stuart England* (Cambridge: Cambridge University Press, 1980), esp. 130–36.

11. P. E. Russell, "English Seventeenth-Century Interpretations of Spanish Literature," *Atlante* 1 (April 1953):70.

12. See Herbert S. Murch's massively researched edition of *The Knight* (New York: Henry Holt, 1908), esp. xxxvii–lvi, lxviii–lxix.

13. Barbara Matulka traces such an evolution for Juan de Flores's fifteenth-century *Grisel y Mirabella* in *The Novels of Juan de Flores and Their European Diffusion*, 169–77, 212–19. *Amadis* underwent a similar development (O'Connor, *Amadis de Gaule*, 133).

14. *Edward I* included "the sinking of Queene Elinor, who sunck at Charingcrosse, and rose againe at Potters-hith now named Queenehith" (Chambers, *Elizabethan Stage*, 3:460). On *The Bold Beauchamps*, see ibid., 3:461, and for *Edward the Fourth*, 4:10–11.

15. See Rudolph Schevill, "On the Influence of Spanish Literature upon English in the Early 17th Century," *Romanische Forschungen* 20

(1907):618; Murch's edition of *The Knight*, xxxv; Gayley, *Beaumont, the Dramatist*, 325–31; John Doebler's edition of *The Knight* (Lincoln: University of Nebraska Press, 1967), xiv, n. 11.

16. Citing Burre's letter, Murch argues for composition in 1610 or early 1611 in his edition of *The Knight* (xi–xv); Oliphant follows Murch in *The Plays of Beaumont and Fletcher* (169–76). Burre may, however, simply refer to his acquisition of the play.

17. Chambers, *Elizabethan Stage*, 2:52, 42.

18. One difficulty with the allusion to *The Travailes of the Three English Brothers* is the Citizen's suggestion that it has been playing at the Red Bull theater, since the quarto advertizes the Queen's Men at the Curtain. According to Chambers, however, the Red Bull was extant around 1606, and both houses "are specified as occupied by the Queen's men in their patent of 15 April 1609" (ibid., 2:446–47).

19. The major internal challenge to 1607 remains the Citizen's command to "read the play of the *Foure Prentices of London*" (4.47–48), for the earliest extant edition of Heywood's play is 1615. As Doebler notes in his edition of *The Knight* (xiii), however, at least one (now lost) earlier edition must have existed "if the possibility of reading it occurs in a play published in 1613." In his epistle to the 1615 quarto, Heywood speaks of the play as written "some fifteene or sixteene yeares agoe" (Chambers, *Elizabethan Stage*, 3:340).

20. Shelton's letter is quoted from *The History of Don Quixote of the Mancha, Translated from the Spanish of Miguel de Cervantes by Thomas Shelton*, ed. W. E. Henley, 2 vols., Tudor Translations, no. 13 (London: David Nutt, 1896), 1:3; publication details and support for Shelton's use of the 1607 Brussels edition can be found in James Fitzmaurice-Kelly's introduction, 1:xix–xxxiii. In Spain, *Don Quixote* enjoyed immediate popularity: pirate editions soon appeared; by July 1605 it was in its fifth printing. See Melveena McKendrick, *Cervantes* (Boston: Little, Brown & Co., 1980), 207–8.

21. The "Curious Impertinent" episode from part 1 of *Don Quixote* also proved influential on the English stage, though it was available, separately, in French by 1608; see A. S. W. Rosenbach's "The Curious-Impertinent in English Dramatic Literature before Shelton's Translation of Don Quixote," *Modern Language Notes* 17 (June 1902), esp. 357–67.

22. Edward Wilson, "Cervantes and English Literature of the Seventeenth Century," *Bulletin Hispanique* 50 (1948):35, 37. Others who see a direct influence include Fitzmaurice-Kelly (Tudor Translations Shelton, 1ᴵvii), Rosenbach ("The Curious Impertinent," 365), McKendrick (*Cervantes*, 271), and Gurr (Fountainwell edition of *The Knight*, 3).

23. Lee Bliss, "*Don Quixote* in England: The Case for *The Knight of the Burning Pestle*," *Viator* 18 (1987):361–80.

24. See also John Doebler's "Beaumont's *The Knight of the Burning*

Pestle and the Prodigal Son Plays," his edition of *The Knight* (xiv-xix), and Gurr's Fountainwell Texts edition (5–6).

25. See also Inge Leimberg's "Das Spiel mit der Dramatischen Illusion in Beaumont's *The Knight of the Burning Pestle*," *Anglia* 81 (1963):159–61.

26. See Doebler's article, n. 24; Alexander Leggatt's *Citizen Comedy in the Age of Shakespeare* (Toronto: University of Toronto Press, 1973), chap. 3; and R. W. Van Fossen's Revels *Eastward Ho* (Manchester: Manchester University Press, 1979).

27. Ronald F. Miller, "Dramatic Form and Dramatic Imagination in Beaumont's *The Knight of the Burning Pestle*," *English Literary Renaissance* 8 (Winter 1978), esp. 80–83, and Sheldon P. Zitner's Revels edition of *The Knight* (Manchester: Manchester University Press, 1984), 36, 41–42.

28. Boundaries may have begun to blur earlier: at least in the printed text, the status of Tim and George, who become Rafe's squire and dwarf, remains a mystery. Miller discusses later uncertainties about the innkeeper and Nick the Barber ("Dramatic Form and Dramatic Imagination," 76–78).

29. David A. Samuelson's discussion of Rafe's attempt to make a single story out of the Citizens' requested scenes is acute ("The Order in Beaumont's *Knight of the Burning Pestle*," *English Literary Renaissance* 9 [Spring 1979]:313–15).

30. See Jackson I. Cope, *The Theater and the Dream* (Baltimore: Johns Hopkins University Press, 1973), 206–10.

31. Merrythought may recall the crafty parasite in *Ralph Roister Doister,* but in personality, singing humour, and structural importance he is an independent creation. His name seems intended to evoke instead the language of Renaissance medical discussions of physical well-being. See George Walton Williams, "Shakespeare's metaphors of health: food, sport and life-preserving rest," *Journal of Medieval and Renaissance Studies* 14 (Fall 1984):190; Williams cites examples from 1558 to 1738 of a proverbial jingle summarizing man's three best "physicians": "Doctor Diet, Doctor Quiet, and Doctor Merryman" (191).

Chapter Four

1. See chap. 2, nn. 1 and 4 for possible earlier collaboration. According to Cyrus Hoy's analysis, the dramatists worked nearly equally on *Cupid's Revenge:* Hoy assigns Beaumont 1.1, 1.3, 2.1–2, 2.4–5, 3.1–2, 4.1, 4.5, 5.1, and Fletcher 1.2, 1.4, 2.3, 2.6, 3.3–4, 4.2–4, 5.2–3 ("Shares [III]," *SB* 11 [1958]:90, 101–2). Fredson Bowers concurs, though he has renumbered some scenes in his edition of the play (*Dramatic Works,* 2:323). In *Philaster,* Hoy believes "Beaumont's is the controlling hand," and he assigns Beaumont 1.2, 2.1, 2.3–4 (to Pharamond's entrance), 3,

4.3, 4.6, 5.1–3 (to King's exit), 5.5, and Fletcher 1.1, 2.2, 2.4 (from Pharamond's entrance), 4.1–2, 5.3 (from King's exit), 5.4 ("Shares [III]," 95–96, 104). See also Robert K. Turner's edition of *Philaster*, in *Dramatic Works*, 1:369.

2. *The Faithful Shepherdess* has no Stationers' Register entry, and the first quarto is undated. The death of one dedicatee, Sir William Scipwith on 3 May 1610, and the brief partnership of its publishers (December 1608 to January 1610), suggest a 1609 or very early 1610 printing (see Hoy, *Dramatic Works*, 3:485). References in Beaumont's prefatory verses to waxlights and a boy dancing, along with the presence of Field, Chapman, and Jonson as other encomiasts, indicate the Revels children as the company. Both John H. Astington in "The Popularity of *Cupid's Revenge*," *Studies in English Literature* 19 (Spring 1979):218, and Andrew Gurr in his edition of *Philaster*, xxi–xxii, assume that Fletcher's *Faithful Shepherdess* preceded *Cupid's Revenge*. While this tidily places individual failures before joint success, Fletcher's tragicomedy may well be the later play, performed (plague permitting) in the winter or spring of 1608–9 at either Blackfriars or Whitefriars (see Chambers, *Elizabethan Stage*, 3:221–22).

3. Chambers, *Elizabethan Stage*, 2:53–61.

4. F. P. Wilson, *The Plague in Shakespeare's London* (Oxford: Clarendon Press, 1927), 124–25. Thomas Dekker in his 1609 *Worke for Armourours* says the playhouses stand with doors locked and their flags taken down, although Wilson notes that some playing, perhaps at the private houses, seems to have been allowed (126).

5. James E. Savage, "The Date of Beaumont and Fletcher's *Cupid's Revenge*," *English Literary History* 15 (December 1948):293; see also Savage's "Beaumont and Fletcher's *Philaster* and Sidney's *Arcadia*," *English Literary History* 14 (September 1947):194–206.

6. On the play's success, see Astington, "The Popularity of *Cupid's Revenge*," 218–29.

7. At roughly the same time, Beaumont and Fletcher were probably also writing the spicy romantic comedy *The Coxcomb* for the same boys' troupe (see chap. 3, n. 2, and chap. 6).

8. For its success at Oxford, see Chambers, *Elizabethan Stage*, 3:276. Daniel was connected both with the Sidney family, in the 1590s, and with the Blackfriars theater, as both dramatist and censor in 1604–5; see *Elizabethan Stage*, 3:272–74, and Irwin Smith, *Shakespeare's Blackfriars Playhouse: Its History and Its Design* (New York: New York University Press, 1964), 190–92, 514–15.

9. The first version of Sidney's romance, the "Old" *Arcadia*, circulated widely in manuscripts reflecting various stages of revision. At some point Sidney began a major reworking, and at his death he had rewritten books 1–2 and completed most of a wholly new book 3. This, the "New" *Arcadia*, was printed posthumously (1590) from a manuscript belonging

to his friend Fulke Greville; chapter divisions were added by the printer. In 1593 the "New" *Arcadia* was reprinted together with the "Old" *Arcadia*'s completion of the story (i.e., "Old" books 3–5, printed from the now-lost manuscript Sidney had presented to his sister, the countess of Pembroke). In this bizarre, composite form *The Countess of Pembroke's Arcadia* remained, through numerous editions, one of the period's most popular books. Borrowings for *Cupid's Revenge* were established by Savage in "Beaumont and Fletcher's *Philaster* and Sidney's *Arcadia*."

10. The spelling "Timantus" establishes the 1593 *Arcadia* as the text probably used for *Cupid's Revenge,* rather than the more recent, "corrected" reprints of 1598 and 1605. This character appears in the appended "Old" *Arcadia,* but among the printed editions only 1593 reads "Timantus." Use of the 1593 edition may also explain the apparent confusion about the status of *Cupid's Revenge*'s central family: at times they are referred to as king, queen, princess, and prince, but at others as members of a ducal family. In the "Old" *Arcadia* the main plot's Basilius and his wife Gynecia were duke and duchess; in the revised *Arcadia* they became king and queen and their daughters princesses. When "Old" *Arcadia*'s books 3–5 were added to the "New" in 1593, titles and names were changed to conform with those in the revised version. Some instances escaped correction, and Beaumont and Fletcher's mixed usage could stem from the remaining confusions.

11. Cf. Palamon's prayer to Venus in the Fletcher-Shakespeare *Two Noble Kinsmen,* 5.1.69–135, where for the huntress Venus mortals are merely "in herds thy game" and love grotesquely animates even arthritic old men of eighty to behave as fools. As G. R. Proudfoot notes in his edition (Nebraska: University of Nebraska Press, 1970), this late collaboration "is not best approached as a sequel to *The Winter's Tale* and *The Tempest*" (xxiv).

12. Sir Philip Sidney, *An Apologie for Poetrie,* in *Elizabethan Critical Essays,* ed. G. Gregory Smith, 2 vols. (1904; reprint, London: Oxford University Press, 1937), 1:199.

13. Eugene M. Waith, *The Pattern of Tragicomedy in Beaumont and Fletcher* (New Haven: Yale University Press, 1952), 14.

14. Both Gurr in his edition of *Philaster,* xxv, and John F. Danby in *Poets on Fortune's Hill* ([London: Faber & Faber, 1952], chap. 6, esp. 154–57) find Sidney to be Beaumont and Fletcher's primary inspiration, though they differ about the dramatists' use of this model.

15. Savage, "*Philaster* and Sidney's *Arcadia,*" esp. 204–6. Savage's article persuasively answers the claim for Alonso Perez's continuation of Montemayor's *Diana* (books 7–8) as sole source made by T. P. Harrison in "A Probable Source of Beaumont and Fletcher's *Philaster,*" *PMLA* 41 (June 1926):294–303. In his edition of *Philaster* (xxvii), Andrew Gurr concurs with Savage about sources but not about date: Gurr sets composition

as "in or after May 1609" (xxviii) and thus challenges Savage's claim, for post 24 September 1610, in "The 'Gaping Wounds' in the text of *Philaster*," *Philological Quarterly* 28 (October 1949):455.

16. Waith, *Pattern of Tragicomedy*, 6.

17. Quotations from *The Faithful Shepherdess* and its epistle are taken from Cyrus Hoy's edition in *Dramatic Works*, vol. 3.

18. Guarini's *Compendio della poesia tragicomica* appeared with *Il Pastor Fido* in the 1602 edition; though Fletcher (and others) knew it, it seems not to have been translated in the seventeenth century. G. K. Hunter discusses Guarini's influence in "Italian Tragicomedy on the English Stage," in *Dramatic Identities and Cultural Tradition: Studies in Shakespeare and His Contemporaries* (New York: Barnes & Noble, 1978), 133–56; see also chap. 2, n. 7 of the present study.

19. See also Waith, *Pattern of Tragicomedy*, 10.

20. In Beaumont's plays, *The Woman Hater*'s Oriana is held in a brothel and treated as a strumpet; in act 3 of *The Knight of the Burning Pestle*, Jasper's unheralded, bizarre threat to kill Luce to "test" her devotion shows a similar compulsion to place virgin heroines on the wrack. The reverse wooings in *The Faithful Shepherdess* recall Oriana's of Gondarino or, a more perverse case, Bacha's of Leucippus in *Cupid's Revenge*.

21. The first reference to *Philaster*, by John Davies of Hereford in epigram 206 of *The Scourge of Folly* (entered in the Stationers' Register 8 October 1610), is to its second title: "*Love lies ableeding*." See also Gurr's edition, xxvi.

22. For a fuller discussion, see Lee Bliss, "Defending Fletcher's Shepherds," *Studies in English Literature* 23 (Spring 1983):295–310.

23. Much of this paragraph's discussion is indebted to Hunter, "Italian Tragicomedy on the English Stage," 140–47, 153.

24. Gurr, introduction to *Philaster*, xxxv.

25. Possibly, *Cymbeline* helped inspire *Philaster*. Although neither can be firmly dated, there are some obvious parallels. Ashley H. Thorndike's opposite thesis, in *The Influence of Beaumont and Fletcher on Shakspere* (Worcester, Mass.: Oliver B. Wood, 1901), has not been generally accepted; Gurr reviews the controversy in his edition, xlv–1, and argues the plausibility of simultaneous production in 1609, when the theaters reopened. On the influence of *Hamlet, Othello*, and *Twelfth Night*, see Lee Bliss, "Three Plays in One: Shakespeare and *Philaster*," *Medieval and Renaissance Drama in England* 2 (1985):153–70.

26. Danby, *Poets on Fortune's Hill*, 203; see also Robert Ornstein, *The Moral Vision of Jacobean Tragedy* (Madison: University of Wisconsin Press, 1965), 171–78, and Clifford Leech, *The John Fletcher Plays* (Cambridge, Mass.: Harvard University Press, 1962), 84.

27. The apt designation of this tone as a "middle mood" nicely suggests the Guarinian ideal of a fusion of apparently opposite genres; the

term is Una Ellis-Fermor's in *Jacobean Drama* (1936; reprint, New York: Vintage Books, 1964), 201–26.

28. Peter Davison, in "The Serious Concerns of *Philaster*," *English Literary History* 30 (March 1963):1–15, argues for the play's preoccupation with a specific contemporary political issue, the split between King and Parliament; see also M. G. M. Adkins, "The Citizens in *Philaster:* Their Function and Significance," *Studies in Philology* 43 (April 1946):203–12. In his edition (li–lviii), Gurr sensibly suggests a more general sympathy with Dion's criticism of the king in 4.4.

29. Waith, *Pattern of Tragicomedy,* 17.

30. The term, though not the argument, is Arthur C. Kirsch's in *Jacobean Dramatic Perspectives* (Charlottesville: University Press of Virginia, 1972), esp. 43–44.

31. *Philaster* exists in two versions: Q1 appeared in 1620 and Q2 in 1622. They differ primarily in their opening and closing sections, and Q2 has always been considered the authoritative text; see Gurr's edition, lxii–lxxix, and Turner's edition in *Dramatic Works,* 1:369–97. Q1's truncated final scene tidies up the conclusion and, by providing husbands for Bellario and Galatea, stresses its resemblance to romantic comedy. Q2 elaborates the Dion-Euphrasia "recognition" but pointedly refuses to round off the story with multiple weddings or a satisfying fate for Bellario. Q2's ending exemplifies Beaumont and Fletcher's originality and the kind of generic transformations that produced their distinctive tragicomic structure and tone.

32. *The Works of Francis Beaumont and John Fletcher,* ed. Glover and Waller, 1:xii (roman for italic font).

Chapter Five

1. In his Regents Renaissance edition, Howard B. Norland hazards "late 1610 or early 1611" (xi); Robert K. Turner notes general agreement for "about 1610" (*Dramatic Works,* 2:3). Andrew Gurr is unusual in thinking the tragedy "probably" followed both *Philaster* and *A King and No King* (Fountainwell edition, *The Maid's Tragedy,* 1).

2. Chambers, *The Elizabethan Stage,* 4:45.

3. Ibid., 3:224–25.

4. There is no major challenge to Hoy's distribution in "Shares (III)," *SB* 11 (1958):94, where he assigns Fletcher 2.2, 4.1, and 5.1–2. Although only about one fifth of the play, they include Aspatia's grief, Melantius's conversion of his sister, the killing of the king, and Melantius's justification. Thomas Fuller's anecdote, if true, implies joint plotting: "Meeting once in a tavern, to contrive the rude draft of a tragedy, Fletcher undertook to kill the king therein; whose words being overheard by a listener . . . he was accused of high treason; till the mistake soon appearing,

154 FRANCIS BEAUMONT

that the plot was only against a dramatic and scenical king, all wound off in merriment" (*The Worthies of England*, 1662, ed. John Freeman [London: George Allen & Unwin, 1952], 439).

5. Gurr, ed., *The Maid's Tragedy*, 2.

6. In "On the Sources of *The Maid's Tragedy*," *Modern Language Notes* 31 (December 1916):502–3, William Dinsmore Briggs suggests Harmodius and Aristogiton in Valerius Maximus's *Factorum ac dictorum memorabilium, libri IX* (3.8.1).

7. Beaumont and Fletcher elaborate and rechoreograph. In his edition of *The Maid's Tragedy*, Norland notes that the result is "more clearly patterned into stages, which are marked by a double turn and a reversal of positions" (xiv, n. 14). On the rhetorical training in the art of declamation that produced these much-admired scenes of impassioned debate on sensational topics, see Waith, *The Pattern of Tragicomedy*, 86–98.

8. Verbal parallels are collected by D. M. McKeithan in *The Debt to Shakespeare in the Beaumont-and-Fletcher Plays* (1938; reprint, Folcroft, Pa.: Folcroft Press, 1969), 44–50.

9. Harry Levin, "An Echo from *The Spanish Tragedy*," *Modern Language Notes* 64 (May 1949):300–302. For the content of Aspatia's description, see Ovid, *Heroides*, 10. As Michael Neill notes in " 'The Simetry, Which Gives a Poem Grace': Masque, Imagery, and the Fancy of *The Maid's Tragedy*," *Renaissance Drama*, n.s. 3 (1970):121, n. 21, Beaumont and Fletcher's third masque song may be imitated from the epithalamion that concludes Jonson's *Haddington Masque*.

10. See Norland's edition of *The Maid's Tragedy*, xv, and G. P. V. Akrigg, *Jacobean Pageant, or The Court of King James I* (Cambridge, Mass.: Harvard University Press, 1962), 371–76.

11. See C. L. Barber, *The Idea of Honour in the English Drama, 1591–1700* (Gothenburg: Elanders Boktryckeri, 1957), 37, 330–36. See also Norland's edition, xv.

12. On *Coriolanus*'s relevance to current political issues, see W. Gordon Zeeveld, "*Coriolanus* and Jacobean Politics," *Modern Language Review* 57 (July 1962):321–34. For its analysis of the idea of honor, see D. J. Gordon, "Name and Fame: Shakespeare's *Coriolanus*," in *Papers, Mainly Shakespearian*, ed. G. I. Duthie, Aberdeen University Studies, no. 147 (London: Oliver & Boyd, 1964), esp. 46–55, and Norman Rabkin, *Shakespeare and the Common Understanding* (New York: Free Press, 1967), 131–44.

13. Gurr, ed., *Maid's Tragedy*, 4. Making Amintor the protagonist, though the commonest way to force this play into some acceptably "tragic" mold, results in a work too easily ridiculed and dismissed, a "tragedy" constructed around a man who can suffer but not act. For opposite critical judgments based on this assumption, see Waith, *The Pattern of Tragicomedy*, 21, and Ornstein, *The Moral Vision of Jacobean Tragedy*, 171, 177.

14. Leech, *The John Fletcher Plays,* 109. Leech's remark is truer for *A King and No King* and Fletcher's plays, but he rightly sees the danger in emphasizing external determinants.

15. Neill notes the prominence given the masque: in performance it would probably take up over half of act 1 and is "roughly comparable in length to an early Jonson Masque" (" 'The Simetry, Which Gives a Poem Grace,' " 112, n. 8).

16. In " 'This For the Most Wrong'd of Women': A Reappraisal of *The Maid's Tragedy,*" *Renaissance Drama,* n.s. 13 (1982):131–56, William Shullenberger observes that Night challenges "the values whose imagistic and mythic center is the sun, and whose social center is the king" (138). For Shullenberger, Evadne is the tragic protagonist, and the masque's loose ends are tied when she binds and murders the king.

17. Inga-Stina Ewbank, " 'These Pretty Devices': A Study of Masques in Plays," in *A Book of Masques,* ed. T. J. B. Spenser and S. W. Wells (Cambridge: Cambridge University Press, 1967), 418.

18. See Shullenberger, " 'This For the Worst Wrong'd of Women,' " 134.

19. "Adolescent intensities" is Danby's term, though for him its relevance is confined to the proto-Cavalier "world of James I and fermenting civil war" (*Poets on Fortune's Hill,* 165, 181–83).

20. George Campbell Macaulay long ago noted that "Surely if these authors were such devoted royalists, and aimed so constantly at exhibiting their loyalty on the stage, it is strange and even unaccountable that so few sovereigns are represented in their plays as a sovereign would desire to be represented, and that so many are set up as objects of contempt and hatred" (*Francis Beaumont: A Critical Study* [1883; reprint, New York: Lemma, 1972], 135). Twice in the Restoration, and possibly in a lost third version, Edmund Waller rewrote act 5 to turn the play into acceptably monarchist tragicomedy: in each the converted Evadne leaves Rhodes instead of killing the king, and Lysippus talks Melantius out of his revenge. See Arthur Colby Sprague, *Beaumont and Fletcher on the Restoration Stage* (1926; reprint, New York: Benjamin Blom, 1965), 58–62, 178–86.

21. Cp. Calderwood on a similar retreat to private meanings in "*Coriolanus:* Wordless Meanings and Meaningless Words," in *Essays in Shakespearean Criticism,* ed. James L. Calderwood and Harold E. Toliver (Englewood Cliffs, N.J.: Prentice-Hall, 1970), 554.

22. Other features of 5.3 suggest *Lear'*s presence. Like Lear with Cordelia, Amintor, holding Aspatia's body and begging the gods to restore her, seeks through folk science to discover life (5.3.233–35). When Amintor dies in his arms, Melantius repents "the greatnesse of / My heart . . . it will not burst at need" (5.3.272–73).

23. On this aspect, see Danby, *Poets on Fortune's Hill,* 184–206.

Chapter Six

1. Chambers, *The Elizabethan Stage*, 3:225.

2. George Walton Williams, introduction to *A King and No King*, in *Dramatic Works*, 2:174–75.

3. Quotations are from *"The Cyropaedia"* . . . *and "The Hellenics"* . . . *of Xenophon*, trans. Rev. J. S. Watson and Rev. Henry Dale (London: George Bell & Sons, 1876), 134–35. Temperance and discretion are the virtues most praised in Cyrus and his Persian commanders. Another index of familiarity with Xenophon is the "ghost" character Mandane who appears in the stage directions to 2.1 of *A King and No King* (first removed by Dyce); see *Dramatic Works*, 2:177. Arbaces's title, "King of Iberia," may suggest a memory of the *Arcadia* stories (bk. 2, chaps. 13, 15) used for *Cupid's Revenge*.

4. Separate elements of the Panthea-story, including Araspes's and Cyrus's discussion of love, were gathered together in the eleventh "novel" of William Painter's *The Palace of Pleasure* (1566–67; rev. ed. of the whole, 1575) and in a sixteenth-century play acted by the Children of the Chapel Royal, *The Warres of Cyrus* (Q 1594).

5. Robert K. Turner suggests another resemblance at 5.2.66–69, in *A King and No King* (Lincoln: University of Nebraska Press, 1963), xiv–xv.

6. The episode in Montemayor lacks the titillation of *A King and No King*, 4.4, but if the dramatists knew it they might have seen possibilities in the exchange between Abyndaraez and Xarifa: he makes a garland and "putting it upon my head, I sat downe againe crowned, and conquered"; she places the garland on her head and says that if she were crowned "Queene and Ladie" of the world, he "shouldest leese nothing by it." See *A Critical Edition of Yong's Translation of George of Montemayor's "Diana" and Gil Polo's "Enamoured Diane,"* ed. Judith M. Kennedy (Oxford: Clarendon Press, 1968), 170. A version of this tale appears in the Italian *Dugento Novelle del signore Celio Malespini* (2.36).

7. *Thierry and Theodoret* is largely by Fletcher and Massinger, but Beaumont may have contributed (see chap. 3, n. 1); it has been variously dated 1607–13. Whatever the order of composition, some variation on the incest theme links these two plays with each other and with Fletcher's comedy *The Captain* (1609–12), where a daughter's incestuous proposal to her father adds spice to the Lelia subplot. The comedy of braggart courtiers who either receive or are threatened with beatings, so prominent in the Bessus plot of *A King and No King*, also appears in *The Captain*, in *Thierry and Theodoret*, and in Fletcher's *The Honest Man's Fortune* (1613). Relevant for Arbaces is Caratach's rebuke to the boastful victor in Fletcher's *Bonduca* (1609–14): "Discretion / And hardie Valour are the twins of

Honour, / And nurs'd together, make a Conquerour: / Divided, but a talker" (1.1.21–24; *Dramatic Works,* 4:157).

8. In his Regents Renaissance edition (xv), Turner suggests the paradoxes of Shakespeare's *All's Well That Ends Well* ("he's guilty and he is not guilty"; "thou art a knave and no knave").

9. In "Shares (III)," *SB* 11 (1958):91, 102, Hoy assigns Fletcher 4.1–3, 5.1, and 5.3.

10. *The Works of Francis Beaumont and John Fletcher,* ed. Glover and Waller, 1:xli (arabic and italic font reversed).

11. Lawrence B. Wallis, *Fletcher, Beaumont & Company* (New York: King's Crown Press, 1947), 195.

12. The first quotation is from Appleton, *Beaumont and Fletcher,* 41; the second from Waith, *The Pattern of Tragicomedy,* 28. In "The Danger Not the Death: The Art of John Fletcher," in *Jacobean Theatre,* ed. J. R. Brown and B. Harris (New York: St. Martin's Press, 1960), Philip Edwards, too, treats *A King and No King* as seminal: protean characters increasingly fit the jolts and surprises of the plot, and the whole becomes an episodic "series of strong scenes, a succession of situations" (172–73).

13. In "An Essay of Dramatic Poesy" (1668), Dryden extols the English for having invented and perfected "a more pleasant way of writing . . . than was ever known to the ancients or moderns . . . which is tragi-comedy," and he elsewhere praises "that excellent play, *The King and No King.*" See *Essays of John Dryden,* ed. W. P. Ker, 2 vols. (Oxford: Clarendon Press, 1926), 1:70, 65. For Edmund Waller's transformation of *The Maid's Tragedy,* see chap. 5, n. 20. *Philaster* was drastically altered for *The Restauration,* probably in 1683; it was again "Revised, and the Two last Acts new Written" by Elkanah Settle in 1695 (Sprague, *Beaumont and Fletcher on the Restoration Stage,* 187–202, 281).

14. By the eighteenth century, changes in dramatic theory and practice altered at least one view of *Philaster*'s genre. In the adaptation performed in 1763, George Colman the Elder tidied up the "ribaldry and obscenity" and eliminated the "unmanly," unheroic elements. Since the original happy ending remains largely intact, the defense of *Philaster, A Tragedy* in the "Advertisement" is of interest: "If to move the passions of pity and terror are the two chief ends of tragedy, there needs no apology for giving that title to the play of Philaster. If Lear, Hamlet, Othello, . . . notwithstanding the casual introduction of comic circumstances in the natural course of the action, are tragedies; Philaster is so too" (*Philaster, A Tragedy,* separately printed "for John Bell," 1778, p. 7).

15. Waith, *Pattern of Tragicomedy,* 42.

16. This structural model was suggested by Arthur Mizener in "The High Design of *A King and No King,*" *Modern Philology* 38 (November 1940):150, and elaborated by Robert K. Turner, Jr., in "The Morality

of *A King and No King,*" *Renaissance Papers* (1961), 93–103 (also the basis for Turner's Regents Renaissance edition's analysis).

17. Finkelpearl sees the play as a "satiric comedy" whose hero, like Philaster, is mocked for "intemperance and vanity" ("Beaumont, Fletcher, and 'Beaumont & Fletcher,' " 156, 158).

18. The dilemmas of the four central lovers comment on each other; the emphasis is on how one event corresponds to another rather than on what happens next. In this sense the play's design is "static, determined not so much by the laws of cause and effect as by the rules of artful arrangement. This peculiarity of the design may be another reason why, even before the happy ending, tragedy does not seem inevitable" (Waith, *Pattern of Tragicomedy,* 35).

19. Rooted in Greek philosophy and its redaction in some of the most popular Roman literary authorities, like Ovid, "libertine naturalism" in the Renaissance ranged from the deeply felt skepticism of Montaigne to a witty, local use of its tenets to invert the conventional morality that assumed a "Law of Nature" coinciding with and validating the "Law of Nations" of civilized society. For the classical background, see Arthur O. Lovejoy and George Boas, *Primitivism and Related Ideas in Antiquity* (1935; reprint, New York: Octagon Books, 1965), esp. chap. 13, and, for the Renaissance, Hiram Haydn, *The Counter-Renaissance* (1950; reprint, Gloucester, Mass.: Peter Smith, 1966), passim; more specific is Louis I. Bredvold, "The Naturalism of Donne in Relation to Some Renaissance Traditions," *Journal of English and Germanic Philology* 22 (October 1923):471–502.

20. For further discussion, see Michael Neill, "The Defense of Contraries: Skeptical Paradox in *A King and No King,*" *Studies in English Literature* 21 (Spring 1981):319–32. Such paradoxes were commonplace in the humanist tradition; for what it is worth, they also appear in *The Warres of Cyrus* (see n. 4).

21. Wishing for pure comedy in requesting Bessus to narrate the late war's events, Panthaea describes Beaumont and Fletcher's perfect audience: "if my brother were in any danger, / Let not thy tale make him abide there long, / Before thou bring him off, for all that while / My heart will beate" (2.1.110–13).

22. For a view of the play as more specifically and topically satiric, see William C. Woodson, "The Casuistry of Innocence in *A King and No King* and its Implications for Tragicomedy," *English Literary Renaissance* 8 (Autumn 1978):312–28.

23. Neither comedy can be securely dated. On arguments for dating and the probable distribution of shares, see chap. 3, n. 2; on the possibility of an earlier joint comedy, *Love's Cure,* see chap. 2.

24. Others find the subplot to be without irony and too close to

tragicomedy for the play's good; see Waith, *Pattern of Tragicomedy*, 20, and Appleton, *Beaumont and Fletcher*, 45.

25. Appleton, *Beaumont and Fletcher*, 96; Donald J. Rulfs, "Beaumont and Fletcher on the London Stage, 1776–1833," *PMLA* 63 (December 1948):1246, n. 4.

26. Moorecraft's transformation recalls Merrythought's success with his wife and Venturewell in *The Knight of the Burning Pestle*. The usurer's moral rounds out his play's celebratory mood: "I purchasde, wrung, and wierdraw'd for my wealth, lost, and was cozend: for which I make a vowe . . . Ile finde a constant meanes to riches without curses" (5.3.53–56).

27. In *Beaumont and Fletcher on the Restoration Stage*, Arthur Colby Sprague quotes Leigh Hunt on the witty raillery in 1.1: "this scene, witl the airs that the lady gives herself, the readiness and sprightliness of he replies, and the lasting style of the prose, is an anticipation of the writin of Congreve" (xx).

28. That the Lady's and Loveless's courtship provides witty, inflt ential confrontations is more significant than its conclusion. Beaumoi and Fletcher are usually credited with bringing a new feminism to Englis comedy, as *The Coxcomb* suggests. In *The Woman's Prize* (1611) Fletche inverts the pattern of *The Scornful Lady* as well as, very self-consciously Shakespeare's *The Taming of the Shrew*: here, Petruchio's second wife tamt the tamer.

Chapter Seven

1. "To The Reader," ll. 36–43, in *The White Devil*, ed. John Russell Brown (London: Methuen, 1960), 4.

2. *The 'Revels' History of Drama in English*, vol. 4, *1613–1660*, ed. Philip Edwards et al. (London: Methuen, 1981), 183; for an extended analysis of Fletcher's influence, see 183–213.

3. Robert Markley, " 'Shakespeare *to thee was dull*': The Phenomenon of Fletcher's Influence," in *From Renaissance to Restoration: Metamorphoses of the Drama*, ed. Robert Markley and Laurie Finke (Cleveland: Bellflower Press, 1984), 89–125. Encomia are by nature adulatory; Markley notes that the features particularly praised suggest an unconscious mining of Fletcher for support of traditions the encomiasts themselves wished to uphold. See also P. W. Thomas, *Sir John Berkenhead, 1617–1679: A Royalist Career in Politics and Polemics* (Oxford: Clarendon Press, 1969), 134–35.

4. In 1633 Sir Henry Herbert, master of the revels, suppressed performance of Fletcher's *The Woman's Prize* until it had been "purgd of oaths, prophaness, and ribaldrye"; he apparently intended to scrutinize all revived plays, "ye rather that in former time the poetts tooke greater liberty than is allowed by mee." See Bowers, *Dramatic Works*, 4:3–4.

5. "An Essay of Dramatic Poesy," in *Essays of John Dryden*, ed. W. P. Ker, 2 vols. (Oxford: Clarendon Press, 1926), 1:81.

6. Joe Lee Davis, *The Sons of Ben: Jonsonian Comedy in Caroline England* (Detroit: Wayne State University Press, 1967), 98–99. See also Kirsch, *Jacobean Dramatic Perspectives*, 48.

7. Dale Underwood, *Etherege and the Seventeenth-Century Comedy of Manners* (New Haven: Yale University Press, 1957), 132.

8. In *Ideas of Greatness: Heroic Drama in England* (New York: Barnes & Noble, 1971), Eugene M. Waith finds that of the canon's fifty-odd plays, "all the tragedies and tragicomedies and even some of the comedies are relevant to the development of heroic drama" (149).

9. Richard Flecknoe, *A Short Discourse of the English Stage*, in *Critical Essays of the Seventeeth Century*, ed. J. E. Spingarn, 3 vols. (Oxford: Clarendon Press, 1908–9), 2:92.

10. "An Essay of Heroic Plays" (1672), in *Essays of John Dryden*, 1:150. Dryden's belief "that serious plays ought not to imitate conversation too nearly" suggests why Beaumont and Fletcher were also stylistically influential, despite their lack of rhyme (148).

11. Related to the growth of tragicomedy was that of tragedy with a happy ending; this form, with its emphasis on "poetic justice," provided the underpinnings of Restoration heroic drama. On the adaptations, see Cecil V. Deane, *Dramatic Theory and the Rhymed Heroic Play* (1931; reprint, London: Frank Cass, 1967), 51.

12. Preface to *Troilus and Cressida* (1679), in *Essays of John Dryden*, 1:220; for Dryden's remarks on *A King and No King*, see 1:212.

13. Complete editions continued to appear, but the general attitude remained one of split praise for their passages of lyric beauty and condemnation for the often "revolting" matter in which this poetry was embedded. Leigh Hunt bowdlerized forty-seven plays and presented the public with *Beaumont and Fletcher; or, the Finest Scenes, Lyrics, and other Beauties of these two Poets, Now first Selected from the Whole of their Works, To the Exclusion of whatever is Morally Objectionable* (cited from Wallis, *Fletcher, Beaumont & Company*, 73).

14. *Coleridge on the Seventeenth Century*, ed. Brinkley, 655–56.

15. "Ben Jonson," in *The Sacred Wood: Essays on Poetry and Criticism* (1920; reprint, London: Methuen, 1960), 116. Eliot defines such poetry's speciousness as "a clever appeal to emotions and associations which they have not themselves grasped; it is hollow" (ibid.).

16. The critical history of Beaumont and Fletcher's reputation in the last three centuries can be traced in greater detail in Wallis's *Fletcher, Beaumont & Company*, 3–125. Wallis's own bias is clear in his subtitle: "Entertainers to the Jacobean Gentry."

Selected Bibliography

Dates of first publication are cited in the Chronology, as well as the seventeenth-century first folio (34 previously unpublished plays, plus Beaumont's *Masque*) and the second folio (52 plays). The following is a selected chronological list of partial and complete editions, as well as twentieth-century single editions. Almost all anthologies of Renaissance drama contain at least one Beaumont-Fletcher play; no attempt has been made to list these.

PRIMARY SOURCES

The Works of Francis Beaumont and John Fletcher. 7 vols. London: Jacob Tonson, 1711. Reprints 1679 folio.

The Works of Francis Beaumont and John Fletcher. Edited by Mr. Theobold, Mr. Seward, and Mr. Sympson. 10 vols. London: J. & R. Tonson & S. Draper, 1750. First attempt at a critical text; preface by Seward.

The Dramatick Works of Beaumont and Fletcher. [Edited by George Colman the Elder.] 10 vols. London: T. Evans & P. Elmsley, 1778. Based on the 1711 edition; reprints prefaces of 1647, 1711, and 1750.

The Dramatic Works of Ben Jonson, and of Beaumont and Fletcher. Edited by Peter Whalley and George Colman. 4 vols. London: J. Stockdale, 1811. Volumes 2–4 are devoted to Beaumont and Fletcher; reprints Colman's 1778 text.

The Works of Beaumont and Fletcher. Edited by Henry Weber. 14 vols. Edinburgh: F. C. & J. Rivington, 1812. Based on the 1647 and 1679 folios, using Monk Mason's *Notes. The Faithful Friends* appears first in this edition.

The Works of Beaumont and Fletcher. Introduction by George Darley. 2 vols. London: George Routledge & Sons, 1839. Weber's text of 1812.

The Works of Beaumont and Fletcher. Edited by the Reverend Alexander Dyce. 11 vols. London: Edward Moxon, 1843–46. Best edition of its time; reprints documents from Beaumont's life.

The Best Plays of Beaumont and Fletcher. Edited with an introduction and notes by J. St. Loe Strachey. Mermaid Series. 2 vols. London: Vizetelley & Co., 1887. Ten plays.

The Works of Francis Beaumont and John Fletcher. Variorum Edition. General editor, A. H. Bullen. 4 vols. London: G. Bell & Sons, 1904–12. Twenty plays; never completed.

The Works of Francis Beaumont and John Fletcher. Edited by Arnold Glover
    and A. R. Waller. Cambridge English Classics. 10 vols. Cambridge:
    Cambridge University Press, 1905–12. Folio of 1679 with appendix
    of variants in first folio and quartos.
Select Plays by Beaumont and Fletcher. Edited by Ernest Rhys. London: J.
    M. Dent & Sons, 1911. Six plays.
Beaumont and Fletcher. Edited by Felix E. Schelling. New York: American
    Book Co., 1912. Four plays.
The Dramatic Works in the Beaumont and Fletcher Canon. General editor,
    Fredson Bowers, 6 vols. to date. Cambridge: Cambridge University
    Press, 1966–. Standard modern edition; old spelling.
Grammar Lecture. British Museum, Sloane MS.1709, folios 12–22. Avail-
    able in Mark Eccles's "Francis Beaumont's *Grammar Lecture.*"
The Lyric Poems of Beaumont and Fletcher. Edited by Ernest Rhys. London:
    J. M. Dent & Co., 1897.
The Knight of the Burning Pestle. Edited by Herbert S. Murch. New York:
    Henry Holt & Co., 1908.
———. Edited by John Doebler. Regents Renaissance Drama Series.
    Lincoln: University of Nebraska Press, 1967.
———. Edited by Andrew Gurr. Fountainwell Drama Texts. Berkeley:
    University of California Press, 1968.
———. Edited by Michael Hattaway. New Mermaids Plays. London:
    Ernest Benn, 1969.
———. Edited by Sheldon P. Zitner. Revels Plays. Manchester: Man-
    chester University Press, 1984.
Philaster. Edited by Andrew Gurr. Revels Plays. London: Methuen, 1969.
———. Edited by Dora Jean Ashe. Regents Renaissance Drama Series.
    Lincoln: University of Nebraska Press, 1974.
The Maid's Tragedy. Edited by Howard B. Norland. Regents Renaissance
    Drama Series. Lincoln: University of Nebraska Press, 1968.
———. Edited by Andrew Gurr. Fountainwell Drama Series. Berkeley:
    University of California Press, 1969.
A King and No King. Edited by Robert K. Turner, Jr. Regents Renaissance
    Drama Series. Lincoln: University of Nebraska Press, 1963.

SECONDARY SOURCES

1. Bibliographies
"Francis Beaumont and John Fletcher." In *The Later Jacobean and Caroline
    Dramatists: A Survey and Bibliography of Recent Studies in English Ren-
    aissance Drama.* Edited by Terence P. Logan and Denzell S. Smith.

Lincoln: University of Nebraska Press, 1978. Items largely restricted to 1923–76; some helpful annotations.

Tannenbaum, S. A. *Beaumont and Fletcher (A Concise Bibliography).* Elizabethan Bibliographies, no. 3. New York: Samuel A. Tannenbaum, 1938. Especially useful for nineteenth century and location of excerpted selections, scenes, and songs.

2. Books and Articles

Adkins, Mary Grace Muse. "The Citizens in *Philaster:* Their Function and Significance." *Studies in Philology* 43 (April 1946):203–12. Argues the play is an exception to "aristocratic sympathies" usually attributed to B and F and assigns this aspect to B.

Appleton, William W. *Beaumont and Fletcher: A Critical Study.* London: George Allen & Unwin, 1956. General study of B and F, including F's other independent and collaborative work.

Astington, John H. "The Popularity of *Cupid's Revenge.*" *Studies in English Literature* 19 (Spring 1979):215–27. Accepts Savage's dating and argues the play's popularity convinced King's Men to employ B and F for *Philaster.*

Baldwin, T. W. "The Three Francis Beaumonts." *Modern Language Notes* 39 (December 1924):505–7. Differentiates between the dramatist, his father, and the relative who became master of Charterhouse.

Bliss, Lee. "*Don Quixote* in England: The Case for *The Knight of the Burning Pestle.*" *Viator* 18 (1987):361–80. Examines various ways *Don Quixote* might have been known in England by 1607.

———. " 'Plot mee no plots': The Life of Drama and the Drama of Life in *The Knight of the Burning Pestle.*" *Modern Language Quarterly* 45 (March 1984):3–21. Critical study of the play; in revised form part of chapter 3 of this book.

———. "Three Plays in One: Shakespeare and *Philaster.*" *Medieval and Renaissance Drama in England* 2 (1985):153–70. Argues *Philaster's* debt to *Hamlet, Othello, and Twelfth Night.*

———. "Tragicomic Romance for the King's Men, 1609–1611: Shakespeare, Beaumont, and Fletcher." In *Comedy from Shakespeare to Sheridan,* edited by A. R. Braunmuller and J. C. Bulman, 148–64. Newark: University of Delaware Press, 1986. Explores similarities and contrasts between Shakespeare's late plays and B and F's major collaborations.

Bond, R. Warwick. "On Six Plays in *Beaumont and Fletcher,* 1679." *Review of English Studies* 11 (July 1935):257–75. Summarizes work on sources, dating, authorship for six plays intended for discontinued Bullen's Variorum edition, including *Love's Cure.*

Briggs, William Dinsmore. "On the Sources of *The Maid's Tragedy.*"

Modern Language Notes 31 (December 1916):502–3. Proposes story of Harmodius and Aristogiton as partial source.

Bryher [Winifred Ellerman]. "A Note on Beaumont and Fletcher." *Life and Letters Today* 36 (January 1943):5–9. A general defense of the plays and playwrights.

Chambers, E. K. *The Elizabethan Stage*. 4 vols. 1923. Reprint (with corrections). Oxford: Clarendon Press, 1951. Invaluable reference work.

Danby, John F. *Poets on Fortune's Hill: Studies in Sidney, Shakespeare, Beaumont & Fletcher*. London: Faber & Faber, 1952. Chapters 6–7 argue B and F's debasement of the Great House Elizabethan literary tradition into "adolescent intensities" popular with a proto-Cavalier court.

Davison, Peter. "The Serious Concerns of *Philaster*." *English Literary History* 30 (March 1963):1–15. Proposes struggle between James I and Parliament over the Great Contract as play's serious political background.

Doebler, John. "Beaumont's *The Knight of the Burning Pestle* and the Prodigal Son Plays." *Studies in English Literature* 5 (Spring 1965):333–44. Discusses this "genre," including *Eastward Ho,* and B's inversion of the pattern.

Eccles, Mark. "A Biographical Dictionary of Elizabethan Authors." *Huntington Library Quarterly* 5 (April 1942):281–302. Largely on John Beaumont, but also corrects and supplements Gayley's biography of the dramatist.

———. "Francis Beaumont's *Grammar Lecture*." *Review of English Studies* 16 (October 1940):402–14. Reprints and discusses this early work.

Edwards, Philip. "The Danger Not the Death: The Art of John Fletcher." In *Jacobean Theatre,* Stratford-upon-Avon Studies, no. 1, edited by John Russell Brown and Bernard Harris, 159–77. New York: St. Martin's Press, 1960. Largely on F's later plays, but discusses *A King and No King.*

Ellis-Fermor, Una. *The Jacobean Drama: An Interpretation.* 1936. Reprint. New York: Vintage Books, 1964. Chapter 11 emphasizes romance elements and nonrealistic approach to character and plot in B and F's influential new dramaturgy.

Finkelpearl, Philip J. "Beaumont, Fletcher, and 'Beaumont & Fletcher': Some Distinctions." *English Literary Renaissance* 1 (Spring 1971):144–64. Distinguishes B from F and argues for B as moralist and critic rather than panderer to the age's decadence.

———. "The Role of the Court in the Development of Jacobean Drama." *Criticism* 24 (Spring 1982):138–58. Argues against idea that court taste or influence affected drama under James I.

———. " 'Wit' in Francis Beaumont's Poems." *Modern Language Quarterly* 28 (March 1967):33–44. Suggests that B learned from Jonson to reject false wit and ostentatious rhetoric.

Fletcher, Ian. *Beaumont and Fletcher.* Writers and Their Work, no. 199.

London: Longmans, Green & Co., 1967. Brief, sensible study, mostly of the collaborative work.

Frost, David L. *The School of Shakespeare: The Influence of Shakespeare on English Drama 1600–42.* Cambridge: Cambridge University Press, 1968. Chapter 6 analyzes the nature and quality of B and F's borrowings and imitations.

Gayley, Charles Mills. *Beaumont, the Dramatist.* 1914. Reprint. New York: Russell & Russell, 1969. Standard biography; enthusiastic but sometimes inaccurate.

Griffiths, L. M. "Shakespearian Qualities of *A King and No King.*" *Poet-Lore* 3 (April 1891):169–77. Praises character delineation and moral treatment.

Harrison, T. P. "A Probable Source of Beaumont and Fletcher's *Philaster.*" *PMLA* 41 (June 1926):294–303. Argues for Perez's continuation of Montemayor's *Diana* as source.

Hoy, Cyrus. "The Shares of Fletcher and his Collaborators in the Beaumont and Fletcher Canon." *Studies in Bibliography* 8–9, 11–14 (1956–61). Most recent, sophisticated attempt to ascribe shares, though least helpful in distinguishing F from B.

Kirsch, Arthur C. *Jacobean Dramatic Perspectives.* Charlottesville: University Press of Virginia, 1972. Chapter 3 argues that self-conscious rhetorical and theatrical artifice undermines B and F's tragicomedy and tragedy but produced comedies of merit.

Lawrence, J. W. "The Riddle of *Philaster.*" *Times Literary Supplement,* 17 November 1921, 751. Explains Q1 as transcript of prompt book for a 1st version, by F and anon. hack, for a boy's company, and Q2 as B's revision for King's Men. Unconvincing.

Leech, Clifford. *The John Fletcher Plays.* Cambridge, Mass.: Harvard University Press, 1962. Also discusses the B and F collaborations.

Leimberg, Inge. "Das Spiel mit der Dramatischen Illusion in Beaumont's *The Knight of the Burning Pestle.*" *Anglia* 81 (1963):141–74. Extensive plot summary, but also analyzes satiric and metadramatic elements.

Levin, Harry. "An Echo from *The Spanish Tragedy.*" *Modern Language Notes* 64 (May 1949):297–302. Suggests 2.2 of *Maid's Tragedy* modeled on "painter's scene" in 1602 additions to Kyd's play.

Macaulay, George Campbell. *Francis Beaumont: A Critical Study.* 1883. Reprint. New York: Lemma, 1972. Early defense of B and attempt to differentiate him from F; has been superseded on questions of authorship and dating.

McKeithan, Daniel Morley. *The Debt to Shakespeare in the Beaumont-and-Fletcher Plays.* 1938. Reprint. Folcroft, Pa.: Folcroft Press, 1969. Extensive, not always convincing, collection of certain and possible borrowings.

Mason, John Monck. *Comments on the Plays of Beaumont and Fletcher.* 1797.

Reprint. New York: Garland, 1972. Comments on and suggests emendations to 1750 edition of Theobald, Seward, and Sympson and to anonymous edition of 1778.

Maxwell, Baldwin. *Studies in Beaumont, Fletcher, and Massinger.* Chapel Hill: University of North Carolina Press, 1939. Essays touching on B's work treat a source for *The Knight,* dating of *The Scornful Lady,* the "hungry knave" character, and the attitude toward duelling in B and F.

————. " 'Twenty Good-Nights'—*The Knight of the Burning Pestle* and Middleton's *Family of Love.*" *Modern Language Notes* 63 (April 1948):233–37. Argues that allusion in *Knight* (2.62–63) and Jasper's "coffin trick" may be intentional parody.

Miller, Ronald F. "Dramatic Form and Dramatic Imagination in Beaumont's *The Knight of the Burning Pestle.*" *English Literary Renaissance* 8 (Winter 1978):67–84. Excellent study of how satire dissolves into exploration of the creative imagination.

Mincoff, Marco. "The Social Background of Beaumont and Fletcher." *English Miscellany* 1 (1950):1–30. Studies B and F in relation to the shift in taste, themes, and audience beginning ca. 1610.

Mitford, John. *Cursory Notes on Various Passages in the Text of Beaumont and Fletcher.* London: John Russell Smith, 1856. Suggests possible emendations to Dyce's edition of 1843–46; includes comments on Dyce's *A Few Notes on Shakespeare.*

Mizener, Arthur. "The High Design of *A King and No King.*" *Modern Philology* 38 (November 1940):133–54. Argues for emotional rather than narrative structure and for theatrical skill unconcerned with character or morality.

Neill, Michael. "The Defence of Contraries: Skeptical Paradox in *A King and No King.*" *Studies in English Literature* 21 (Spring 1981):319–32. Especially interesting on philosophical implications of the play's paradoxes.

————. " 'The Simetry, Which Gives a Poem Grace': Masque, Imagery, and the Fancy of *The Maid's Tragedy.*" *Renaissance Drama,* n.s. 3 (1970):111–35. Excellent study of how the masque's imagery is worked out in the rest of the play.

Oliphant, E. H. C. *The Plays of Beaumont and Fletcher.* New Haven: Yale University Press, 1927. Authorship study, with attempt to determine shares for all plays in "B and F" canon.

————. "Three Beaumont and Fletcher Plays." *Review of English Studies* 12 (April 1936):197–202. Takes issue with R. W. Bond on dating three plays, including *Love's Cure.*

Ornstein, Robert. *The Moral Vision of Jacobean Tragedy.* Madison: University of Wisconsin Press, 1965. Chapters 6–7 discuss B and F briefly and *The Maid's Tragedy* at greater length.

Rulfs, Donald J. "Beaumont and Fletcher on the London Stage, 1776–1833." *PMLA* 63 (December 1948):1245–64. Useful survey of revivals and changing taste in drama.

Samuelson, David A. "The Order in Beaumont's *Knight of the Burning Pestle.*" *English Literary Renaissance* 9 (Spring 1979):302–18. Interesting discussion of relations among competing "plots."

Savage, James E. "Beaumont and Fletcher's *Philaster* and Sidney's *Arcadia.*" *English Literary History* 14 (September 1947):194–206. Establishes *Arcadia* as source for *Cupid's Revenge;* indicates characteristic B and F stock types borrowed from Sidney and carried on in *Philaster.*

————. "The Date of Beaumont and Fletcher's *Cupid's Revenge.*" *English Literary History* 15 (December 1948):286–94. Argues on internal evidence for 1607 or early 1608.

————. "The 'Gaping Wounds' in the Text of *Philaster.*" *Philological Quarterly* 28 (October 1949):443–57. Contends that Q2 represents B and F's original play and Q1 the censored version probably performed; suggests date of late 1610.

Shullenberger, William. " 'This For the Most Wrong'd of Women': A Reappraisal of *The Maid's Tragedy.*" *Renaissance Drama*, n.s. 13 (1982):131–56. Argues for masque's thematic importance and for Evadne as tragic protagonist.

Sprague, Arthur Colby. *Beaumont and Fletcher on the Restoration Stage.* 1926. Reprint. New York: Benjamin Blom, 1965. Best survey of frequency of revival and nature of later adaptations.

Thorndike, Ashley H. *The Influence of Beaumont and Fletcher on Shakspere.* Worcester, Mass.: Oliver B. Wood, 1901. Suggests B and F influenced Shakespeare's romances, esp. *Cymbeline.*

Tomlinson, T. B. *A Study of Elizabethan and Jacobean Tragedy.* Cambridge: Cambridge University Press, 1964. Chapter 11 argues for B and F's contribution to "decadence" of Jacobean tragedy.

Turner, Robert K., Jr. "The Morality of *A King and No King.*" *Renaissance Papers*, 1961, 93–103. Analyzes morality-play structure and interrelation of symbolic and narrative levels; forms basis for introduction to Turner's edition.

Upton, Albert W. "Allusions to James I and His Court in Marston's *Fawn* and Beaumont's *Woman Hater.*" *PMLA* 44 (December 1929):1048–65. Argues for extreme political topicality.

————. "The Authorship of *The Woman Hater.*" *Philological Quarterly* 9 (January 1930):33–42. Argues, against earlier critics, that B was primarily responsible for this play.

Waith, Eugene M. *The Pattern of Tragicomedy in Beaumont and Fletcher.* New Haven: Yale University Press, 1952. Fullest study of whole "B and F" canon; emphasizes stylization of experience and relates their work to art of declamation and classical *controversiae.*

Wallis, Lawrence B. *Fletcher, Beaumont & Company: Entertainers to the Jacobean Gentry.* New York: King's Crown Press, 1947. Most complete
study of dramatists' reputation; some speculative analyses of plays'
effect on original audience.
Ward, Charles E. "A Note on Beaumont and Fletcher's *Coxcomb.*" *Philological Quarterly* 9 (January 1930):73–76. Suggests the play con-
sciously subverts the usual tales of a cuckolded husband and the trial
of his wife by a friend.
Wilson, Harold S. "*Philaster* and *Cymbeline.*" In *English Institute Essays
1951.* New York: Columbia University Press, 1952, 146–67. Argues
against Thorndike's contention that B and F influenced Shakespeare.
Wilson, John Harold. *The Influence of Beaumont and Fletcher on Restoration
Drama.* Columbus: Ohio State University Press, 1928. General survey
of popularity, borrowings, and imitations.
Woodson, William C. "The Casuistry of Innocence in *A King and No King*
and Its Implications for Tragicomedy." *English Literary Renaissance* 8
(Autumn 1978):312–28. Argues B and F catered to Globe's middle-
class audience by seeming to espouse Puritan beliefs in one plot, while
actually subverting this pattern elsewhere.

Index

Amadis de Gaule, 58
Astington, John H., 57
Aubrey, John, 1
Aurelio e Isabella, 22

Beaumont, Francis, early years, 3–5;
family Catholicism, 8; literary and
theatrical beginnings, 5–8; marriage,
11; playwriting career, 9–16, 57;
reputation and influence, 1–3, 57,
132–38; use of public and private
theater traditions, 14–16, 19, 36,
55, 133–34

WORKS—NON-THEATRICAL:
Commendatory verses, 7, 12
Elegies, 11
Epistles to Jonson, 7, 11, 13
Grammar Lecture, 4
*Masque of the Inner Temple and Gray's
Inn*, 2, 6, 12, 16, 142n43
Salmacis and Hermaphroditus, 4, 5, 12,
137

WORKS—PUBLICATION AS
   COLLABORATIONS:
*Comedies and Tragedies Written by
Francis Beaumont and John Fletcher,
Gentlemen* (1647 folio), 10;
commendatory verses to, 1, 2, 86,
110, 133; content of, 2, 132
Fifty Comedies and Tragedies . . .
(1679 folio), 124, 132, 136

WORKS—THEATRICAL:
Coxcomb, The, 2, 33, *122–27*, 130;
date and sources, 122; parodic use
of genre types, 122–23, 124–25;
shares, 123, 146n2
Cupid's Revenge, 13, 15, *56–69*, 70–
80; *passim*, 84, 87, 90, 91, 95,
97, 102, 114, 120, 122; date, 57;
establishment of B-F characters,
67, 69, 73, 113; failure of generic
blend, 61, 62–65, 68–69; shares,
149n1; sources, 57–62
King and No King, A, 73, 87, 106,
107–21, 124, 135, 138; date,
107; relation to preceding plays,
116–17, 118, 120; shares, 110,
157n9; sources, 107–110;
tragicomic form, 110–13, 118–20
Knight of The Burning Pestle, The, 1,
2, 7, 12, 14, 16, 20, *33–55*, 56,
58, 90, 121–22, 123, 124, 127,
133, 137, 138; date, 40–41;
Induction, 34–37; satire in, 37–
39, 42–43, 51, 54; sources, 34–
42, 46
Love's Cure, 17–19, 23, 143n1
Maid's Tragedy, The, 87–106, 110,
114, 115, 121, 124, 138; date
and shares, 87, 153n4; Masque of
Night, 92–93, 99, 101–3, 104,
105; political and social issues,
88–89, 94–96, 98–100; self-
reflexivity, 103–6; sources, 87–
88; tragic form, 89–90, 99, 106
Philaster, 56, 57, 67, 69, 71, 72,
73–86, 87, 88, 90, 91, 95, 102,
104, 106, 109, 110, 111, 113,
114, 118, 121, 122, 124, 138;
date, 57; shares, 149n1; sources,
73; tragicomic form, 73, 76, 80,
82, 85–86, 124, 153n31
Scornful Lady, The, 13, 33, *127–31*,
133, 134; date, 122; shares, 127,
146n2
Woman Hater, The, 7, 12, 14, *19–
32*, 33, 34, 35, 41, 56, 65, 73,
122, 123, 132, 137; Fletcher's
contribution, 143n4; generic

dissonance, 20, 22, 27–30, 32; parodic use of sources, 22–25; theatrical self-consciousness, 19–20, 23–24; unconventional heroine, 30–32, 123

WORKS—THEATRICAL, attributed to:
Beggars' Bush, 13, 33, 145–46n1
Captain, The, 33, 145–46n1
Four Plays in One, 7, 141n21
History of Madon, King of Britain, The (lost), 146n3
Love's Pilgrimage, 13, 145–46n1
Noble Gentleman, The, 145–46n1
Tragedy of Thierry and Theodoret, The, 13, 109, 145–46n1

Beaumont, Sir Henry, 3, 4, 13
Beaumont, Sir John, 3, 4–5, 8, 11; *Metamorphosis of Tobacco*, 4, 12
Bentley, Gerald Eades, 9, 11
Blackfriars theater (Children of the Revels), 5–8; *passim*, 14–16, 40, 41, 58, 122; audience for, 3–4, 14, 20, 35–39, 42, 58; transfer to King's Men, 56–57, 146n2. *See also* King's Men

Cervantes Saavedra, Miguel de: *Don Quixote*, 39–42, 122
Chapman, George, 6, 7, 9, 10, 11, 12, 17, 18, 89, 129, 132; works mentioned: Byron plays, 12, 89; *Eastward Ho*, 6, 20, 24, 37; *Gentleman Usher, The*, 17; *Sir Giles Goosecap*, 17; *Widow's Tears, The*, 18, 27, 28, 126, 129
Cokayne, Sir Aston, 2
Coleridge, S. T., 136
Comedy, 52, 55, 132; City comedy (Citizen Comedy), 14, 16, 20, 30, 34, 37, 38, 45, 55, 63–65, 76–78, 113, 122–23, 127–28, 134; Humours comedy, 19, 22, 51, 129; Romantic comedy, 21, 45, 55, 74, 76, 82, 115, 120, 123, 127, 129, 134. *See also* Satire
Cotton, Charles, 2

Danby, John F., 73
Daniel, Samuel: *The Queenes Arcadia*, 58
Day, John: *Ile of Guls*, 36, 39, 58, 60; *Travailes of the Three English Brothers* (with Rowley and Wilkins), 41
Dekker, Thomas, 10, 132; *Guls Hornebooke, The*, 35
Deloney, Thomas: *Gentle Craft, The*, 38; *Jack of Newbury*, 38
Diodorus, Siculus: *Bibliotheca historica*, 108
Donne, John, 3, 9, 10, 11, 38
Drayton, Michael, 4, 5, 11
Dryden, John, 8, 133, 135

Eliot, T. S., 136

Fauchet, Claude: *Lez Antiquitez Gauloises et Francoises*, 109
Field, Nathan, 6, 7
Finkelpearl, Philip J., 2, 3–4, 137
Flecknoe, Richard, 135
Fletcher, John, early connection with Beaumont, 1–3, 6–7; professional playwright, 10, 11, 15, 132, 134, 136–37

WORKS: *(See also* Beaumont, Francis, WORKS—THEATRICAL)
Faithful Shepherdess, The, 1, 6, 7, 12, 14, 16, 36, 56, 69–73, 78, 122; date and theater, 150n2; establishment of character-types, 70, 71, 73; thematic patterning in, 70; theoretical defense of, 70–71
Honest Man's Fortune, The, 121

Fuller, Thomas: *The Worthies of England*, 15, 153n4

Gayley, Charles Mills, 137
Gayton, Edmund: *Pleasant Notes upon Don Quixot*, 35–36
Giovio, Paulo (Paulus Jovius), 23; *De Piscibus romanis*, 23
Guarini, Giambattista, defense of tragicomedy, 70–71; *Il Pastor Fido*, 58, 69, 72, 73

Gunpowder Plot, The, 8

Heliodorus: *Aethiopian History*, 58, 60
Henry, Prince of Wales, 9, 10
Herodotus, 108
Herrick, Robert, 110
Heywood, Thomas, 10, 132; works
  mentioned: *Bold Beauchamps*, 39; *Edward IV*, 39; *Four Prentises of London, The*, 38; *If You Know not Me*, 39
Hoy, Cyrus, 17, 18
Hunter, G. K., 72

Induction. *See* Beaumont, Francis, *The Knight*
Inns of Court, 3–5, 14, 37; *see also* Blackfriars, audience

James I, King of England, 8, 10, 13, 56, 78, 88, 136; *see also* Satire
Jonson, Ben, 4–15; *passim*, 17, 20, 22, 29, 36, 38, 43, 73, 132, 133; works mentioned: *Alchemist, The*, 41; *Bartholomew Fair*, 6; *Catiline*, 7, 11; *Cynthia's Revels*, 6, 12, 15, 61; *Eastward Ho*, 6, 20, 24, 37; *Epicoene*, 6, 7, 22, 41, 127; *Every Man in His Humour*, 17; *Every Man out of His Humour*, 4, 15; *Sejanus*, 6, 7; *Volpone*, 6, 7, 11, 14

King's Men, 9, 11, 13–15, 56, 57, 58, 73, 107, 122
Kyd, Thomas: *The Spanish Tragedy*, 49, 50, 88

Lisle, George, 1
Lyly, John, 134; works mentioned: *Gallathea*, 6; *Loves Metamorphosis*, 61; *Mother Bombie*, 109

Macaulay, George Campbell, 137
Maine, Jasper, 1
Markham, Gervase: *English Arcadia, The*, 58
Marston, John, 3–14; *passim*, 18, 20, 28, 129; works mentioned: *Dutch Courtesan, The*, 18–19, 23, 28, 37,

129; *Eastward Ho*, 6, 20, 24, 37; *Fawn, The*, 27, 129; *Malcontent, The*, 6, 73
Massinger, Philip, 2, 17, 18, 57, 132
Masuccio (of Salerno): *Il Novellino*, 109
Middleton, Thomas, 21; works mentioned: *Blurt, Master Constable*, 17, 23; *Your Five Gallants*, 41
Montaigne, Michel de, 18
Montemayor, Jorge de: *Diana* (Alonso Perez's continuation), 69, 73, 109
Moseley, Humphrey, 2, 10–11
Mucedorus, 49
Munday, Anthony, 34, 37
Murch, Herbert S., 37

Palmerin romances, 38, 58
Paul's, Children of, 6, 19
Peele, George: *Edward I*, 39; *Old Wives Tale, The*, 39
Perez, Alonso. *See* Montemayor, Jorge de
Plutarch, 108

Restoration drama: comedy, 126, 128, 129, 130, 132, 133–34; heroic drama, 133, 134–35
Revels, Children of the. *See* Blackfriars
Romance, burlesque of, 46, 49–51, 54, 57, 123, 124; chivalric romance, 37–38, 46, 49–51, 54–55; revival of, 57–58; citizen romance, 38–39; pastoral romance, 69, 73, 78; *see also* Cervantes; *Palmerin* romances; Sidney

Satire, 8, 9, 19, 20; *Coxcomb, The*, 124; *Knight, The*, 37–39, 42–43, 51, 54; *Philaster*, 78; *Woman Hater, The*, 26–30; *see also* Blackfriars; Comedy, city; James I
Savage, James E., 57
Shakespeare, William, 10, 11, 14, 15–16, 19, 21, 57, 72, 129, 132, 133, 134, 135; works mentioned: *All's Well That Ends Well*, 88; *Antony and Cleopatra*, 23; *Coriolanus*, 89; *Hamlet*, 23, 27, 73, 82, 87, 96; *Henry IV*, part 1, 46, 49, 88, 121; *Henry IV*,

part 2, 124; *Julius Caesar*, 87, 88;
King Lear, 101, 106; *Macbeth*, 50;
Midsummer Night's Dream, A, 39, 44,
70; *Much Ado About Nothing*, 26,
129; *Othello*, 23; *Troilus and Cressida*,
88; *Twelfth Night*, 76; *Two Noble
Kinsmen, The*, 16
Sharpham, Edward: *Cupid's Whirligig*,
61
Selton, Thomas, 40–41
Shirley, James, 86
Sidney, Sir Philip, 14; *Apologie for Poe-
tric, An*, 68, 107; *Arcadia*, 16, 57–
62, 63, 67, 69, 70, 71, 72, 73, 87;
"Old" and "New" *Arcadia*, 150n9;
text for *Cupid's Revenge*,, 151n10

Timoneda, Juan de: *El Patrañuelo*, 109
Tragedy, B-F development of, 89–90,
105–6, 119; *see also* Beaumont, Francis, *Cupid's Revenge* and *Maid's Tragedy, The*
Tragicomedy, B-F development of, 15–
16, 20, 57, 73, 85–86, 105, 110–
11, 118–19, 125, 132; English beginnings, 72–73, 143–44n7,
152n18; Fletcher's pastoralism, 70–
72, 122

Vega, Alonso de la: *Tolomea*, 109

Waith, Eugene M., 68, 111
Webster, John, 132
Whitefriars theater, acquisition by Chil-
dren of the Revels, 56–57, 146n2
Wilkins, George: *Miseries of Enforced
Marriage, The*, 41; *Travailes of the
Three English Brothers, The* (with Day
and Rowley), 41
Wily Beguiled, 36, 147n7

Xenophon: *Cyropaedia*, 107, 108